Fashion

+

Music

LAURENCE KING

Published in 2016 by
Laurence King Publishing Ltd
361-373 City Road
London EC1V 1LR
e-mail: enquiries@laurenceking.com
www.laurenceking.com

Text © 2016 Katie Baron
Illustrations © the copyright
holders; see page 208
Designed and produced by Laurence
King Publishing Ltd, London.

Katie Baron has asserted her
right under the Copyright,
Designs and Patents Act of 1988
to be identified as the author
of this work.

All rights reserved. No part of
this publication may be reproduced
or transmitted in any form or
by any means, electronic or
mechanical, including photocopy,
recording or any information
storage and retrieval system,
without prior permission in writing
from the publisher.

A catalogue record for this book is
available from the British Library.

ISBN: 978-1-78067-748-4

Design: Intercity
Picture research: Evi Peroulaki
Commissioning editor: Sophie Drysdale
Senior editor: Rosanna Lewis

Cover image: Madonna photographed
by Tom Munro for *L'Uomo Vogue*, 2014

Printed in China

**Fashion
Creatives
Shaping
Pop Culture**

Fashion

+

Music

Katie Baron

Contents

006 **Foreword**
by Professor Frances Corner OBE

008 **Introduction**

011 **B. Åkerlund**
+ Madonna, Beyoncé, Britney Spears, Lady Gaga, Laleh

020 **William Baker**
+ Kylie Minogue

030 **Judy Blame**
+ Boy George, Neneh Cherry, Massive Attack, Björk, Iggy Pop, Baaba Maal

041 **Jeffrey Bryant**
+ Pet Shop Boys, Goldfrapp, Lady Gaga

050 **Es Devlin**
+ Pet Shop Boys, Kanye West, Lily Allen, Miley Cyrus

061 **Franc Fernandez**
+ Lady Gaga, Scissor Sisters, Sam Sparro, Fischerspooner, Kelela, Vic Mensa

070 **Nicola Formichetti**
+ Lady Gaga, Brooke Candy, Color Code

080 **Jean-Paul Goude**
+ Grace Jones

092 **Andrea Lieberman**
+ Puff Daddy, Jennifer Lopez, Gwen Stefani, Mary J. Blige

103 **Anastasia Marano**
+ M.I.A., Azealia Banks, Santigold

112 **Jordan Mooney**
+ Sex Pistols, Adam and the Ants

122 **Arianne Phillips**
+ Madonna, Lenny Kravitz, Courtney Love

132 **Antony Price**
+ Roxy Music, Duran Duran

142 **Michael Schmidt**
+ Cher, Debbie Harry, Tina Turner, Britney Spears, Rihanna, Lady Gaga, Madonna, Aerosmith

152 **Jo and Pat Skinny**
+ Pulp, Blur, Suede, Republica, The Longpigs

162 **Stevie Stewart**
+ Kylie Minogue, Britney Spears, Girls Aloud

172 **Jenke-Ahmed Tailly**
+ Beyoncé

182 **Johnny Wujek**
+ Katy Perry, Shakira, Nicki Minaj

192 **Kansai Yamamoto**
+ David Bowie, Lady Gaga

204 **Index**

208 **Acknowledgements/Picture Credits**

Foreword

As a child of the 1970s, my first experience of fashion came not from the catwalks of Milan or Paris but from the stages of *Top of the Pops*. For me, what artists such as David Bowie and Debbie Harry wore was of real significance. Now, the designers and influencers of tomorrow are themselves following social media's most popular figures, mostly musicians, with stars generating huge and diverse audiences. We now have unprecedented access to how these artists live and what they wear when performing as well as in their (admittedly manicured) downtime – resulting in an even greater influence over the average person's fashion choices, and in turn over their own self-imaging.

This is compounded by the fact that the line between music and fashion is becoming increasingly blurred. Rihanna launched her collection for River Island in 2013; ex-Oasis frontman Liam Gallagher has his own label, Pretty Green; Pharrell Williams co-founded the labels Billionaire Boys Club and ICECREAM; and pairs of Kanye West's exclusive Yeezy sneakers for Adidas routinely sell for beyond £5,000 on eBay. Stylists and designers are often innovators, but it is musicians who regularly allow these styles to proliferate, thanks to their credible embodiment of lifestyle ideals – including their ability to connect or even reroute notions of gender, race and sexuality on the global stage.

While the more avant-garde catwalk designs are routinely mocked in the non-fashion media, their adoption by music stars – who are viewed as more legitimate players in fashion's often elitist landscape – allows them to travel from outlier to trend, becoming quasi-uniforms for fans seeking affiliation or affirmation. Musicians can link fashion, lifestyle and identity, taking collections' abstract themes and contextualizing them as social aspiration. Through their personal style, both on- and offstage or screen, music-industry stars remain powerfully able to extend their artistic influence and vision far beyond their music – often making themselves 'immortal' in the process.

In that context, this book is very timely. With Katie Baron's breadth of knowledge and her 15 years of experience not just as a writer and producer but also as a trend forecaster, she is well attuned to the constantly changing, always intersecting world of creative commercial culture. With an eye always on the new and unexpected, who better to analyse the changing and symbiotic relationship between fashion, music and culture?

Professor Frances Corner OBE
Pro-Vice Chancellor, London College of Fashion

Kylie Minogue in Simon Preen's gothic-luxe body-con, in promotional images conceptualized by William Baker for her Kiss Me Once tour (2014).

Introduction

Fashion and music are formidable forces: entrancing, bewildering, identity-affirming, panic-inducing, tribe-forming, arguably life-saving and indisputably two of the finest playgrounds for indulging creative vision. As such, it rarely gets more exciting than when the two collide.

Growing up as I did in the 1980s, the British television show *Top of the Pops* and the advent of *MTV*, seminally wedged in prime-time entertainment, were the two key triggers of my fashion fascination. With fashion and music, one always fuels the other, and it was thrillingly impossible to separate the contents from the package. From the video for Madonna's never-tired club classic 'Get Into the Groove' to wild-child Neneh Cherry performing, nine months pregnant, in bad-boy high-tops, an industrial medallion and a gold Gaultier jacket, the attitude penetrated my consciousness thick, fast and absolutely unforgettably. Later, in common with 99 per cent of creative students, I sought out *The Face*, *i-D* and *Dazed & Confused* magazines for my visual inspiration, my cultural protein. But they weren't where the fascination truly started.

This book is a celebratory exploration of how these twin agents of creative expression have long had a powerful mutual attraction, and of how fashion has consistently amplified our understanding of the band, and in many cases the brand. While the relationship has been in play for some time, it has never been more significant than it is now. In the digital era, powered by visual soundbites, with pop videos, album art, stage looks and street-style shots distributed, devoured and dissected across the globe in nanoseconds, image means everything. Music may be the foundation, but fashion and the larger-than-life personae it creates have become the glue that binds sound, style and attitude, confirming the creative intent and ensuring that the audience remains captivated.

Hip-hop iconoclast Neneh Cherry, from the *Raw Like Sushi* album series of 1989. Styled by Judy Blame, photographed by Jean-Baptiste Mondino.

'We're all visually stimulated, regardless of whether we consider ourselves creative. The original rock stars were religious icons and saints. We all need something to believe in and these stars, with these looks, are essentially rendering themselves immortal.'

Michael Schmidt

From music videos to editorial shoots, and from ad campaigns to stage shows, via the evolution of some of the industry's most significant, often era-defining collaborations, this book focuses on the power of the fashion–music synthesis, as agent for reflection but also for change. A socio-pop-cultural journey through territories including identity, feminism, gender, sexuality (and sexual politics), cultural appropriation and the impact of Internet culture on the way we communicate, concoct, perceive and represent our ideas, it's an essential reference for anyone interested in fashion's role as a medium with which to innovate, communicate and seduce.

Fashion + Music is based on original interviews with nineteen seminal stylists, costumers, designers and art directors – each one conducted in person – plus a host of their core associates. You'll also discover visual material that has never previously been seen or discussed: mood boards, personal photographs and vital 'hidden' reference inspiration. From household names to the industry's most cherished insiders, these are the creatives fuelling the fantasy, giving context to the sound and adding flesh to the bones of much wider pop-cultural agendas.

Katie Baron

B. Åkerlund

+

Madonna, Beyoncé, Britney Spears,
Lady Gaga, Laleh

B. Åkerlund may not refer to herself as a feminist, but her fearless attitude and boundlessly competitive appetite for using fashion to present women at their most awe-inspiring have given rise to a wealth of unforgettable, often identity-defining imagery - enhancing the status of many of the twenty-first century's most influential female pop icons, including Beyoncé, Lady Gaga, Britney Spears and Madonna.

1
Her own best advertisement: B. Åkerlund appears in a campaign for the Swedish eyewear designer Anna-Karin Karlsson in 2015. Photographed by Ekaterina Belinskaya.

Powerful to the point of regal, Åkerlund's women are a superhuman tribe immortalized by their sexual potency, imposing presence and exuberant indifference to convention. They are, in fact, often echoes of the Swedish-born, self-styled 'fashion activist' Åkerlund herself. A flesh-and-blood reverberation of the mesmerizing, maximalist fashion fantasies she creates for album art, music videos and performances, Åkerlund is frequently her own best advert – a 'project' she has been cultivating since moving from Sweden to Los Angeles with her family as a teenager. While her repertoire of work is huge and always expanding – at the time of our meeting, she was directing a fashion show for Swedish sports star Björn Borg's eponymous fashion label, writing a series of alternative children's books and preparing to make her directorial debut with the Swedish pop star Laleh's new music video – her own irrepressibly outré sense of style has always been a one-in-a-million calling card.

2

When she appeared on Sweden's version of the American TV show *Project Runway*, Åkerlund wore 'a futuristic gown by London-based designers Erevos Aether and a custom wig/hat made the size of a small child', as she described it. 'My outfit was not something any normal human would wear; it was a fashion statement to get the audience to wake up and realize it was a fashion competition, not a commercial brand presentation.'

While her look may be continually evolving – for the best part of the last decade she has been many bewitching shades of punk-rock-goth queen – in her teens and early twenties she was a 'thematic dresser', committed to a tsunami of styles with utter devotion: 'I had one year where I wore a different outfit every single day. That was a way to express myself and what styling meant to me. If I dressed in a sari, I'd have the jewellery, the make-up, the hair – I'd go full costume. That was the early years of me not knowing what to do with my creativity because I didn't have the platform I have now to express it. All I had was myself, and I was really shy.'

Now, of course, the platforms and the alter egos with which she has to play are considerably bigger – broad enough and ambitious enough to satisfy both the artists' agendas and her own. One of the first major pop videos she styled and costumed was Lady Gaga's 'Paparazzi' (2009), directed by her husband, Jonas Åkerlund, a Grammy Award-winning film director. Says B. Åkerlund: 'When we [Gaga and I] met I felt like it was almost too close to home to begin with – like looking at myself 15 years ago. It was nothing new to me because I dressed like her, for real, without an audience, but it was a great connection.' The video, conceived as a short film, deals with the trappings of fame, dark *and* glorious. Åkerlund interpreted the treatment sartorially via a brilliantly overwhelming gamut of fashion excess, racing from sci-fi-style corsetry in the form of a metallic leotard by Thierry Mugler (complete with a gilded prosthetic arm) to PVC bondage body-con and a flamenco-style catsuit. A cavalcade of cartoon vixens rolled into one pop star-cum-performance artist, it was ideal territory for Åkerlund's brand of explosive creativity and something of a blueprint for the Amazonian modern dominatrix image that defines her career. The more indelible the impression, the better: 'I know I've succeeded when I create a look for an artist and it turns into something else – a Lego toy, or someone dressed their Barbie doll in the same way. That's when I know I've done a good job.'

2
Cover for Madonna's album *Hard Candy* (2008), styled by Åkerlund.

3
Stills from the Swedish pop star Laleh's 'Colors' music video (2015), which Åkerlund both styled and directed.

4
Brittany Murphy in a still from the Hollywood movie *Spun* (2002), on which Åkerlund cut her heavyweight styling teeth, pre-dating her now maximalist, anti-normcore oeuvre.

Just as Åkerlund's work has morphed into the antithesis of mid-nineties grunge – the anti-gloss aesthetic so prevalent when she first emerged on to the US creative scene and which she herself so astutely realized, albeit with trailer-trash inflections, in the film *Spun* (2002) – her 'more-is-always-more' fashion philosophy is also a flagrant rebuttal of the post-noughties 'normcore' movement: the urbanite trend for wearing consciously bland, average-looking clothes as a badge of big-brand fatigue. Trading furiously in fantasy and flamboyance, self-confessed 'label whore' Åkerlund desires to rail against mediocrity at every level, making her perfect for an industry whose lifeblood is conspicuity. But her methodology runs deeper than superficial shock tactics. Regardless of how fast the look has to be put together ('people have no idea how quick we often have to work in music'), her 'dream bigger, think larger than life, be the best you can be' mantra defines her approach to achieving long-lasting traction, even when that places her at a potentially difficult crossroads within the contentious landscape of modern feminism. After all, crafting the ultimate women, in glorious symbolic form, does not come without hard work, or even pain.

B. Åkerlund

Echoing the vision of the legendary French art director Jean-Paul Goude (see page 80), who coined the term 'French Correction' to describe extending or accentuating his muses' body parts (and his own) in his fantastical images to create the ultimate being, Åkerlund, too, is interested in pushing her presentation of women to extremes to display them at their most scintillating. It is a simple but logical concept: impressive equates with memorable, and memorable, inside pop culture's wondrous bubble, equates with virtual immortality. 'My job is to make them the people they're meant to be, looking as good as they can possibly be – effectively making them larger than life,' says Åkerlund. 'And yes, I have made many people cry. It's not something I'm proud of, but if they cry I know it's really good. Yes! Then the look is totally achieved. I'm sorry to all the women I've hurt through the years but they are sexy, strong and powerful and that takes work. I also think it's important for people to know that what you see is hard work, even for the artist.' Her assistants refer to the process as 'the B. Åkerlund experience'. Pushing for extremity is an approach that underpins the Åkerlunds' regular collaborative projects. Jonas Åkerlund says, 'Both B. and I tend to push story and character far; we don't have much of a grey zone. It's resulted in strong impressions and strong characters, which isn't something we planned out, but it works.'

The most striking example of the Åkerlunds' partnership is Beyoncé's O2 adverts announcing her 2013 Mrs Carter world tour. Arguably more extreme than any of Beyoncé's considerable previous visual extravaganzas, the advert portrays her as a queen holding court, gliding through a palatial setting. Åkerlund's heavily researched mood boards for the project reveal a visual smorgasbord of regal references, modern and historic, dizzyingly layered with voluminous bejewelled panelling, lace, capes, collars and a Thierry Mugler corset – interspersed with military source material. The summation is a look somewhere between Marie Antoinette and Queen Victoria, via Alexander McQueen and Victoria's Secret. The showpiece was a custom-made 18-carat-gold overskirt (custom creations and reworked pieces are an Åkerlund speciality) that the stylist/costume designer describes as being 'like hell on earth to actually wear'. Proving that pain is no barrier to art, the duo have reprised their relationship many times since, including short films for four tracks from Beyoncé's lauded self-titled 'visual album' of 2013: 'Pretty Hurts', 'Superpower', 'Haunted' and 'Partition'.

5
Åkerlund's moodboard for the O2 ad is a smorgasbord of regal and military references, characteristically heavily researched.

6
Madonna performs at the annual Super Bowl halftime extravaganza in 2012, styled by Åkerlund.

5

+ Madonna, Beyoncé, Britney Spears, Lady Gaga, Laleh

A similarly insatiable appetite for visual research came into play when Åkerlund worked on Madonna's Roman Empire-themed performance for the Super Bowl halftime show in 2012. Åkerlund describes the halftime show – now a multimedia, globally televised behemoth in which minute details are as important as the sweeping overview – as requiring a superhuman effort that left her spent for three months following the event. 'Before we even looked at the clothes, I did extensive research on the history of the empire, including flying to Rome itself.' But the viewing figures would affirm her own retrospective sentiment that the effort was clearly worth it; even Beyoncé's lauded halftime show failed to match Madonna's 112.5 million viewers.

The project presents an almost textbook example of Åkerlund's and Madonna's tireless energy and obsession with details (they now collaborate regularly), indicative of their joint belief in fashion performances that reach for a singularly spectacular visual universe. For the 13-minute show, the pair ('Madonna and I were in contact every single day for three months covering the tiniest of details') dressed not only the star herself (as Cleopatra) but also her associate performers – Nicki Minaj, M.I.A., LMFAO, CeeLo Green – plus every backing singer and band member, racking up approximately 350 outfits. While Åkerlund stresses that there was no specific discussion about using it as a platform to reassert Madonna's dominance in a pop-music field now largely fuelled by considerably younger female stars, the Roman theme would suggest otherwise. Madonna appeared as in charge and sexually energized as ever. 'She simply owned it,' recalls Åkerlund.

7
Promo for Åkerlund's own fashion-orientated creative network, Who You Are.

My job is to make them the people they're meant to be ... I have made many people cry. It's not something I'm proud of, but if they cry I know it's really good ... I'm sorry to all the women I've hurt through the years but they are sexy, strong and powerful and that takes work.

B. Åkerlund

Unsurprisingly, sex and sensuality are also close to Åkerlund's creative heartland ('B. has a black belt in sexy,' quips Jonas) – a core component of any Åkerlund project that is never more visible than in Britney Spears' video for the blistering dance track 'Work Bitch' (2013). 'I don't like things that aren't sexy because sex sells and to me a sexy woman is a powerful woman. As I told Beyoncé, "I'm here and I'm your sex police." My job is to make sure they're sexy.' It's a near-perfect example of fashion's transformative power as the key to 'becoming' (in music terms, unleashing the all-important alter ego). Britney, for whom the track represented a major industry comeback, appears in the middle of the Nevada desert, a dominatrix surrounded by a posse of burlesque dancers. The fashion is part rock chick, part Folies Bergère, amplified with classic-Åkerlund, metallic breastplate-style corsetry that evokes the sense of a woman, as with Madonna, who is both a leader and a survivor. The video asserted Spears' continued influence, despite the fact that the most powerful imagery never made it into the public domain. 'She had a vision about being taped [bound with tape] so I made this outfit of hot pants and a top and when we shot it, it was like unleashing an animal,' recalls Åkerlund. 'But in the end it was taken out, which is kind of sad to me because I remember watching the video and going "Holy shit". She just became so sexual – you could feel it in her whole body. It was amazing, but sadly wasn't in the final cut.'

7

+ Madonna, Beyoncé, Britney Spears, Lady Gaga, Laleh

8

The artwork for Madonna's album *Hard Candy* (2008), on which she has a white-blonde quiff and wears a bespoke boxer's belt emblazoned with a golden letter 'M', is another example of Åkerlund's smart use of fashion-cum-costuming to spotlight a female powerhouse in residence. The brief from Madonna was simply: 'Punk movie star with a royal twist.' In Åkerlund's hand that soundbite-style cue (the interpretation of keywords being indicative of the way the pair often communicate) morphed into an homage to Madonna's infamous tough-love streak, while re-referencing the axis of pleasure and pain that has permeated her career as far back as 'Justify My Love' and 'Erotica'.

Pleasure and pain are apt allusions, for there is also a dark, albeit playful, side to Åkerlund that gives the musicians with whom she collaborates obvious bite. Beyoncé's 'Superpower' (2013) is a key case in point – a story of apocalyptic insurgency that took the artist a million miles from classic R&B styling or her Texan belle roots. Instead, unapologetically fierce and resolutely powerful, she is posed as the leader of the dissidents clad in cut-off shorts and camo jacket in one scene, and balaclava, ripped fishnets, thigh-high boots and miniskirt crafted from parachute material in another.

8
Stills from the video for Lady Gaga's single 'Paparazzi' (2009), a key track from her breakthrough album, for which fashion was instrumental in establishing her artistic agenda.

+ Madonna, Beyoncé, Britney Spears, Lady Gaga, Laleh

9
Campaign images for the creative director Robert Lussier and Åkerlund's own accessories label, Le Snob — both a serious luxury line and a tongue-in-cheek comment on the fashion industry's sense of self-regard. Photographed by Tim Walker.

10
A screen grab from the website for Åkerlund's Who You Are, a virtual network established in 2014 to forge unique creative collaborations.

11
An image from the film *The Cell* (2000), directed by Tarsem Singh — a key influence on Åkerlund's aesthetic as a stylist and costume designer.

10

I push and I push and I think that comes from being in the school of Madonna. She taught me that when you think it's good it could be better and when you think it's better it could be the best. Ultimately, I want to provoke and make people think. I want to beat the system.

B. Åkerlund

Åkerlund's fashion sensibility is now so strong that it is swiftly becoming its own ecosystem. Influenced by the work of artists including the fashion designer John Galliano and the late Japanese costume designer Eiko Ishioka (known for Francis Ford Coppola's *Dracula* and Tarsem Singh's *The Cell*), she is louder and bolder than the vast majority of her peers even in the music business; upon starting out, she was regularly advised by others in the industry to slow down, which she of course ignored. Her mission to whip anything bordering on banality into more exhilarating shape has manifested both in the online platform whoyouare.com – a virtual collective for emerging fashion talent – and in her own accessories and bag line, Le Snob. She describes the latter, featuring bags shaped like champagne bottles, as 'based on a snobby lifestyle – it's all the things you don't need but have to have, which is geared towards what I want and what I think'. It is classic irreverent-yet-honest Åkerlund humour based entirely on the knowledge that fashion is a powerful and seductive tool, but no more and no less; a beast to be tamed but more regularly unleashed as an all-conquering weapon. 'I push and I push and I think that comes from being in the school of Madonna. She taught me that when you think it's good it could be better and when you think it's better it could be the best. Ultimately, I want to provoke and make people think. I want to beat the system.'

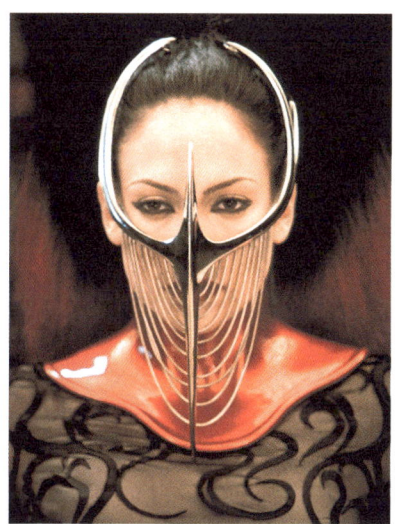

11

William Baker

+

Kylie Minogue

1
Kylie Minogue's landmark album *Fever* (2001). The visual language, conceptualized by Baker, referenced Jean-Paul Goude's partnership with Grace Jones (see page 80).

2
Minogue rides into the stadium for her KylieX2008 tour on a gigantic skull - a very literal symbol of her then recent (death-defying) victory over breast cancer.

William Baker is the consummate contemporary pop impresario: a self-made, multifaceted creative director whose lifelong obsessions with symbology, the escapism of high glamour and the vast, powerful sociocultural reach of music have enabled him - in tandem with his most long-term collaborator, the Australian pop priestess Kylie Minogue - to orchestrate some of the most iconic entertainment-entrenched fashion imagery of the last two decades.

While Baker describes himself professionally as 'essentially an introvert' in need of an extrovert twin to co-author his fantasies, early stories reveal a character beguiled by the power of visual provocation. 'Growing up, pop videos were my culture, and as a massive Boy George fan I was always plastered in make-up. I then became a Madonna fan – even winning a lookalike competition,' he laughs. The British professor of advertising and marketing Dr Jonathan Wilson, who went to school with Baker, affectionately recalls how he was 'always winding people up – he was quite notorious even then, an early master of hype'. Growing up in Manchester's late-1980s/early-1990s 'Madchester' heyday also placed Baker directly in the path of a maelstrom of key indie bands (including Happy Mondays, The Stone Roses and Inspiral Carpets) plus the magisterial sway of legendary club The Haçienda – all steadily reclaiming Britain's alternative youth culture in the face of a heavy half-decade of manufactured pop.

The look – an unprecedented mash-up of rave, retro and football casual – may be all but invisible in Baker's contemporary work, but it demonstrated the power of style and sound in union on a fundamental level. Music presented an obvious ally for his burgeoning appetite for style with substance beyond the cosmetic. 'People still have a rough time coming out, but pop music made it so that it was never a problem for me being gay,' he says. 'When I was 17, I went to Madonna's [Jean Paul Gaultier-costumed] Blonde Ambition tour and it was almost like a religious experience. I loved the combination of high fashion, pop music and drama on stage. There was the now classic suit with the corset and the tits coming out, and she was very outspoken about AIDS, safe sex and the Catholic Church – essentially very controversial. The music didn't necessarily come from a political place, but certainly a social core which had a massive impact on me personally and my understanding of what it meant to be a genuine pop artist.'

3

Madonna and her subsequent ascent to omnipotent cultural icon fuelled Baker's fascination with contextualizing imagery, to the extent that he read the American academic Camille Paglia's book *Sexual Personae* – a study of sexual decadence in Western literary and visual culture – and then embarked on a degree in theology. 'It was essentially about deciphering incredibly powerful imagery, text and visual codes – a discipline that made total sense to me,' he recalls. While studying, Baker worked as a stylist, assisting greats including Judy Blame (one of Boy George's early collaborators; see page 30) and the late Isabella Blow, but insists he was always something of a misfit in traditional fashion circles: 'I obviously had a love for clothes, but not for garments in themselves. Even then they were always just a means to an end, really.'

A Saturday job at Vivienne Westwood's Conduit Street shop in London introduced Baker to his own pop-culture conspirator-cum-personal deity: Kylie Minogue, with whom he would later set a considerable precedent as the first pop star fashion stylist to transition publicly to the role of full creative director. It was the mid 1990s, a period of decadent dramatic excess and glamazon supermodels that personified his belief in amplified, sensational visual messaging. It was also the genesis of the showgirl obsession that he and Minogue would later crystallize into a core creative signature. 'The supermodels were at their height. Kate [Moss] was just starting out, and Naomi [Campbell], Linda [Evangelista], Christy [Turlington], Carla Bruni were all in her [Westwood's] shows in Paris, which created an incredibly glamorous, *Dynasty*-like atmosphere. I loved the glamour and that ridiculously exaggerated version of women. In many ways it was very over the top, almost like drag, but it was built on a very upbeat, aspirational and unpretentious energy. The shows generated a really electric sense of excitement.'

3
'My own personal Jesus': a giant crucifix in the hallway of Baker's own home refers to his years studying theology, his subsequent fascination with iconography and the premise of pop stars as modern deities.

4
The cover of Minogue's album *Light Years* (2000) referenced Mary Magdalene. Photographed by Vincent Peters.

4

> It's such an intense marriage of ideals that being in love is a key analogy. You put them on a pedestal and make them into icons.
>
> William Baker

Like so many of the brightest romances in British fashion history (reference the designer Alexander McQueen and stylist Katy England), Baker and Minogue commenced their courtship over tea, following an impromptu visit by Minogue to Westwood's shop. She was transitioning from Stock Aitken Waterman's teen-pop hit factory to the edgier territory of Deconstruction Records and was famous, but not yet a megastar. 'It felt like fate, and the connection was very real, which is essential for a good creative relationship. It's such an intense marriage of ideals that being in love is a key analogy. You put them on a pedestal and make them into icons. I've had a similar connection with [Jamiroquai star] Jay Kay – a brilliantly colourful, flamboyant character. It's not a sexual connection, but a kind of absorption nonetheless.'

Impossible Princess (1997) was Baker and Minogue's first album together, marking an artist coming of age and to terms with her adult identity, post-soap-opera pop stardom. Reflecting lyrics flush with critical introspection and intimacy and new musical influences including indie rock, folk and drum and bass, the imagery (much of which was shot by Minogue's then boyfriend, the French photographer Stéphane Sednaoui) was rife with experimentalism – including a neon-centric 3D cover. The attitude was more abandoned. The fashion became darker, more directional and enigmatic. The single 'Did It Again' featured a manga-esque Minogue, while 'Breathe' symbolically depicted Minogue virtually barefaced.

Whereas *Impossible Princess* was the transitional rite of passage, *Light Years* (2000) became Baker and Minogue's millennial paean to heroically glamorous iconography – and a glimpse into Baker's preoccupation with crafting a modern deity. The album cover, photographed through the cinematically seductive lens of the German photographer Vincent Peters, features Minogue draped in a blue Jeremy Scott chiffon swimsuit, backlit by a vast halo-effect sunset. 'It wasn't an absolutely conscious thing at the time,' Baker explains, 'but I can certainly now see my background coming in; the album cover was a very religious-looking [Mary] Magdalene-referencing image of Kylie. Even that blue is a colour that I always associate with Mary. Fashion-wise, there were lots of echoes of the work Stella McCartney was doing at Chloé – lots of golden skin and really healthy-looking girls – but essentially it was intentionally very regal, with a strength but also a sense of purity.'

The hot pants were just something she had in the back of a drawer, which she'd worn to some kind of pimps, nerds and tourists party, but they became part of a plan to focus on her key assets in order to pull away from the half-successes of the Deconstruction era. It's funny that they've become so iconic – we were literally selling her arse.

William Baker

5
Minogue wearing the now-famous gold hot pants in the music video for 'Spinning Around' (2001), devised to reboot her career.

6
Stills from the music video for 'Can't Get You Out of my Head' (2001), a Ballardian-esque hybrid of 'dystopian melancholy and euphoria' directed by Dawn Shadforth, and another exercise in crafting an icon.

And what of the now almost mythological gold hot pants featured in the Dawn Shadforth-directed disco-pumped 'Spinning Around' video? 'There are a few things with Kylie that are very accidental and a few things that are very planned,' Baker confesses. 'The hot pants were just something she had in the back of a drawer, which she'd worn to some kind of pimps, nerds and tourists party, but they became part of a plan to focus on her key assets in order to pull away from the half-successes of the Deconstruction era. It's funny that they've become so iconic – we were literally selling her arse,' he half-jokes.

6

If *Light Years* indelibly returned Minogue to the pop spotlight, it was *Fever* (2001) that completed the resurrection. Its most enduring track, visually and sonically, remains 'Can't Get You Out of my Head' – a track also directed by Shadforth that she describes as 'obsessional' and that Baker cites as a unique moment of collective, synergetic clarity: 'We were all on fire, extremely hungry. It was the point at which we stopped caring about being cool, and that's when it started to really work.' Baker recalls it as another deliberate exercise in re-crafting the icon, which Shadforth suggests came from some key visual frissons. The video's most memorable sequences depict Minogue wearing a now iconic white hooded jumpsuit (designed by the British costumier Fee Doran, aka Mrs Jones) in a white room surrounded by a troop of robotic dancers, all sheathed in red minidresses and visors. While the latter was a direct reference to German electro-pop icons Kraftwerk, the overall tableau was inspired by Shadforth's time on the Costa del Sol. Says Shadforth: 'I was interested in the [J.G.] Ballardian, dystopian feel of that place. The sun and the blue sky and all these developments but then the feeling of sterility and loneliness within this perceived sixties utopian dream. It seemed to be a great visual counterpoint to the cool Kraftwerk production/ New Order-ish production – that kind of melancholy and euphoria, the feeling of passion married with iciness. All the very best pop songs have those two elements. The dress had an extreme sexiness that I hadn't conceived of but it was framed in a world that was verging on clinical – the perfect effect.'

The track was a critical shift away from 'smiley Kylie' to a more nuanced identity. Baker says, 'It's such a strong electronic track but also very sparse and quite erotically charged. Jean-Paul Goude's [page 80] powerfully stark work with Grace Jones was a big inspiration, and the jumpsuit, again, had almost religious implications.' The album cover – designed by Tony Hung – toys with a similar vein of sexy-playful 1980s electronica.

> **Much of the time we've worked together she's been happy for me to project my fantasies on to her; she was a willing, complicit muse.**
>
> William Baker

I was interested in the [J.G.] Ballardian, dystopian feel of that place. The sun and the blue sky and all these developments but then the feeling of sterility and loneliness within this perceived sixties utopian dream. It seemed to be a great visual counterpoint to the cool Kraftwerk production/ New Order–ish production - that kind of melancholy and euphoria, the feeling of passion married with iciness. All the very best pop songs have those two elements.

Dawn Shadforth, director

7

8

7
Kylie's album *Body Language* (2003), underscored by the artist's preoccupation with Paris. Photographed by Mert and Marcus.

8
A poster for Minogue's KylieX2008 tour.

9
Minogue during the KylieX2008 tour in an otherworldly set piece that subtly references Jesus' crown of thorns - another reference to survival and resurrection.

The flirty, more languidly sexy follow-up, *Body Language* (2003), was the first album for which Baker consciously commandeered more directional fashion labels, albeit heavyweight brands. Following the Fever Tour (2002), which kick-started a long-running relationship with the Italian fashion giant Dolce & Gabbana, Baker romanced other super-brands including Chanel and Balenciaga, both of which at the time rarely lent to musicians, and also Helmut Lang. 'It was a really creative time for us, to be able to have that massive dressing-up box at our disposal,' recalls Baker. Brigitte Bardot references flew, bolstering Minogue's own Parisian preoccupation. As the albums took hold, so did the tours. Intimate and Live (1998); Fever, which Minogue describes as a tour in which she felt 'somehow elevated and felt otherworldly, I was able to become a character I hadn't been before'; the Showgirl tour (2005–6); KylieX2008; and Aphrodite (2011) delivered a platform for Baker to craft more expansive, theatrical versions of their previous fascinations and acted as a new repository for real-life obsessions. 'I think the tours are the purest expression of our relationship because they so clearly show what she does, as a performer, and what I do in terms of creating the worlds she's performing in. Much of the time we've worked together she's been happy for me to project my fantasies on to her; she was a willing, complicit muse. Plus, of course, she's an actress – that's her background. The showgirl had a walk, for instance. It echoes how when we worked with [the photographer duo] Mert and Marcus on the *Body Language* album cover they actually referred to the character in the picture as a third person, as if a separate entity.'

Over the years we have built a language, which I feel is our own. Music and fashion, music as fashion, fashion as expression - it's so important because it's able to pinpoint a moment in time without any dialogue.

Kylie Minogue, pop star

10

11

12

13

14

15

16

The KylieX2008 tour is especially pertinent – heralding Minogue's return to the stage following breast cancer in the mid-noughties. For Baker, the creative reaction was to showcase a warrior sensibility symbolic of physical victory. Standout visuals from or related to the tour include her entering the stadium riding a gigantic skull, a body-con-style dress with storm-trooper breastplates and a latex suit attached to a snaking gaggle of wires (a subtle semi-religious reference to Jesus' crown of thorns and Minogue's perceived indestructibility). 'I'd begun to see her as less frothy, and more a controller of men. She had literally cheated death and to me she became this very kind of powerful, sexy survivor – much more of a kind of Helmut Newton woman. We started working with Jean Paul Gaultier, things became a little tougher, darker and the male dancers became more homoerotic – possibly the result of my own sense of emasculation received from working with a woman for so long. Like I say, the alter ego, the final vision is really a combination of our concerns or desires.' Minogue affirms the sentiment: 'When we first met I was absorbing myself in London music-and-fashion culture, and he was one of the characters I met along the way. Over the years we have built a language, which I feel is our own. Music and fashion, music as fashion, fashion as expression – it's so important because it's able to pinpoint a moment in time without any dialogue.'

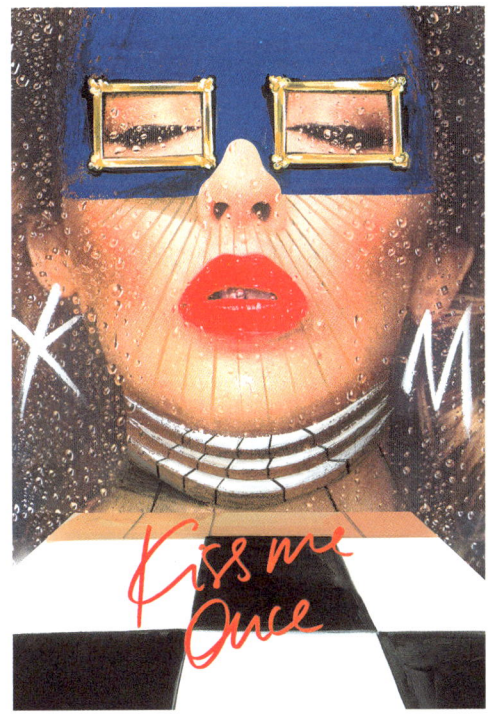

17

> # So much of my emotional identity came from my icons during those awkward phases of adolescence and I think the stuff that Kylie did, no matter how naive at the time or layered up later, ultimately comes from a real place with real meaning within that sense of fantasy.
>
> William Baker

10–16
Images of Minogue in concert, for album art, in editorial imagery and behind the scenes – all conceptualized, styled and photographed by Baker, who describes her as his `complicit muse'.

17
An artwork concept for Minogue's album *Kiss Me Once* (2014), designed (and later photographed) by Baker.

Minogue's album *Kiss Me Once* (2014) still features Baker's influence – he photographed the album cover and was creative director on the tour, but he suggests that the core creative complicity that powered the rich success of the last two decades may be slowing. 'The idea with that cover, which is heavily [Helmut] Newton-inspired, was to project a strong sense of erotica but to shoot her as a woman, not just a gay icon. Kylie loves her gay audience but it's become more her, less about a character now – it's time for her to step out from behind the persona.'

What's certain is that Baker's brand of escapism will continue to drive larger-than-life fantasies destined to inspire others. 'Having a role model is so important, that idea of effectively having your own personal Jesus. So much of my emotional identity came from my icons during those awkward phases of adolescence and I think the stuff that Kylie did, no matter how naive at the time or layered up later, ultimately comes from a real place with real meaning within that sense of fantasy. It's an incredible privilege to be able to continue that legacy.'

Judy Blame

+

Boy George, Neneh Cherry, Massive Attack,
Björk, Iggy Pop, Baaba Maal

Judy Blame is a legend of street-derived DIY styling; a creative hero generally allied to the most flamboyant end of the fashion spectrum. But his kitschy B-movie name (divined in the showy, hedonistic creative crucible that was London's 1980s club scene) and extravagant personal style belie an extraordinary knack for communicating simple, powerful truths, especially when he is working with musicians - icons like Boy George, Neneh Cherry, Björk, Massive Attack and Iggy Pop.

1
Neneh Cherry - one of Blame's most significant creative charges - from the *Raw Like Sushi* album cover series (1989). Photographed by Jean-Baptiste Mondino.

Judy Blame

Musicians trade on Blame's magpie-like creative mentality and honest, artist-driven references to help crystallize their industry personae, via TV shows and stadium outfits, album art, pop videos and more. 'There's a level of respect,' he says. 'If you look at my most iconic pictures they're the simplest ones. When you're working with an entertainer, you don't want to see the outfit before you see them. There are so many instances now where it's so worked out down to the tour T-shirt and the lipstick and the perfume; it's just a way of squeezing a young, funky person dry. That's how I see that kind of pop stardom. It's great, and it's fun, but it's essentially musical cartoons; it's not real people, it's not believable and it's not the way I do things.'

Originally (and still) an accessories designer, Blame remembers fashion/music history back when the two industries were oil and water – parallel worlds circling each other suspiciously – with the glimmer of a union just starting to emerge in nightclubs. Having run away at 17 from home in Devon, deep in the English countryside, Blame chased the punk movement of the late 1970s to London ('England was in a very low place, a lot of strikes, and racial unrest, and then along came this movement that was all about ripping up the past to find a new, different way forward'), followed by a stint in Manchester forging friendships with graphic design visionaries including Malcolm Garrett and Peter Saville. But it was in London's clubs – Blitz, Heaven, Cha Cha – as punk slid into the 'peacock time' New Romantic era of the 1980s that Blame found his most formative framework, developing his own freewheeling, experimental stylistic language and a set of social-cum-professional cohorts that were to define his legacy.

2
Gender-bending 1980s icon Boy George, a key creative partner who deployed Blame's distinctive, club-ready DIY sensibility to powerful and much-mimicked effect. Shown in concert in 1983.

3
A collage of Boy George by Blame, depicting George's infamous speech at the 1984 Grammy Awards, which triggered record-burning outrage from some conservative viewers.

2

+ Boy George, Neneh Cherry, Massive Attack, Björk, Iggy Pop, Baaba Maal

Echoing Vivienne Westwood and Malcolm McLaren's use of fashion to define the riotous, anti-establishment nature of punk, the clubs were incubating new fashion/music crossovers: the avant-garde nightclub host and promoter Steve Strange was developing the pop group Visage, while the gender-bending singer-songwriter Boy George had founded Culture Club. But it was as part of the late stylist Ray Petri's Buffalo Crew – an influential collective of photographers, stylists and other image-makers – that Blame unearthed his appetite for aesthetics built on the unified pillars of fashion, style, sound and attitude. 'Ray taught me that it wasn't just about clothes or visuals but rather life and how you hold yourself. The overall vision was about your attitude and how you present yourself to the world; how you think. I'm quite free-spirited and anarchic in the way that I approach things. Ray helped me to fine-tune that chaos and give it direction.'

The club scene delivered a pivotal friendship with the fashion designer and art director Antony Price (see page 132), one of the first designers to fuse the fashion and entertainment industries, including orchestrating Roxy Music's era-defining sleek art-pop look. (Price asked Blame to create jewellery for his catwalk show after seeing a homemade book of his accessories produced from Polaroid photos.) It also delivered two of Blame's seminal collaborators: Boy George and the Swedish American singer, songwriter and rapper Neneh Cherry.

> **Punk sold newspapers and the New Romantics sold fashion. Once the media clocked on to the column inches made possible by all these crazy kids dressing up, it realized it had found its audience of young people, all over the place. Street culture had been a bit of an elitist gang mentality, bound to magazines like *i–D* and *The Face*. Now it was something altogether bigger, more mainstream.**
>
> Judy Blame

For George, Blame created homespun, oversize and overtly ostentatious pieces of jewellery that were worn on Culture Club's stadium tours and George's controversial 1984 Grammy appearance, featuring an award acceptance speech ('Thank you America, you've got style, you've got taste and you know a good drag queen when you see one') that spurred some of the United States' more conservative viewers to burn the group's records. It also gave Blame his first taste of the mass influence of pop stardom – in particular, the transformative power of fashion as a conduit for a large-scale artist–audience relationship. 'I think George knew it would happen,' recalls Blame. 'In all honesty I didn't – I was so busy buttoning outfits! I'd come up with a hat with shoelaces and we'd play a gig and all the kids would have hats with shoelaces on them. It was great for George because it really gave him a contact with his audience they could feel and I liked the fact that kids could copy it. The punk era was all about being different; the New Romantics brought people into competition with the pop stars in a way, even as followers. In a sense it was their version of running away from home, the thing that helped them to discover what they wanted.'

The launch of MTV in 1981 galvanized the mass media into finally embracing the power of fashion as an extensive commercial tool, way beyond the confines of the catwalk. 'Punk sold newspapers and the New Romantics sold fashion,' says Blame. 'Once the media clocked on to the column inches made possible by all these crazy kids dressing up, it realized it had found its audience of young people, all over the place. Street culture had been a bit of an elitist gang mentality, bound to magazines like *i-D* and *The Face* [with which Judy was affiliated]. Now it was something altogether bigger, more mainstream.'

Judy Blame

4

4–6
The cover of Neneh Cherry's hip-hop influenced single 'Buffalo Stance' (1989), art-directed by David James, riffs on much of Blame's bricolage aesthetic. Stills from the videos for 'Buffalo Stance' and 'Manchild' (also 1989, an homage to Cherry's family life in London and bearing her signature trainers and gold chains) illustrate the potent hybrid of fashion (Blame) and street style (Cherry). The latter features a cameo from Blame himself. Directed by Jean-Baptiste Mondino.

Next up was Neneh Cherry. When they met, in a club, they danced together for three hours solid. Blame describes their relationship as founded on their equally 'shameless' preoccupation with stealing influences, inspiration and references from whatever catches their eyes. 'There was her with her international-ness and me with my I'll-use-anything-and-be-influenced-by-anything attitude. I'd come from more of a fashion background and she was more street, more hip-hop, so it was a question of us mixing the two cultures – just as Ray Petri had done by putting a fabulous-looking black man in a Gucci suit, or a Comme des Garçons jacket on a Rasta. We fitted.'

When they first started working together on promoting Cherry's first single, 'Buffalo Stance' (from the album *Raw Like Sushi* of 1989), she was pregnant with her second child. Her appearance on the UK TV show *Top of the Pops* while heavily pregnant was a watershed moment, much imitated since by lifestyle magazines as a celebrity rite of passage. 'Neneh was an incredibly beautiful woman and we didn't want to promote her like some pop bimbo. She was a strong woman; we showed it off rather than hiding it,' says Blame. 'The director of *Top of the Pops* was shocked silly that I'd put her in a BodyMap stretchy skirt and a little Gaultier jacket, and nor was the record company happy, but what did they want her to go out there in? A tent? Fuck off. She's Neneh Cherry.'

5

6

rge, Neneh Cherry, Massive Attack, Björk, Iggy Pop, Baaba Maal

Judy Blame

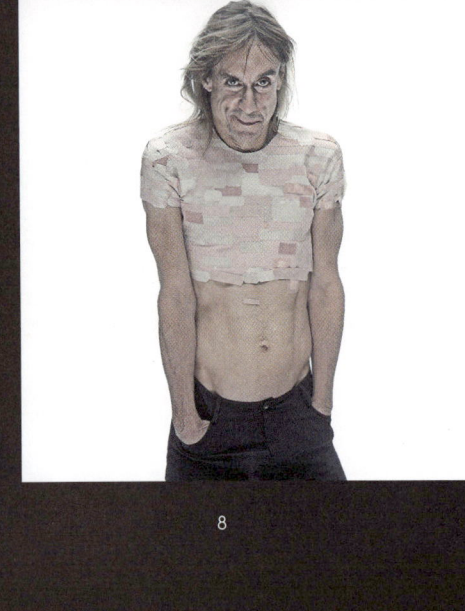

8

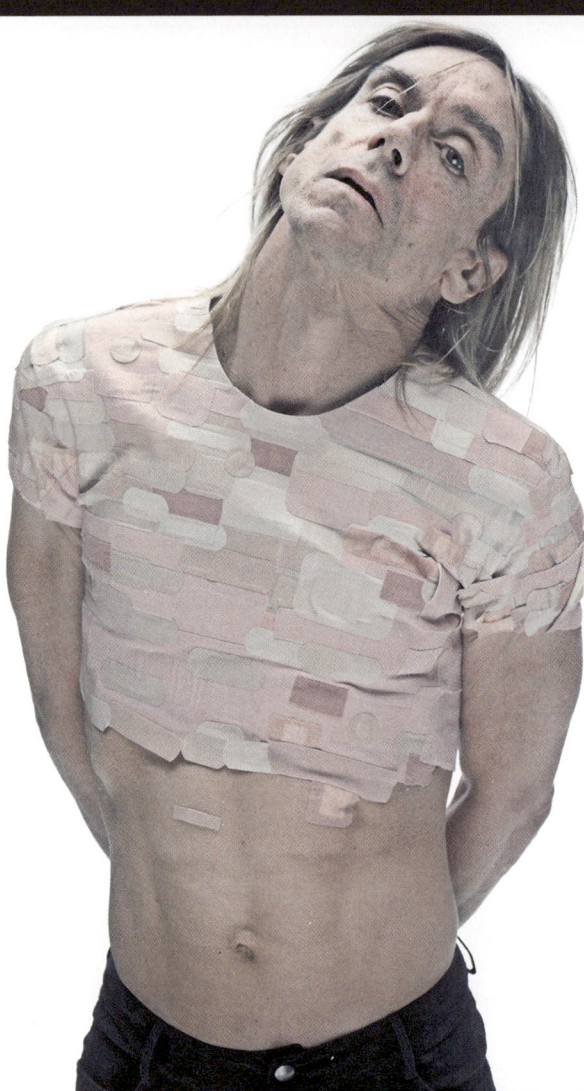

9

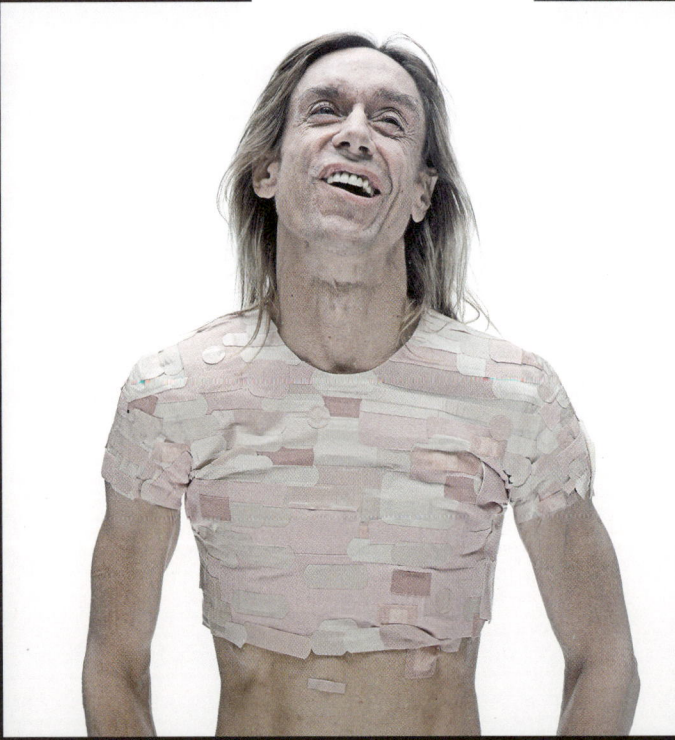

10

Cherry subsequently became a feminist icon of sorts, a trailblazing example of wielding a life and career alongside motherhood – an idea echoed by the album's second single, 'Manchild'. The video, as with many of the Cherry–Blame collaborations, was devised in tandem with photographer Jean-Baptiste Mondino and conveyed an homage to Cherry's family life in west London and the characters it comprised (Blame had practically moved in). Mixing the banality of everyday living with a more surreal flavour indicative of the progressive nature of the artist and track, the blue-screen studio-shot video was inspired by an afternoon in Cherry's back garden, to the extent of featuring her wearing a towel wrapped around her head (exactly as she had come downstairs to the shoot in the hotel where they were staying in Paris), a washing line and cameos by Blame and the artist Barry Kamen, also Buffalo Crew royalty. The fashion highlights the duo's high–low aesthetic: classic French lingerie, a Jean Paul Gaultier jacket ('one of the first designers who would let us borrow the clothes for music videos – a real visionary', says Blame), trainers and gold jewellery – a signature Cherry look. The album cover for *Raw Like Sushi*, a portrait, played on several long-running visual themes for Cherry. Her bandaged fists (a Mondino request) were an homage to Petri, who often featured boxing imagery, but can also be read as a metaphor for her as an empowered woman; a survivor and a victor of sorts. 'It's often about reminding someone of their own identity,' says Blame.

11

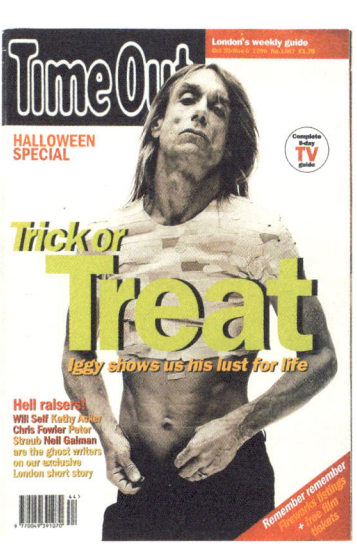

12

8–12
The rock legend Iggy Pop in a shoot for *Time Out* (1996), for which Blame constructed an impromptu T-shirt from plasters. Photographed by Gavin Evans.

Using visuals to crystallize identity became such a key part of Blame's professional lexicon that in some instances fashion took a back seat to the wider game of art direction. During the early 1990s Blame took on a more Petri-style curatorial role for the cult British trip-hop group Massive Attack – connecting them with a slew of burgeoning artists, designers and photographers able to realize their sound, including the photographer Juergen Teller and the filmmaker Baillie Walsh, who directed the video for the iconic track 'Unfinished Sympathy'. 'From working with people like Neneh I realized that I was in fact able to educate other people,' says Blame.

Fashion remains Blame's most demanding mistress, however, and a constant magnet for his own early idols. He describes the US rock star Iggy Pop as one of his favourite musicians to have collaborated with and another key example of his less-is-more, reality-trumps-artifice school of thought. On their first shoot together for *The Face* (1986), despite pulling in rails of clothes from designers including John Richmond and Christopher Nemeth, they eventually used Pop's own beaten-up pair of jeans direct from his suitcase. For a cover of *Time Out* magazine (1996), Blame created just one piece – a T-shirt made entirely from plasters – on the basis that 'it was the simplicity that was everything. He [Pop] is such a genius performer and such a great personality that I just made one thing and it was like a perfect statement.'

13

The Senegalese singer Baaba Maal is another of Blame's collaborative charges – a traditional African artist for whom Blame's street-smart eye and talent for melding apparently contrary influences presented a passport to a wider Western audience. 'I'd put him in what Europeans would consider to be very left-field, mad clothes, such as Yohji Yamamoto and Comme des Garçons, but as an African he could carry them off. It was a really honest match … you just have to be ready to adapt and go with the person, and that's the difference between working with pure fashion and musicians.'

Ultimately, however, it is strong, pioneering women who are his creative nirvana. Björk, too, while only a one-time collaborator, is a shining example of his capacity to conjure iconic imagery with remarkable simplicity – symbolic of the time but able to withstand decades of re-releases. Again in partnership with Mondino, Blame created the image for her acclaimed first album, *Debut* (1993) – now considered a classic music portrait. True to his belief in representing the artist as honestly as possible, Blame had requested that she simply bring her favourite clothes from her own wardrobe. However, when the airline lost her luggage ('she walked into my hotel room carrying just a model of a boat, a little satin Martin Margiela dress and a big pair of boots') they changed plan and re-routed to Margiela's Paris showroom. 'She'd talked a lot about the fact the album was quite techno but she wanted to look like a little animal, so I just yanked that little furry jumper off Martin's rail. Then [the French make-up artist] Topolino came in and put those two sequins under her eyes and that was it – the full stop!' recalls Blame. And so pop music's inimitable cyber pixie was born: a crystal-clear synergy of quiet vulnerability and extrovert determination.

+ Boy George, Neneh Cherry, Massive Attack, Björk, Iggy Pop, Baaba Maal

13
Debut, the now iconic first album cover for the avant-garde Icelandic superstar Björk, is a lucid demonstration of Blame's capacity for communicating powerful truths. Photographed by Jean-Baptiste Mondino.

14
Blame and Mondino reunited with long-time accomplice Cherry on the visual identity of her single 'Everything' (2014).

According to Blame, such is the power of the fashion/music bond that the vast majority of the relationships he has developed with musicians remain open-ended. A man bred on collectives, much like his earlier affiliations on London's club scene and at the heart of the Buffalo Crew, Blame regards it as like the ebb and flow of family. Indeed, for Cherry's unofficial comeback album *The Blank Project* in 2014 (her first solo album for almost two decades), Blame was back with a vengeance – reuniting with Mondino for the first video, 'Everything'. Shot in a cavernous warehouse and filmed in eerie black and white, a singular long-shot focuses on a solitary Cherry, dancing frenetically as the camera gradually creeps closer. Wearing an all-black outfit of leather and stripped fabric that is equal shades Frida Kahlo and Yohji Yamamoto, plus trainers and a string of chunky neck chains, she resembles an urban shaman, magically defiant. The fact that she is now 50, with a look (still co-authored by Blame) and sound as stunning yet attitudinal as the landmark appearance on *Top of the Pops*, consciously serves to confirm her ongoing status as a talisman for sassy women the world over, age irrelevant.

Blame is acutely aware of how, when there is a message to transmit, the job is never really over: 'I don't know you could say we've ever really finished. A lot of us have had pretty bonkers lives, and they don't constantly cross, but there's every likelihood, with most of them, that they'll walk through the door next week and ask for something.'

14

> **I don't know you could say we've ever really finished. A lot of us have had pretty bonkers lives, and they don't constantly cross, but there's every likelihood, with most of them, that they'll walk through the door next week and ask for something.**
>
> Judy Blame

Jeffrey Bryant

+

Pet Shop Boys, Goldfrapp,
Lady Gaga

'I don't hate the mainstream, but I do have an in-built phobia of it. It was always so important to rebel against it, to be different, to force change.' Just as he was in London's hedonistic 1980s club scene, an era that still underscores his idiosyncratic DIY aesthetic, Jeffrey Bryant is anything but standard. Combining a design sensibility that revels in the absurd with a rare mastery of highly complex sculptural garments, this relatively unsung hero of Britain's countercultural elite has been a critical, inspirational, direct link between British clubbing culture and global pop music for more than two decades, fuelling the vision of cult music heroes including Lady Gaga, Pet Shop Boys and Alison Goldfrapp.

1
Epitomizing the experimental, visceral, DIY style born out of the sybaritic London club scene: the Pet Shop Boys in concert (Pandemonium Tour, 2009-11) wearing Bryant-designed coats made from thousands of black plastic straws.

Jeffrey Bryant

While Bryant's extraordinary costume design still rails against homogeneity with every stitch, a legion of pieces devised for some of the music industry's most beguiling iconoclasts have given his work such global mass-media traction that the Andy Warhol Museum in Pittsburgh now sells a Dress-your-Gaga paper doll cut-out book featuring two of Bryant's designs.

The origin of Bryant's visionary work is a rite-of-passage story of escapism plus needs-must innovation, kick-started by punk. Born in South Wales, he worked as a mechanical engineer at Cardiff's steelworks (a job involving skills that would later prove invaluable to the complicated structures of his cartoonish constructions). Punk, as the full sonic–visual package of attitudinal dissent, offered Bryant an alternative perspective and was the catalyst for his first design inventions. Desperate to imitate the wool trousers from Vivienne Westwood's Seditionaries collection (a quintessential punk garment) but allergic to wool, Bryant used his own straight-cut cotton pyjama bottoms as a pattern from which to create the necessary anti-itch lining. His custom DIY design snowballed into making clothes for all his club- and concert-going cohorts, happy to mix his homage handiwork with slices of the real thing. He says, 'We became famous purely by having fantastic clothing. I realized very quickly that outrageousness would make me stand out, putting energy in the battery to push me further.' He migrated to London at the start of the 1980s, following the scent of the New Romantics and bands such as Adam and the Ants ('they were different, because they were so theatrical – other bands would just go on but they played classical music, wore tribal war paint and played characters'). He spent the best part of the next decade refining an experimental aesthetic incubated within the clubs, parties and general sybaritic blur of the city's throbbing underground scene.

An ideal playground for his outré vision, the post-punk club scene, epitomized by Blitz and Hell, offered a world of flamboyance and extremes – a wholly revised breed of rebellion rooted in sartorial one-upmanship, gender-bending life as performance art and an overall sense of 'becoming' that outstripped the stylistically Identikit tribalism of its harder, more aggressive predecessor. Bryant was a constant fixture at the clubs Heaven and Trade and high on the radar of legendary club hosts Michael and Gerlinde Costiff – totemic figures whose stewardship of the scene connected it with a wealth of external international musicians, art directors and music promoters seeking to plug into its unorthodox vibrancy. It was the Costiffs who engineered Bryant's entrance into the world of pop music by introducing him to two of his most enduring collaborators, the British electro-pop duo Pet Shop Boys (Neil Tennant and Chris Lowe).

2

3

+ Pet Shop Boys, Goldfrapp, Lady Gaga

4

2
The 1990s pop group Deuce, wearing reflective suits by Bryant.

3
Bryant models his own outrageous designs in a series of acid-house-era images that took him from clubs to music videos, thanks to directors and producers hankering to plug into the scene's vibrancy.

4
The Pet Shop Boys video 'Was It Worth It?' (1991), in which Bryant appeared, was drawn directly from the London club Kinky Gerlinky, whose performers Bryant routinely costumed.

5
Michael and Gerlinde's World: Pages from a Diary (2013) – a retro-documentary of the world of the legendary London club hosts Michael and Gerlinde Costiff, who introduced Bryant to the Pet Shop Boys.

Bryant started off as a performer in their video 'Was It Worth It?' (1991), based on the Costiff-run nightclub Kinky Gerlinky (described by the Costiffs as a place of 'unashamed glamour, where Bryant would often costume the performers to help them stand out among stiff competition'). Bryant secured the video gig by showing Tennant and Lowe a book filled with photos of 'drag queens in mad clothes' (all him), dressed in whatever materials he could appropriate. Says Tennant: 'What makes Jeffrey different is that he likes making things, while fashion now is mostly about buying things. Jeffrey makes things constantly; he's a totally compulsive person. There's an element of spontaneity in a theatrical, workshopped tradition, plus an aesthetic based entirely and enduringly on a Poundland level of frugality.' Bryant himself wore a white wig and giant platforms built into red vinyl trousers – an idea borrowed from David Bowie's Kansai Yamamoto (see page 192) period, rebooted for the acid house era.

The following year, when the club/dance music group Deee-Lite performed at the Brixton Academy in south London, they assembled a 20-strong group of London's nightclub A list for their 'Groove Is in the Heart' encore, including Bryant and a Naomi Campbell-esque drag queen, Winston, whose Bryant-created dress the lead singer, Lady Miss Kier, swiftly commandeered for herself. The transition from performer to designer was unmarked and organic, recalls Bryant: 'There was no real difference. I was doing it in clubs, and then I was doing it on camera. It effectively gave me an apprenticeship. I had a back catalogue of pictures from my club days to present to people, and that's what they wanted to re-create in pictures and videos, what they wanted artists to look like.' His clothes became emblematic of a tribe in demand, a nocturnal subcultural gang whose notoriety had morphed them into a hot pop-culture commodity. As the stylist and designer Judy Blame (see page 30) recalls of the period, 'Punk sold newspapers and the New Romantics sold clothes.'

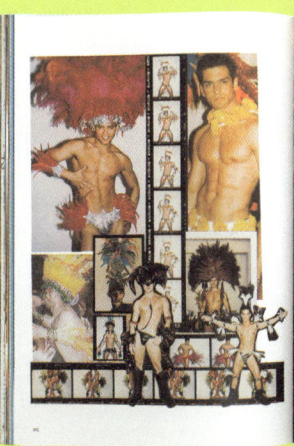 

5

As the 1990s hit, after an unsatisfactory late 1980s flirtation with the body-beautiful monochrome minimalism championed by the iconic US fashion photographer Bruce Weber (an aesthete whose sumptuous black-and-white lifestyle imagery defined the identities of a host of American brands including Calvin Klein, Ralph Lauren and Abercrombie & Fitch, not to mention a trilogy of black-and-white pop videos for the Pet Shop Boys), Bryant returned to his default desire for showmanship. He created looks for the camp dance-pop act Right Said Fred, the urban London boy band East 17 and the bubble-gum pop group Deuce. For Cyndi Lauper's European tour in 1994, he provided oversize faux-fur coats in wildly clashing colours (pieces retrieved directly from his mates), the influence of which notably re-emerged on the autumn–winter 2014 catwalk of the French label Balmain.

But it was during a reunion with the Pet Shop Boys in 1999 for their Nightlife tour that Bryant found his most enduring creative groove. Plugging into their mutual affinity for otherworldly characters encircled by a surreal flamboyance, their alliance has given rise to a vast catalogue of experimental costuming bearing a sci-fi-like agelessness. The pieces have both framed and exalted the Pet Shop Boys – the overlords of lyrically smart, touching and often witty pop – and rendered their shows as famous as their music.

> **It's true that my work could be considered very in your face, but ultimately it's like a joke or the delivery of an exceptionally important line in a play. The first look of any outfit is the most important thing; you either win or you lose. If it's dismissed, I've failed.**
>
> Jeffrey Bryant

One of the heroes remains the 'straw jacket' (2013) – a coat constructed from thousands of high-shine black drinking straws protruding aggressively like a geological explosion. Another is what Bryant refers to as the 'radiator/flat-pack jacket' – an origami-style jacket that pumps up like wings and then recoils to an unassuming footprint, like a paper bag. A third is his cuboid-esque puffer jacket constructed from a series of boxy, Lego-like inflatables that are worn on Lowe's arms – a slightly reimagined version of which was worn by the dancers in the Pandemonium tour of 2009–11. All were pre-existing concepts that Bryant had been toying with privately, which made the cut thanks to their impressive ingenuity and extraordinary visual resonance. 'They [the Pet Shop Boys] were so excited by the ideas that they were going to wear them even if they didn't, strictly speaking, illustrate the music or fit in. From then I simply evolved them,' recalls Bryant. What connects such pieces, and also separates Bryant's work from the cheaper clichés of drag or the standard theatrics that emerged, less successfully, from other corners of the 1980s club scene, is a highly nuanced sense of the outrageous that he describes as 'calculated, appropriate extremes'. Such extremity is also at the heart of the rich and recognizable lexicon of the Pet Shop Boys, who view it as a transformative tool essential to propelling the key pop myth. Tennant says: 'Extreme is part of our iconography, as I personally admire the artifice of performance, the creation of a persona as a way to really engage the audience, and this is why costume is so important. Chris and I have never felt it was necessary to suppose we were presenting our real selves entirely; we've always dressed up to become the Pet Shop Boys.'

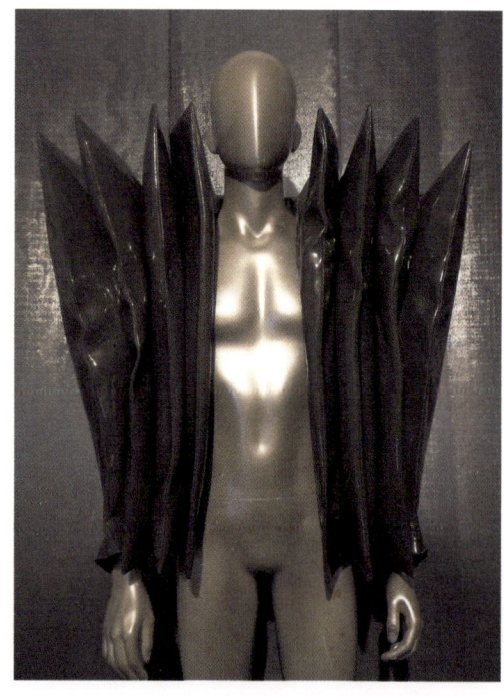

6

+ Pet Shop Boys, Goldfrapp, Lady Gaga

7

Instead, suggests Bryant, the focus is on creating clothes/outfits/looks that come with a tailored visceral impact – pieces to be seen within the context of a specific multisensory staging in order to render them most exhilarating. As sexually ambiguous, era-unspecific 'wearable sculptures', they are also well placed to stand the test of time. He describes a particular moment in the Electric tour (2013–14), devised by the acclaimed set and costume designer Es Devlin (see page 50), which begins with a transparent onstage screen showing just a single spark glowing in the pitch darkness. The spark runs into a hat shape, which slowly turns upwards, transforming into a tunnel. As Tennant urges 'Turn it on', the electricity and the techno soundtrack start, showing the duo illuminated against the darkness wearing the straw jacket and large signature cone hats. Bryant says, 'That's when the screaming starts, which is incredibly pleasing for me – very rewarding in terms of understanding the power of the total look. It's true that my work could be considered very in your face, but ultimately it's like a joke or the delivery of an exceptionally important line in a play. The first look of any outfit is the most important thing; you either win or you lose. If it's dismissed, I've failed.'

6
The origami-esque 'radiator' jacket created for Pet Shop Boy Chris Lowe, which pumps up and recoils – a classic example of Bryant's sartorial engineering.

7
Neil Tennant on stage in the iconic 'straw jacket'.

> Extreme is part of our iconography, as I personally admire the artifice of performance, the creation of a persona as a way to really engage the audience, and this is why costume is so important.
>
> Neil Tennant, musician and singer-songwriter

8
The disco-ball helmet: another linchpin piece within the Pet Shop Boys' visual ecosystem, which Bryant refers to as 'the random jigsaw of absurdity' and Tennant as 'the admirable artifice' of their extreme iconography.

9
Cube headpieces worn on the Pet Shop Boys' Pandemonium tour in Barcelona (2009).

10
Suits made of foil - a material typical of Bryant's unashamedly frugal, scavenger-like sensibility - originally rejected by Tennant and Lowe, migrated to the duo's dancers instead.

+ Pet Shop Boys, Goldfrapp, Lady Gaga

9

Suits too, for Tennant at least, are something of a Bryant/Pet Shop Boys signature, thanks to their loaded sartorial symbolism. Unlike the sexually charged sleekness of Antony Price's suits for the pop stars Roxy Music and Duran Duran, suits and dance music do not mix, or so conventional wisdom goes, making them the ultimate fashion statement for a pop band renowned for intelligent, subversive commentary. They are part of the legacy begun on the Pet Shop Boys' Performance tour (1990), devised by the operatic director David Fielding, that saw the duo arrive onstage on surfboards in bright yellow suits. Bryant explains, 'It was so absurd it was fantastic. That was effectively the starter and everything after must be a continuation.' For their Electric tour (2013–14), under Devlin's direction, the dancers wore Bryant-devised high-vis orange shirts, suits and shoes (plus mixing-bowl headpieces), while the Fundamental tour (2006–7) included a set piece in which the male backing singers wore suits – one a bold floral style made from blanket fabric, the other covered in a pixel-like pattern. It is another example of the make-and-do design typical of Bryant's scavenger mentality, a hangover from the 1980s that often surfaces in the multitude of backing-dancer outfits (such as a series of 'bouncing foil suits') that regularly include Tennant's and Lowe's rejects.

Other trademarks include mirrors – a fascination Bryant attributes to the eccentric British artist and jeweller Andrew Logan that's most exuberantly expressed in Lowe's reflective silver bomber jacket and disco-ball helmet for the Electric tour – and a major penchant for splicing references (eras, styles and genres) to create what Bryant refers to as 'the random jigsaw of absurdity'. The best examples are Tennant's 'Captain Pugwash' jacket worn for their Pandemonium tour (2009–11) – a three-way marriage of an Elizabethan jacket, a contemporary Louis Vuitton raised 'can' shoulder and holographic nightclub-orientated vinyl strips – and a dress for the avant-garde British musician Alison Goldfrapp's Head First tour (2010) that involved marrying a Junya Watanabe-style ruff collar with an old Thierry Mugler dress resembling candy-coloured Chinese lanterns. Bryant and Goldfrapp subsequently reprised their partnership with the creation of the 'Video-tape Cape' – a black wrap of high-shine reflective videotape, inspired by Goldfrapp glimpsing a single strand of tape hanging from a tree while driving past in a taxi.

10

047

Jeffrey Bryant

+ Pet Shop Boys, Goldfrapp, Lady Gaga

> **What makes Jeffrey different is that he likes making things, while fashion now is mostly about buying things. Jeffrey makes things constantly; he's a totally compulsive person. There's an element of spontaneity in a theatrical, workshopped tradition, plus an aesthetic based entirely and enduringly on a Poundland level of frugality.**
>
> Neil Tennant

12

It is Bryant – and particularly his legion of visual oddities invoked in tandem with the Pet Shop Boys – who has arguably laid a core blueprint for latter-day art-centric megastars. They include Lady Gaga, an artist who has regularly adopted a similarly radical, performance-art relationship to fashion to catapult herself, across numerous personae, into a stratosphere far beyond the vast majority of her peers. Bryant has even contributed to that oeuvre, with three key looks commissioned by her former creative director, Nicola Formichetti (see page 70): a completely transparent net outfit featuring black velvet chevron zigzags, a lace chevron dress worn to a Mac Cosmetics presentation (later copied for a scene in US TV show *Glee*) and a latex yellow-and-black dress with razor-sharp extruded shoulders, created purely for her to strut through Heathrow airport. (The last outfit had an alternative version with trousers and a full mask reminiscent of those worn by the late club icon and performance artist Leigh Bowery.) While Gaga wore the looks only for fleeting moments, their places in the pantheon of pop-culture history were fixed in nanoseconds, thanks to the rampant, instantaneous dissemination of social-media conversation.

Whether obvious to later generations or not, Bryant's work remains a lucid illustration of the continuing influence of the 1980s club scene on pop-music videos, album art and stage personae. Not only is there a slow filtration of refracted, co-opted ideas – as can be traced through the work of acclaimed designers such as the 1980s-obsessed Kim Jones (reference his two-tone bomber jackets for Louis Vuitton and the Aztec detailing within his own early-noughties collection) – but also concepts are lifted wholesale directly from the dance floor and on to the backs of pop stars. As much about transferral as appropriation, Bryant's designs have successfully bathed a host of stars in the glow of dramatic residual glamour and the unadulterated ambience of the artfully, timelessly and pleasingly absurd.

13

1

2

Es Devlin

+

Pet Shop Boys, Kanye West,
Lily Allen, Miley Cyrus

1
The pop star Lily Allen on stage during her Sheezus tour (2014). Devlin's combination of visual dynamism, wit and honesty — the costuming referenced Allen's preoccupation with new motherhood — is typical of her creative approach.

2
Meta fashion: The Pet Shop Boys at the closing ceremony of the London 2012 Olympic Games, wearing Devlin-directed, Gareth Pugh-designed costumes that reprised Pugh's costuming of the ballet *Carbon Life* (2011).

3
Kanye West during his joint Watch the Throne tour (2011-12) with fellow rap superstar Jay Z. Devlin's frequent collaboration with West showcases her rare capacity for conjoining fashion, space and sound within one holistic narrative, marrying art and pop culture.

3

For digital-era pop stars dogged by the decline of traditional music sales but elevated exponentially by the viral spread of millions of social-media screen grabs, live performances have never been more important. A linchpin within that world is the set and costume designer Es Devlin OBE. Straddling the worlds of opera, dance, theatre and spectacular public events (she designed the Olympics closing ceremony in London in 2012 and is devising the opening event for Rio 2016), she has become an integral brain within the stage-crafted visions of pop stars including the Pet Shop Boys, Kanye West, Lady Gaga, Miley Cyrus and Lily Allen.

4
Kanye West and Jay Z performing during their Watch the Throne tour (2011–12)

5
A stage concept developed in tandem with art iconoclasts Jake and Dinos Chapman for the hardcore punk band Wire was the design that led Kanye West to Devlin's door.

Devlin is a storyteller whose connection to fashion, and its co-dependent relationship with space and sound, comes with deep and multifarious roots. While she cites visiting the English National Opera (ENO) aged 12 as the touchpaper that ignited her passion for theatrical design, populist media was also a major influence – rousing an access-all-areas approach to creativity and an unusually meritocratic stance concerning the great high–low cultural divide within the arts. 'Some pop music clearly doesn't merit anything, but then some opera doesn't either, just as some fashion doesn't warrant looking at twice and some does. It's not genre that defines whether you should look again. The point of anything you look at in terms of art is that, once you've seen it, your mind will not be able to look at the world, or apply itself to any task, in the same way.' For Devlin, the flip side of ENO was the weekly ritual of watching TV music shows, compounded by the arrival of MTV in the early 1980s. 'Because everybody watched the same programmes,' she says, 'the next day when you came into school it became a forum, a focus of debate. I remember, for instance, that Frankie Goes to Hollywood's "Relax" T-shirt really shocked people [the related single was banned from BBC and MTV airplay for sexually explicit lyrics], which then became a kind of manifesto. Subliminally you don't know how you're being hard-wired, but the music and the image, including the fashion, came together so you were naturally imbibing both with the same receptors without really being conscious of it.'

Devlin's key, ongoing collaborations with the cult British electro-pop duo Pet Shop Boys and the pop megastar Kanye West have solidified her domination of the sweet spot between art and pop culture, via fictionalized worlds anchored in intense, amplified characterization. When West initially approached Devlin in 2005 for his Touch the Sky tour, it was to reimagine an idea that had already been developed in tandem with the British artists Jake and Dinos Chapman for the hardcore punk band Wire – a concept that involved placing each musician inside an individual box plugged directly into an electrocardiogram (ECG) machine that visualized their heartbeats mid-performance. She has worked with West on all his subsequent tours: Glow in the Dark (2008), a concept that revolutionized the rap genre by placing West on stage alone; Watch the Throne with the rapper Jay Z (2011); and Yeezus (2013).

While Devlin is at pains to point out that she has no direct influence over West's clothes, she also affirms that in the staged space the creative connection between the sartorial and the spatial are indivisible: the star and his environment are always to be understood as one giant, moving visual sculpture in which an assumed identity must be channelled from all sides. It is an approach she traces back to her original theatre training (after studying on the Motley Theatre Design Course in London, in 1995 Devlin won the biennial Linbury Prize for stage design): 'When you're creating a tableau and you have furniture and people in it, it's all considered one picture – it's all part of your tools.' The Glow in the Dark tour placed West within a barren, alien wilderness. Devlin describes it as a potentially prophetic moment (his mother died unexpectedly during the tour) that elicited a very truthful spark of connection. A visceral illustration of a man alone, embedded in a palpable sense of pathos, West appeared messianic but also vulnerable. 'The word "need" is key to anything I find in music. Whenever I'm really looking at why a song moves me I look at: why did it need to be written? What need is really occurring? If you can really gain access to someone's need and vulnerability or pain, then something very powerful happens.'

6
A screen-shot close-up of the bespoke, diamond-encrusted Maison Martin Margiela balaclava conceived to peg Kanye West as a renegade rap star as comfortable with artistic symbolism as with (standard) status symbols.

7
Louis Vuitton's `Series 3' exhibition (2015). Devlin has collaborated with the French megabrand since the seminal holographic spring-summer 2015 catwalk show - a direct result of her epic but nuanced stage productions.

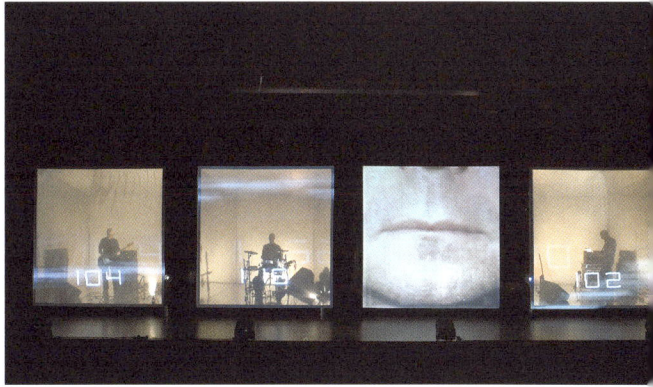

5

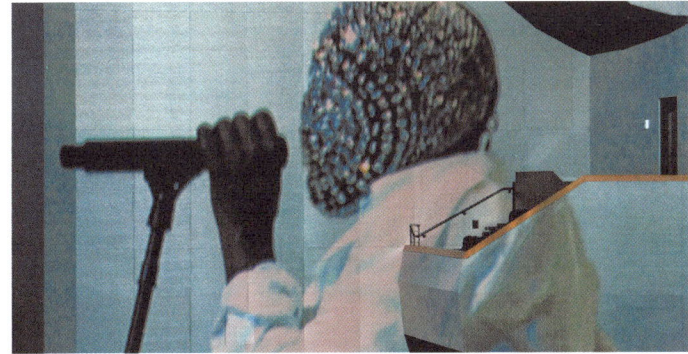

6

7

During West's three-show, mixed-album Revel residency in Atlantic City in the United States (December 2012), it was his attire – a leather sci-fi-meets-streetwear kilt, demonstrably more sober than standard rap bling – and in particular his use of elaborate masks that informed the staging. The abstracted physicality of his headwear – including balaclavas by the avant-garde fashion house Martin Margiela (one encrusted with diamonds, the other made from feathers) – served to disguise but also to differentiate West as a maverick rap star prepared to drop the stage entourage and embrace symbolism over status symbols in order to rewrite the script. The masks 'became these extraordinary characters, a whole look that personified those shows', recalls Devlin, who projected arctic scenes (partly referencing the frozen landscape of Chanel's autumn–winter 2010 show) that heightened the sense of an otherworldly, isolated, superhuman voyager and echoed the scenario for Glow in the Dark.

 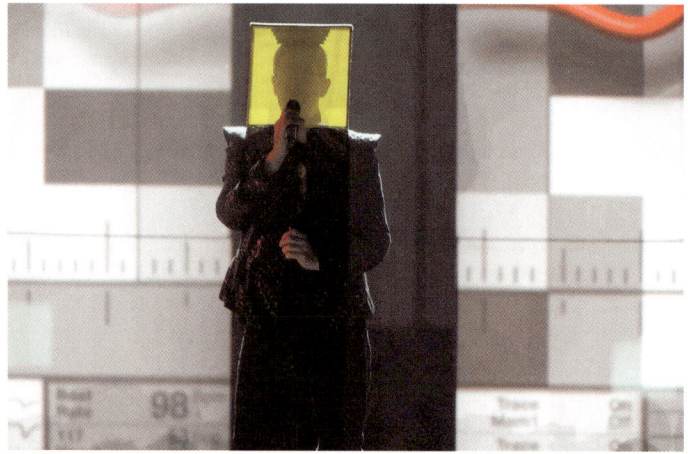

It's my instinct to use costume to veer away from the truth. The starting point of any song is often the personal experience, and then you turn it into something bigger and more brilliant.

Neil Tennant, musician and singer-songwriter

8
Neil Tennant of the Pet Shop Boys wears a Devlin-designed Minotaur head during the Electric Tour (2013), symbolic of the contemporary pull between man and machine, primal desire and made artifice that is inherent to the group's work.

9, 11
The Pet Shop Boys assume more Devlin-devised headgear for their Pandemonium tour (2009).

A similar sense of abstraction, metaphor and tantalizing transhumanism is visible in Devlin's work with the Pet Shop Boys – a duo renowned for their cerebral approach to pop music to the extent that in 2014 they debuted *A Man from the Future*, an electronic/orchestral/choral tribute to the computer-science pioneer Alan Turing. The Pet Shop Boys are Devlin's most significant collaborators to date in terms of crafting full-spectrum design odysseys, from extraordinary headpieces and outfits tantamount to art objects to immersive stage environments. She has directed sets and costumes (many of the latter in tandem with the duo's stylist, Jeffrey Bryant (see page 41), plus a host of talented 'makers') for three key tours: Fundamental (2006), Pandemonium (2009) and Electric (2013). It is largely Devlin, whom Tennant describes as 'someone with the rare ability to make the whole vision happen, creating shows not concerts', cranking up the exuberant visual storytelling that consciously teeters between the daft and the profound.

For Pandemonium, Devlin created a set subsumed in box-like shapes. It extended to the cast, rendering the backing dancers as cuboid-headed Lego people. At one stage, the singer, Neil Tennant, wore a gauze-fronted box on his head, while the keyboard player, Chris Lowe, was encased in a hooded jacket made from mirrored slabs of loosely tessellated triangles. The concept delivered a sense of visual absurdity attuned to the band's preference for music rooted in the transcendental power of storytelling rather than the limited literal truth of outright confession (a methodology applied even to the many songs with a strong autobiographical underlay). Like their album artwork at the time, the concept was influenced by the German artist Gerhard Richter's '4900 Colours' exhibition at London's Serpentine Gallery in 2008, featuring a series of works displaying bright monochrome squares randomly arranged in a grid formation. The anonymous-looking pixel-like squares evoke Richter's desire to evade definition and achieve a sense of boundlessness – a sentiment echoed by Tennant, who describes costuming as protection from the probing vulnerability of raw autobiographical material: 'It's my instinct to use costume to veer away from the truth. The starting point of any song is often the personal experience, and then you turn it into something bigger and more brilliant.'

10
More from the London 2012 Olympics closing ceremony, with the Pet Shop Boys. Devlin describes the band's characters as 'like asexual beings; they allow you to design them as if they are works of art.'

11

For the closing ceremony of the London 2012 Olympics, featuring the Pet Shop Boys, Devlin suggested that the avant-garde British designer Gareth Pugh reimagine the fierce geometric costumes he originally designed for the ballet *Carbon Life* (2011). The duo, and a group of dancers who toured the set pedalling orange bikes, morphed into a cast of Lego-like sculptural beings, with signature 'cone heads', a recurring theme across the Pet Shop Boys' career (originally created by the operatic director and designer David Fielding for their 'Can You Forgive Her?' music video in 1993). Devlin says, 'The characters they create are almost like asexual beings; they allow you to design them as if they are works of art.'

For the Electric tour the following year, one of the most significant design aspects was the Minotaur heads, developed with the prop and costume maker Robert Allsopp, who also created the costuming for Kate Bush's comeback shows Before the Dawn in 2014. The concepts for Electric were circuitry and the division between man and machine – primal desire versus constructed artifice. 'The whole thesis of Pet Shop Boys' music is that the more you abstract away from humanity, the more you synthesize and process everything,' explains Devlin. 'When you do get a pure human voice rising through that manufactured encasement, and it touches you, it becomes that much more significant. The Minotaur was essentially to recognize the divine and the beast,' explains Devlin.

Es Devlin

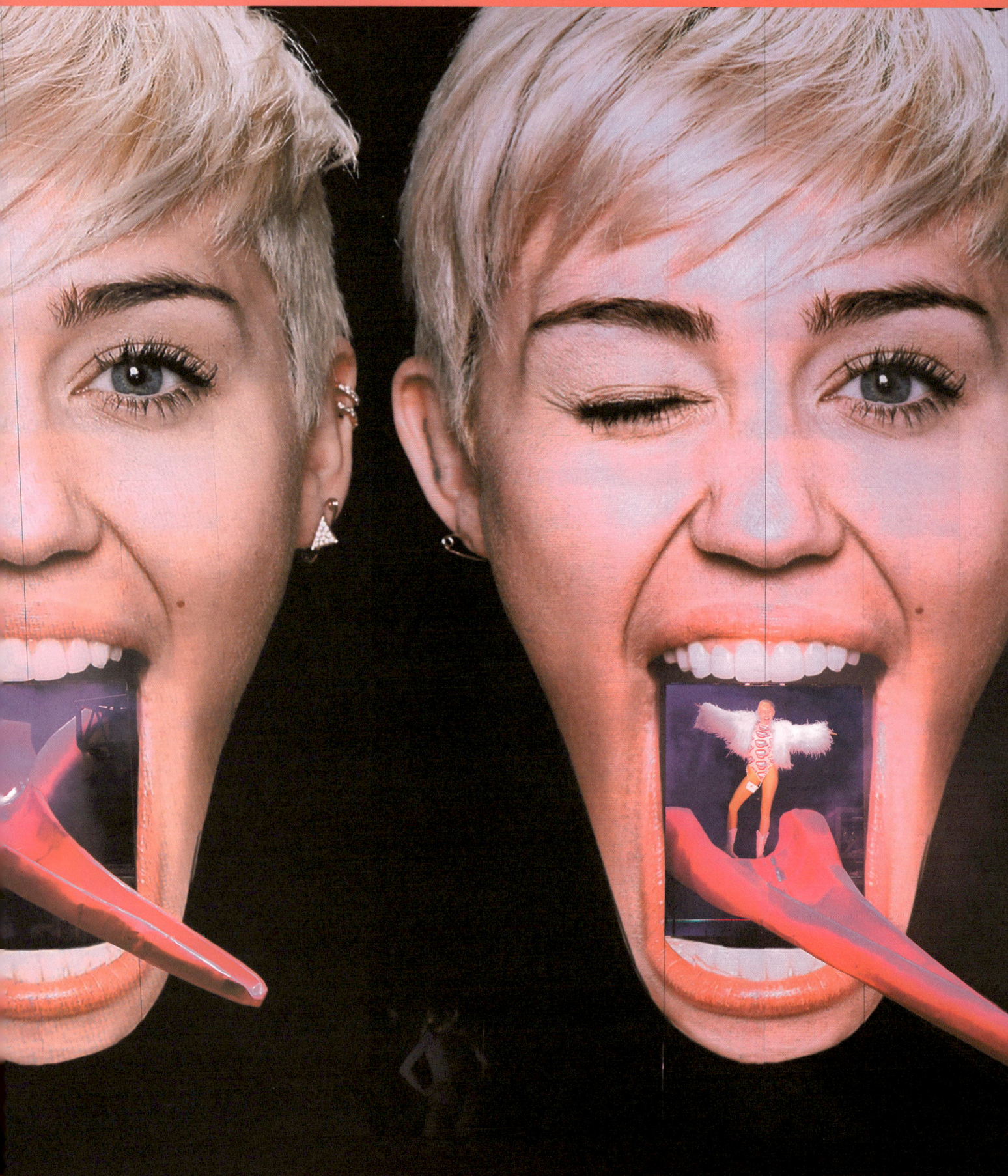

+ Pet Shop Boys, Kanye West, Lily Allen, Miley Cyrus

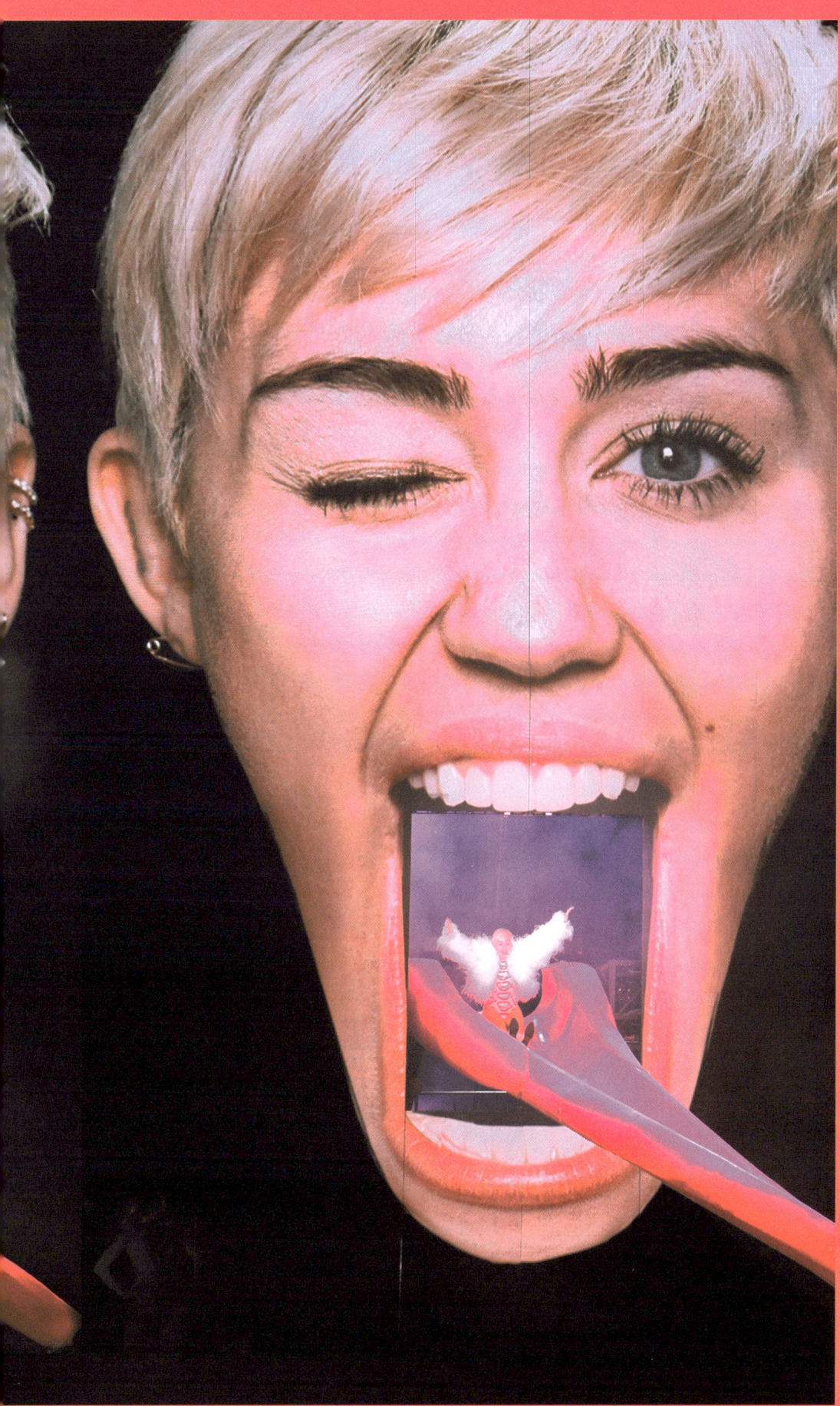

12
Devlin's work with the Disney popstrel-turned-provocateur Miley Cyrus, for her Bangerz tour (2014). The design illustrates Devlin's sentiment that articulating personally understood emotional truths is as critical as commenting on profound but exclusive moments.

13

13
Lily Allen's Sheezus tour (2014),
for which Devlin collaborated with
the acclaimed prop and costume
maker Robert Allsopp.

14
Devlin co-orchestrated the
landmark spring-summer 2015 Louis
Vuitton catwalk show with the
brand's internal creative team,
affirming her role as an elite
crossover artist.

Allsopp was also recruited for Lily Allen's Sheezus tour (2014) to create supersize heads of dogs and pigeons for her backing dancers – a surreal tableau conjuring the banality of daily life (including video content of a suggestively leaking pair of baby milk bottles) that echoed, says Devlin, Allen's preoccupation with the very slippery topic of 'how to try and return to the identity of the pop star once you've become a mother'.

The American pop star Miley Cyrus is another artist for whom Devlin has helped devise a visual identity to support a state of transition: the Bangerz tour (2014), in collaboration with tour director Diane Martel. 'The sound of that entire campaign, her total output, was basically her murdering [Cyrus' Disney character] Hannah Montana,' says Devlin, who created a giant protruding tongue (Cyrus' then trademark gesture) as a symbol of the star's personal crusade to kill off her sanitized child-star persona, just as David Bowie had extinguished Ziggy Stardust at the height of his fame. 'The arc of the show has her sliding down her own notoriety [the tongue] to come in and then exiting by flying out of a door in the sky, seen as a kind of *Truman Show* universe, the hermetically sealed bubble of fame.' For Devlin, Cyrus standing in the gape of the tongue wearing a feather boa (or looking up at a gargantuan model of her dog) while wearing her stripy chaps against a backdrop of striped video projections was 'poetry in motion', suggesting that defining moments in pop culture need not always be based in profundity. They can also be found in articulating more common, universally understood personal truths: 'To call it a moment in history is too grand, but it's certainly a moment where there's a focus – people's gaze is on this person, and you're trying to make the various elements converge to say something that is honest about the moment and what's happened to this particular human in the present cultural context.'

It is no coincidence that Devlin, a self-confessed mischief-maker who revels in humour and irreverence, is drawn to bold, often controversial characters. Attitudinally, she describes both Cyrus and West as twenty-first-century punks, owing to their abject disregard for convention, established hierarchy and (counterintuitively, considering their line of work) popularity – something that is reflected in their sartorial choices. With Cyrus, much of the over-the-top, cartoonishly inflammatory staging for Bangerz invoked Martel, stylist Lisa Ratnic and Cyrus' joint penchant for ratchet fashion – a ghetto-trash style consciously pushing against the barriers of tastefulness, perfectly in sync with Cyrus' hedonistic bid to annihilate her pristine past. With West, the sense of anarchy is based on his certainty of personal identity. Devlin recalls a conversation discussing his appearance at the star-studded annual Met Ball in New York in 2013, for which the theme was Punk: Chaos to Couture: 'I was sketching ideas with Virgil Abloh [West's creative director], working with torn prints of the *Watch the Throne* artwork, and it was getting a bit pastiche. Kanye took one look and said, "I'm KANYE WEST. I AM punk: I can't be nothing BUT punk. Getting out your safety pins and tearing your posters is nice, but it's retro chic, it ain't punk. These guys who truly have no fear, that's punk."'

To call it a moment in history is too grand, but it's certainly a moment where there's a focus - people's gaze is on this person, and you're trying to make the various elements converge to say something that is honest about the moment and what's happened to this particular human in the present cultural context.

Es Devlin

Devlin describes the creative process between herself and many of the artists she works with as one of constant osmosis in which ideas flow both ways, observing that artists can become conduits of vast currents of energy that pass between them and their audience – up to 80,000 fans per night during a stadium tour. Re-framing and re-energizing Devlin's gestures, instincts and knowledge, both learned traditionally and acquired informally, the process is as appealing to brands as it is to artists. In 2013 it led to a collaboration with the luxury French megabrand Louis Vuitton, a business whose bid to remain commercially dominant is hugely underscored by its assumed guise as a patron of the arts. For its spring–summer 2015 show, staged in Paris in its new Louis Vuitton Foundation – a gleaming multi-purpose arts building designed by Frank Gehry – Devlin collaborated with Faye McLeod and Ansel Thompson [Louis Vuitton's visual creative director and senior designer, respectively]. A retro-futuristic, tech-enhanced landscape of orbiting, holographic images expressed the creative director Nicolas Ghesquière's dual infatuation with 1970s-style muses and cutting-edge innovation. As the venue morphed into a planetarium, a coterie of slowly rotating, moon-like faces recited lines, in perfect unison, lifted and adapted from David Lynch's foreboding sci-fi epic *Dune* (1984). The eerie overall effect suggested memories from the future, or projections from an unconfirmed past, and – as with all Devlin's projects – communicated a multi-tiered melange of people, place and identity. 'Ultimately I try and find a truth in anything I do, while pushing for originality. If what you're doing isn't moving it on in some way, then why are you doing it?'

14

1

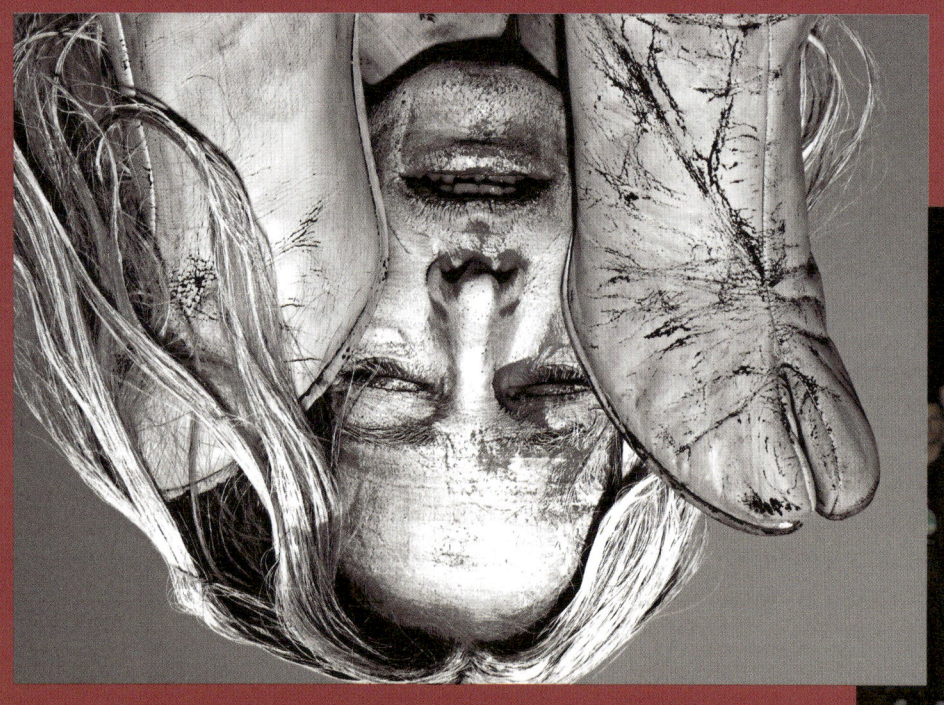

2

3

In the Wild West of the social-media-saturated era, making, consuming and distributing visual imagery has become a landscape in which many of the old rules concerning taste, appropriation and even originality no longer apply. Leading a new generation of pop-culture creatives bent on embracing that shift is Franc Fernandez - a self-taught fashion designer, artist, art director and stylist whose work has bolstered the identities of musicians including Lady Gaga, Scissor Sisters, Sam Sparro, Fischerspooner, Kelela and Katy Perry.

Franc Fernandez

+

Lady Gaga, Scissor Sisters, Sam Sparro, Fischerspooner, Kelela, Vic Mensa

1-3
Life according to Fernandez: the experimental video treatment for Sam Sparro's `Pink Cloud' (2010), styled and directed by Fernandez; an archive-reinventing advertorial for the subversive fashion house Maison Martin Margiela in *Blend* magazine in 2011, based on the premise of disruptive outsiders; and Lady Gaga in Fernandez's infamous, industry-baiting `Meat Dress' (2010).

To collaborate with Fernandez is undoubtedly to harness a brave new world of near-feral visual communication, but while a constant stream of references pulled from just about anywhere (including Instagram and Tumblr) are his creative bread and butter, some robust cultural baselines are also essential to his perspective. First is his Argentinian heritage (Fernandez's family moved to Sylmar, a tough district on the periphery of greater Los Angeles, when he was 8 years old), which he suggests has nurtured a substantial in-built appreciation of style that shows obvious effort. 'I think that in Latin cultures it's far more important that you present yourself with care. You don't go lazy, ever. Especially when you're older, when fashion becomes a compensation for youth!'

4-5
A Fernandez-designed suit worn by the hip-hop artist Vic Mensa to the 2015 MTV Video Music Awards: a political statement on the hugely contentious topic of police brutality and oppression in the United States.

Second is that transnational childhood leap – a shift in environment that has enabled Fernandez to observe cultural nuances as the eternal insider–outsider; a limbo-land of alien creative curiosity with usefully mixed perimeters. 'I was the kid that looked white but was Latino, so I wasn't white enough for the white kids, and the Latino kids were mainly Mexican, so an Argentine kid wasn't Latino enough for them,' recalls Fernandez. It is no coincidence that his key influences include the progressive American hip-hop group Outkast, in particular a fixation on its theatrical frontman Andre 3000, and also the stylist Andrea Lieberman (see page 92), who was instrumental in transforming Gwen Stefani from frontwoman of the Californian rock group No Doubt into a neo-skater hip-hop pop icon. 'With Outkast, part of the fascination relates to the fact that I've been a huge fan of hip-hop all my life, but they were also the first group that made me feel like I didn't have to be a black kid like them to enjoy them. They were innately eccentric in a way that was cool – that was the way to connect, to be inclusive. Andre 3000 often wasn't the macho stereotype; on occasions he'd be wearing pink bell-bottoms or golfers' plus fours.'

I don't like the obvious symbols of provocation - I'll never use skulls or crosses or guns; something like the meat dress is a far more interesting point of contention.

Franc Fernandez

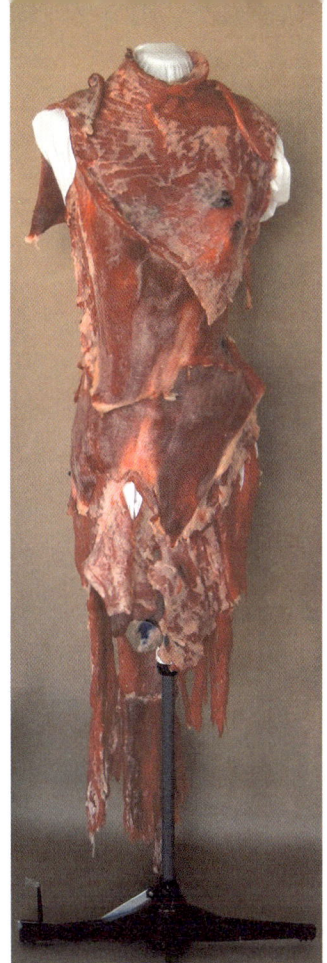

Fernandez's teenage years cultivated his DIY skills, particularly making hats, and his predilection for alternative positioning: 'I deliberately picked something that wasn't competitive – at the time I was the only milliner that would make non-functioning fashion hats in LA.' But it was the omnipresent accomplice of social media that dispatched the first bite of the pop-music cherry, via a formidable series of debut commissions after Fernandez struck up a conversation with Lady Gaga's then creative director Nicola Formichetti (see page 70) on the social network Myspace. Formichetti borrowed a selection of geometric hats made from balsa wood for the Japanese edition of Vogue Hommes and other millinery that 'looked as though it had been stretched by the wind – quite Hussein Chalayan-esque' for performances. Next, Fernandez was asked to design a full jewellery ensemble for the (award-winning) video of Gaga's single 'Bad Romance' (2009) – the track that ensured her trajectory to superstardom. Loosely briefed to make something in the vein of an 'Ibiza gay pride float parade', Fernandez custom-created a flexible, torso-skimming latticework of white crystal and diamond costume jewellery with matching mask/crown, using materials that he 'literally got from a downtown faux-jeweller and wired together'.

However, it was the next commission that catapulted him into the heart of the media's lion's den: the infamous meat dress (painstakingly crafted from real slices of meat) Gaga wore to the MTV Video Music Awards (VMAs) in Los Angeles in 2010. Surreal, subversive and typically Gaga, it was a massive media sensation whose intentions divided commentators en masse: an artistic statement with a feminist agenda (women as meat) or an anti-fashion dig at the now sensation-hungry (style over content) fashion and music industry themselves? The only certainty is that it has inaccurately cast Fernandez as a sartorial enfant terrible hellbent purely on mass provocation. While he is undoubtedly comfortable with fuelling controversy ('although I don't like the obvious symbols of provocation – I'll never use skulls or crosses or guns; something like the meat dress is a far more interesting point of contention'), the dress was also a more simplistic symbol of his preference for making the seemingly impossible a physical reality; having developed the original request for a meat purse into a full-blown dress, Fernandez – resourceful as ever – drafted in the family butcher to bring it to life.

Irrespective of the root of the provocation, there is always substance behind the style. Countering the political apathy of which his generation is so frequently accused, Fernandez's instinct for using pop culture to telegraph social concerns fast, and far, was affirmed by his collaboration with the American hip-hop artist Vic Mensa, via the MTV VMAs in 2015. Mensa wore a Fernandez-designed suit with portraits of victims of police brutality or oppression, adding fuel to a considerable fire then burning up the US media.

6
Lady Gaga's meat dress of 2010 – a work so provocative that cultural commentators were divided as to whether it was part of a feminist agenda or a dig at the sensation-desperate media itself.

7
A still from Gaga's award-winning 'Bad Romance' music video (2009), for which Fernandez created the artist's body-skimming jewellery, after meeting creative director Nicola Formichetti via Myspace.

While the static image is clearly very important, I do design for experience. I don't mind that it then disintegrates. It's about creating the thing that you only remember.

Franc Fernandez

+ Lady Gaga, Scissor Sisters, Sam Sparro, Fischerspooner, Kelela, Vic Mensa

Making garments with a legacy beyond their initial wearing also extends to Fernandez's penchant for creating work that must be seen to be appreciated – indicative that a life lived increasingly through screens has conversely augmented a desire for experiences that cannot be replicated or distilled purely into a visual soundbite. He embraces every idea, skill or concept on the digital *and* physical spectrum with the same energy ('I'm agile digitally but I'm also badass at hand sewing'). Not atypically, at the time of our meeting Fernandez was immersed in creating a suit to be set on fire mid-performance. 'While the static image is clearly very important, I do design for experience. I don't mind that it then disintegrates. It's about creating the thing that you only remember – instances where you can take as many pictures of the show [as you like] but it's ultimately about how you feel.'

8
Fernandez's artwork for Kelela's single 'The High' (2014), featuring an experimental projection-mapping technique.

9,10
The Scissor Sisters (9) performing in Fernandez-designed latex suits inspired by Tony Scott's postmodernist vampire movie *The Hunger* (1983; 10).

Falling in love with someone in that environment - half of it is visual.

Franc Fernandez

Such transitory show work has included a raft of stage wear for the American glam-rock/disco group Scissor Sisters, including an unforgettable masculinized version of a burlesque outfit for frontman Jake Shears – a latex suit with panels for his limbs and backside that could be systematically stripped off. Fernandez describes the suit as being 'so consciously clichéd as to be cool'. He also devised a series of vampiric 'dark, elegant and very sexy' dresses for the group's frontwoman, Ana Matronic, inspired by the cult horror film *The Hunger* (1983) starring David Bowie and Catherine Deneuve. Visuals that are less overtly provocative (but have no less impact) have come with the creative direction for a new collaborator, the American Ethiopian R&B/grime singer-songwriter Kelela. For her first headline gigs in Los Angeles and New York in 2014, Fernandez devised an opening visual treatment (echoed on the artwork for her single 'The High') in which she stands alone onstage, on a white box, wearing all white, as circular pools of abstract imagery including marble and rings of fire are projected over her. Reminiscent of the way the French creative Jean-Paul Goude (see page 80) would preface Grace Jones' live shows with extraordinarily atmospheric scene-setting, the ephemeral treatment aims, according to Fernandez, to prime the audience for seduction: 'Falling in love with someone in that environment – half of it is visual.'

9

10

065

Franc Fernandez

That sense of augmenting visual impact through shifting vistas is also channelled in the video treatment Fernandez devised for the Australian synth-pop/nu-disco artist Sam Sparro's single 'Pink Cloud' (2010) – an amalgamation of scenes showing Sparro undergoing various 'monster make-up tests' reminiscent of the Blitz club era's extreme costuming (see pages 32 and 42). But Kelela's refusal to echo or borrow directly from any other tribe or era of performance (exactly the reason, she says, she is working with Fernandez) presents a more unusual story. To date, the style that the pair is developing together is a deliberate mix of sometimes unlikely stylistic references, best described as a refined version of streetwear (the independent unisex label Phlemuns is a key early collaborator). According to Kelela, it is all part of a new vision of multiplicity that is not generally associated with the standard pop marketing machine, which prefers easy-to-categorize aesthetics – especially for women. Kelela says, 'I'm interested in creating things that are a bit problematic, so that you can't just skip on over them.' She cites Missy Elliott's video for 'The Rain (Supa Dupa Fly)' (1997), in which Elliott is dressed in a bin-bag suit, as the ultimate subversion. 'I like the idea of being covered up one day, then in a translucent mesh dress the next. I think we need a bit more of that kind of disruptive vision now, especially with female artists, and I think that's coming through Franc.'

The concept of constructing an eclectic fashion style that may be identifiable enough to be imitated or recognized in years to come also syncs with Fernandez's over-arching philosophy for developing visual worlds (garments, album art, stage treatments) that are based on references sought, rehashed and reframed from the conveyor-belt feed of social media. According to Fernandez, success depends on engaging naively but sensitively in order to appropriate ideas in a way that transforms them into something original. 'Trawling Tumblr is something that confirms that the inspirations you have are important and valid,' says Fernandez, 'and it's a place where there actually needs to be a certain kind of respectful irreverence. It's important not to keep the same context because then you're just creating a Disneyland – by making something exactly the same, you're essentially feeding an unhealthy nostalgia for the image you saw. Nostalgia holds you down. Respect comes from a transparency about your sources, effectively like asking your friend [if you can] borrow their clothes; there has to be an agreement that you tell people where/who they're from.'

11
The rapper Iggy Azalea in a leather jumpsuit featuring illustrations influenced by one of Fernandez's favourite blogs on chola culture. The image later appeared on the same blog, a sign of the rampant, circular nature of influence in Internet culture.

On occasion that evolution of ideas has included Fernandez's work actually feeding the hungry beast of social media from which it came – not perpetuating the same idea but providing a freshly twisted form of inspiration. The most vivid example is a fitted leather two-piece chola playsuit embellished with illustrations that he made for the Australian rapper Iggy Azalea. Inspired by one of his favourite blogs full of Los Angeles chola references, he refiltered the concept via his own mood board and was then, after Azalea's performance, able to see images of her onstage back on the same blog. The same is true of Björk's Instagram image of Kelela onstage mid-projection-mapping visual treatment: the original idea was in part actually inspired by the avant-garde Icelandic pop star's own visual concepts. When the inspiration becomes the inspired, 'it's the biggest possible thank you,' says Fernandez.

12
Stills of Fernandez's extreme 'monster make-up' treatment for Sam Sparro's 'Pink Cloud' music video (2010), a concept that borrowed from the visual feast of London's Blitz club era.

13
A screen grab from Fernandez's own Tumblr offers a rich glimpse into his frenetic world of disparate influences and inspirations.

14
The chola blog Fernandez referenced for his project with Azalea.

+ Lady Gaga, Scissor Sisters, Sam Sparro, Fischerspooner, Kelela, Vic Mensa

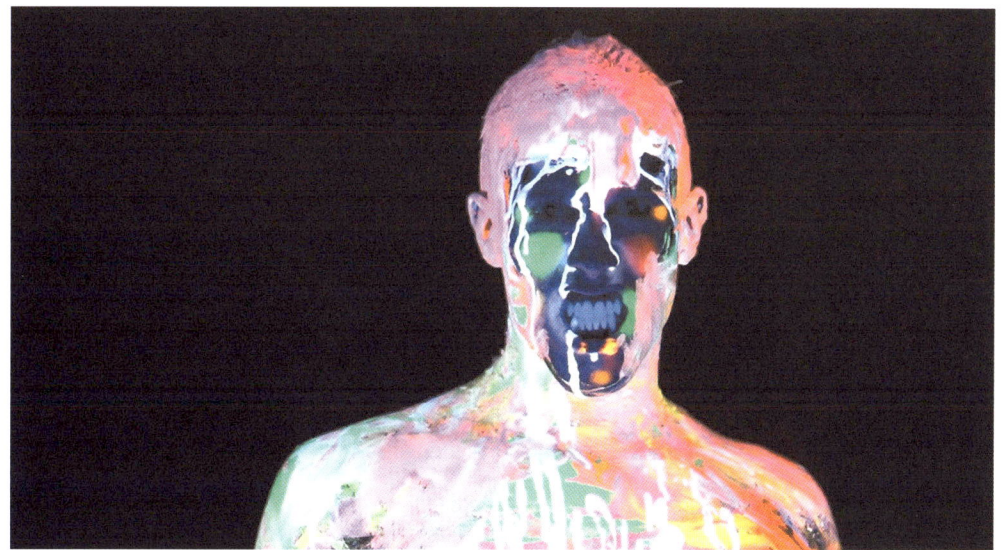

12

13

14

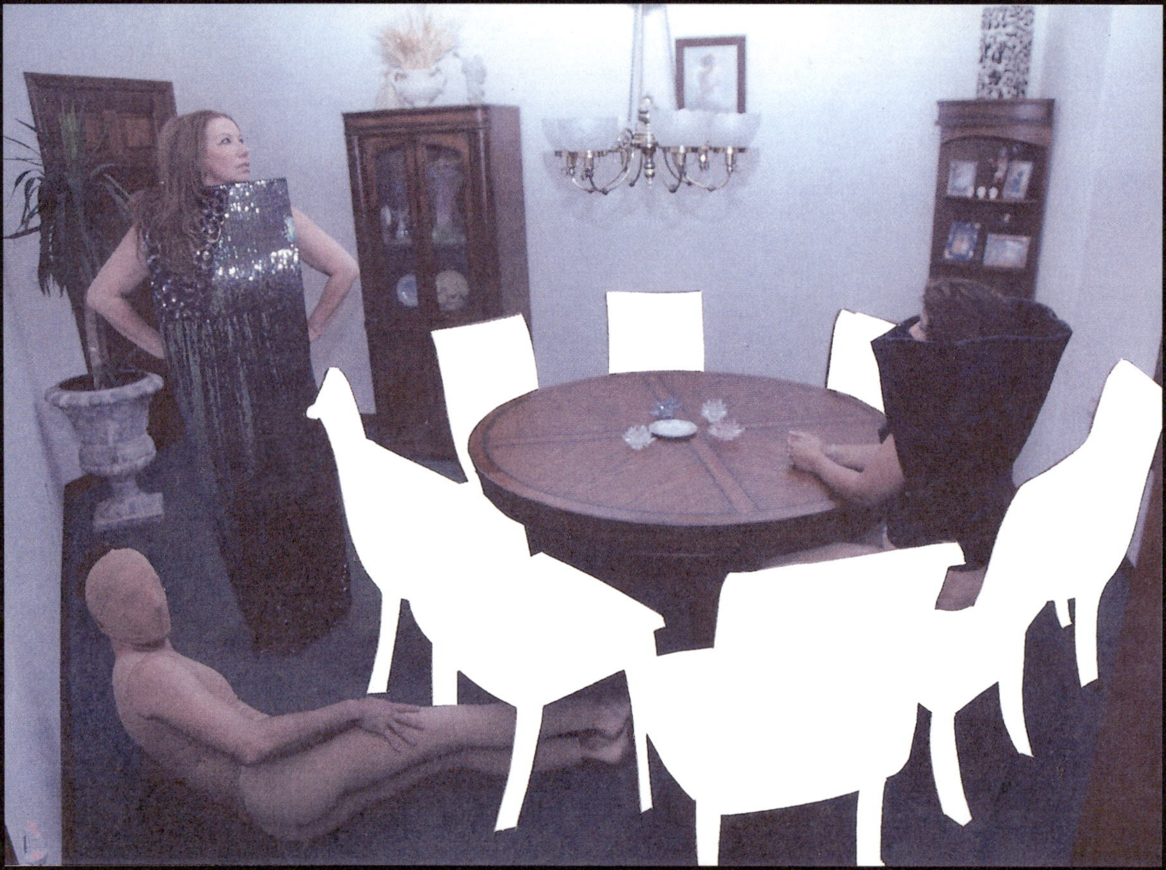

Franc Fernandez

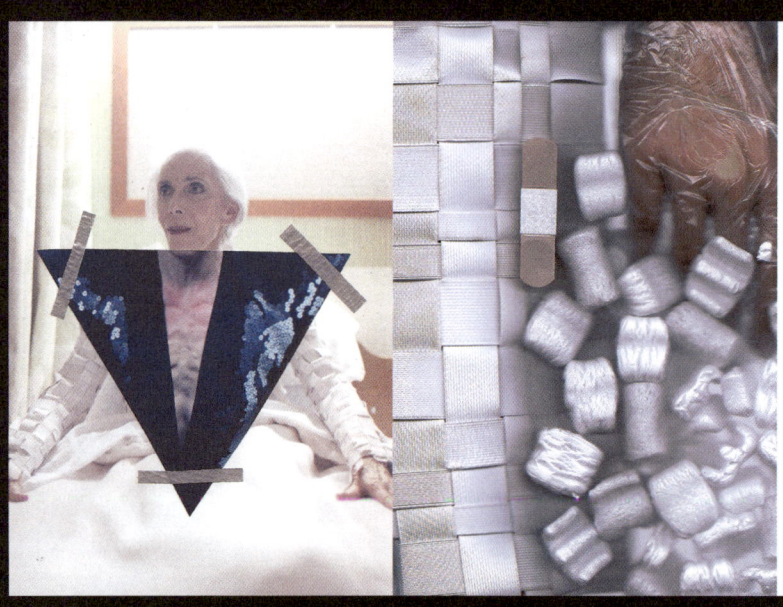

+ Lady Gaga, Scissor Sisters, Sam Sparro, Fischerspooner, Kelela, Vic Mensa

16

Although he is recognized in fashion circles as a committed but approachable dissenter, Fernandez is unlikely to be a creative who later transfers his thinking into a biannual collection. Kelela describes him as the antithesis to her previously difficult fashion experiences: 'I've been turned off by the culture of fashion that I've always perceived as equating being successful with being mean. Franc is familiar with the establishment but also doesn't care about it, which gives the biggest possibilities of all.' Special projects and partnerships with the promise of rolling evolution are far more his speed, and have unsurprisingly made him a magnet for more established creatives similarly allied to championing a disruptive 'outsider' artistic manifesto. One such brand is the famously iconoclastic design house Maison Martin Margiela, which commissioned Fernandez and the photographer/filmmaker Luke Gilford to devise a special advertorial reinterpreting the brand's archive pieces – the perfect platform for Fernandez's insider–outsider fashion stance. The duo cast non-professional models who were mostly friends or fellow creatives whom they found inspiring, including two transgender artists, to deliver a left-field, youth-orientated take on an unconventional but nevertheless global brand. 'I love brands like Margiela because this is an established house that, for the most part, is saying "Fuck you" to fashion,' says Fernandez. 'When everyone else wasn't doing power dressing they were making shoulders and then when everyone started to return to shoulders because of them, they were making shoulders tiny. It's this idea of not looking at other people, ignoring the trend.'

In the past decade, the ability to access visual information has created a spectrum and appetite for image that has historically never existed before. Audiences desire challenging and strange ideas. Notions of beauty have collapsed and aesthetic boundaries have been obliterated. Franc has been a part of defining this new perspective on popular image-making.

Casey Spooner, musician and performance artist

Such is Fernandez's skill at corralling a new attitude towards visual culture that the music-industry creative director Willo Perron engaged him to develop art-direction concepts for Katy Perry's album *Prism* (2013); Casey Spooner – one half of the headline duo within New York electro-pop performance group Fischerspooner – also commissioned Fernandez, to restyle archived stage wear for the group's book *New Truth* (2014). Spooner views Fernandez as a kindred spirit in terms of his willingness to embrace art and pop culture in both its highest and lowest forms without prejudice: 'We share a similar optimism that pop culture can be intelligent and transformative; that something populist can lead and not follow; that great ideas need not be mired in modernist notions of the underground or the avant-garde,' he says. 'In the past decade, the ability to access visual information has created a spectrum and appetite for image that have historically never existed before. Audiences desire challenging and strange ideas. Notions of beauty have collapsed and aesthetic boundaries have been obliterated. Franc has been a part of defining this new perspective on popular image-making.'

15
Fernandez's collaborative project with the photographer/filmmaker Luke Gilford for Maison Martin Margiela featured a host of unorthodox `outsider' models as alternative modern muses.

16
New Truth (2014), a retrospective by the art/pop/performance collective Fischerspooner. It featured some of the group's key performance ephemera archived and restyled by Fernandez, who similarly designs for fleeting moments of performance as much as final products.

Nicola Formichetti

+

Lady Gaga, Brooke Candy,
Color Code

Few fashion professionals genuinely merit the title 'creative director' - at its truest a kaleidoscopic mantle of styling, design, image-making and identity curation - as much as Nicola Formichetti, the original chief creative accomplice to the superstar Lady Gaga, and co-author of the identities of Brooke Candy and Color Code. His multicultural, DIY approach to splicing high fashion, street style, art and pop music has made him arguably the most significant visual communicator of the digital generation.

1
Paper magazine, September 2014, featuring Formichetti's formidable creative conspirator, the rap provocateur Brooke Candy. Photographed by Richard Burbridge.

2
Lady Gaga, with whom Formichetti first migrated from fashion to pop in full, for *i-D* magazine (spring 2011). Photographed by Mariano Vivanco.

3
Color Code, the all-female J-pop group uniting Formichetti's unique 'multicultural mash-up of cute meets fucked-up' in the ultimate pop package.

With an outlook rooted in defiance but bound by inclusivity, the Japanese Italian Formichetti is now steering the taboo-teasing rapper Brooke Candy to places far beyond the genre's macho borders, while also moulding J-pop's newest (alternative) girl band, Color Code. If it looks as though he is making it up as he goes along, he is – to a degree. But while formulae do not apply, four factors are generally always in orbit: a well-honed youth-culture antenna that instinctively keeps him ahead of any curve (his studio is largely staffed by under-30s); early adoption of new media and social communications; a belief in the power of creative communities; and a healthy irreverence for the snobbery of an industry that is wont to sacrifice pioneering creativity on the altar of perceived good taste.

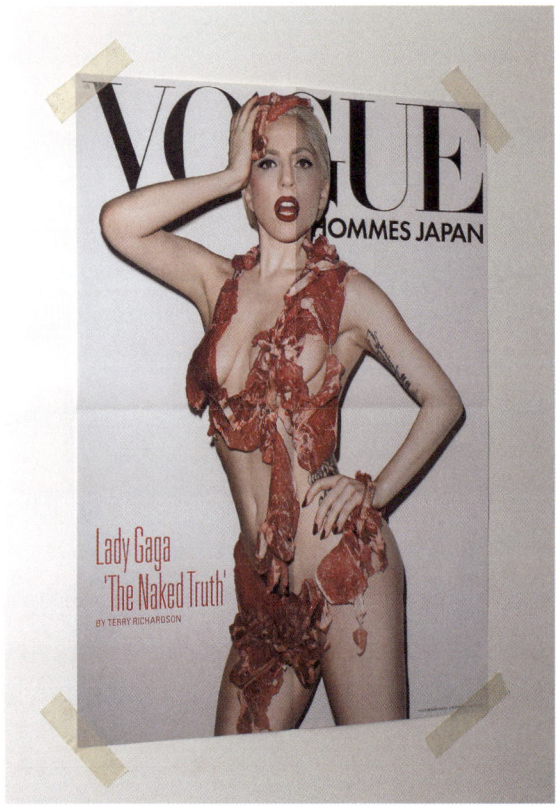

4

5

When Formichetti – a former London club kid who cut his teeth as fashion director of British style bible *Dazed & Confused* magazine – first met Lady Gaga, she was a long way from mega-stardom. As much performance artist as singer-songwriter, Gaga bore echoes of Formichetti's first pop crushes (Madonna, Deee-Lite's Lady Miss Kier and the inhabitants of George Michael's 'Too Funky' video of 1992 – 'people that came in a package with a whole world I could dive into', says Formichetti). She was an irresistible embodiment of his wildest dreams: a talented, intelligent muse-in-waiting capable of rendering his most daring fashion fantasies in flesh and blood, way beyond the printed page he was then mostly dealing with. 'She looked like some of my clubbing friends with this really raw aesthetic, but she wasn't rock or techno or pop. All these things influenced her and that was very important to me. I saw a potential in her that I thought could go to the next level, which wasn't about just making money or being super-famous,' recalls Formichetti. 'The whole Warholian thing she was doing at the time, saying she wanted to be famous', was, he says, less about stardom in the obvious sense and more an echo of Warhol's meddling with the modern meaning of celebrity – the crux of Formichetti and Gaga's shared creative odyssey being to contest the traditional hierarchies of art and pop culture, and especially of fashion.

6

> I never agreed with [high fashion] because it's largely based on fear. It's a scare tactic. They [the industry] scare people with really skinny girls or presenting something unattainable, to drive desire ... which means it can be very one-dimensional. I always felt like I was a fashion punk. I always wanted to take it somewhere else.
>
> Nicola Formichetti

4
Lady Gaga in the original (pre-dress) meat bikini, photographed by Terry Richardson for *Vogue Hommes Japan*, September 2010.

5
Demonstrative of her and Formichetti's appetite for ravaging industry rules, Gaga appears as her male alter ego Jo Calderone in *Vogue Hommes Japan* (autumn-winter 2011), photographed by Nick Knight.

6
Lady Gaga at the 2011 Grammy Awards wearing a surreal, latex-like costume by Hussein Chalayan.

Their first meeting and collaboration was a shoot for *V* magazine in 2009. Gaga, then unknown, arrived already dressed and in full hair and make-up – an enormous editorial faux pas. Formichetti was bewitched. Subsequent projects came thick and fast; they swiftly embarked on exploding the traditional rules of high fashion that even Formichetti, at the time immersed in the creatively daring but cliquey worlds of *Dazed & Confused*, *Vogue Hommes Japan* and *V*, had become attuned to. 'I never agreed with that system because it's largely based on fear. It's a scare tactic. They [the industry] scare people with really skinny girls or presenting something unattainable, to drive desire. It's very mean, very bitchy. And it works in fashion, which means it can be very one-dimensional. I always felt like I was a fashion punk. I always wanted to take it somewhere else.'

Seminal, mischievously boundary-pushing editorial imagery includes the *Vogue Hommes Japan* September 2010 cover shot by Terry Richardson, in which Gaga wears a meat bikini (a concept infamously reprised later the same month when she wore a dress made by Franc Fernandez from raw beef to the 2010 MTV Video Music Awards; see page 61); the *Vogue Hommes Japan* 'True Believer' cover shot by Nick Knight (double cover with the one above) in which she appears as fictional male alter ego Jo Calderone; and the March 2011 cover of *i-D* magazine, photographed by Mariano Vivanco, in which dermal implants, severely geometric hair, bleached eyebrows and a rubberized black Mugler coat summon an unnervingly sophisticated vampiric entity. Videos – in particular 'Alejandro' (2009) directed by Steven Klein, 'Born this Way' (2011) by Nick Knight and 'Bad Romance' (2009) by Francis Lawrence – unfurled a brand-new world around Formichetti of theatre, set design and dance. Their resonance beyond the rarefied world of fashion had him hooked: 'For me they're like pieces of art, because you can talk about those videos with anyone now.' Awards ceremonies, too, became key fodder for fashion-fuelled artistry too extreme to be contained in traditional formats. When she performed 'Born this Way' at the 2011 Grammys in LA, she arrived onstage in an egg-like capsule (carried by servants) designed by the British/Turkish Cypriot designer Hussein Chalayan. Gaga emerged in a gold bandeau top and long skirt made of a material reminiscent of surgical latex, with a high blonde ponytail and black-and-gold make-up. The message was clear: Welcome to the Cult of Gaga.

Another example proving the collaborators' social-media pop prowess is when Formichetti showed his debut collection as creative director of luxury Parisian fashion house Thierry Mugler (a post he held from 2011 to 2013). Gaga served as musical director for the show, which she used as a platform to preview her new music. Their vast body of fans were obliged to access the brand's Facebook page in order to view the live web-stream, instantly modernizing Mugler. Now renowned for spinning superior social-media buzz, Formichetti also uses social platforms (predominantly Instagram and Tumblr) as his core playgrounds for hunting inspiration and recruiting new talent, including his other major Mugler muse – the fully tattooed Rico Genest, aka Zombie Boy. In Formichetti's first project in 2013 as the inaugural artistic director for the Italian fashion brand Diesel, he created Reboot, an initiative that invited consumers to become creators by uploading photos, artwork and videos as visual responses to his briefs. With Formichetti as ringleader, the concept – in acknowledging the millennial appetite for entrepreneurialism (and self-promotion) – mobilized a brand-new legion of fans.

7

Six months later people were begging me, paying me to give her stuff to wear. Now it's industry standard to have a musician or performer associated with your label.

Nicola Formichetti

8

7,8
The videos for `Alejandro'
(2009; dir. Steven Klein), which
introduced Formichetti to the
worlds of theatre design and dance,
and `Bad Romance' (2009; dir.
Francis Lawrence).

9
Lady Gaga performed in and served as
musical director of Formichetti's
first catwalk show as artistic
director of the French fashion
house Thierry Mugler in 2011.

Initially almost every designer refused to collaborate with Gaga and Formichetti, on any level. 'Six months later people were begging me, paying me to give her stuff to wear. Now it's industry standard to have a musician or performer associated with your label,' recalls Formichetti. Alexander McQueen and Miuccia Prada, whom Formichetti describes as 'real risk-takers', were the anomalies; that is why the early videos, such as 'Bad Romance', are so invested with McQueen's exquisite alien-esque beauty, including key looks from his seminal reptilian-oceanic spring–summer 2010 'Plato Atlantis' show. Other industry creatives, too, were as unwilling to play ball – visionaries such as the photographers Nick Knight, Steven Klein and Inez & Vinoodh were the notable exceptions.

Gaga's major trump card was a game-changing embrace of social media (in 2012 she became the first pop star to reach 20 million Twitter followers) – a supremely democratizing spanner in high fashion's elitist works and a massive influence on Formichetti's own methodology. 'I saw her really talking to people, her fans, which I thought was so beautiful, so genuine,' he says. 'At the time for a big pop star to be talking to a kid online was unheard of; for me it was so refreshing.' His early blog posts detailed exactly what Gaga was wearing while making any kind of public appearance. 'Every time she went out we put together an outfit because that was as important to us as walking the red carpet,' Formichetti says. 'At one point we were doing several outfit changes per day.' The posts were a clear predecessor of browse-to-buy blogs – a now ubiquitous e-commerce format that has turned the online diaries of amateur fashion enthusiasts into serious advertising/selling space.

Nicola Formichetti

10
The seminal music video for Brooke Candy's single 'Opulence' – a concept that caused an irreversible shift in Candy's image – was directed by Steven Klein.

11
Look-book images from the autumn-winter 2015 Nicopanda collection bear out Formichetti's flair for hybridizing new-media-influenced visual references, cultural cues and even gender.

> The idea was to make her [Brooke Candy] almost so ugly that she wasn't even recognizable, in order to de-sexualize her and show the talent first.
>
> Nicola Formichetti

Formichetti's first major music project post-Gaga is Brooke Candy, his muse at Diesel who appears in collection presentations and ad campaigns – confirming that his amplified celebrity has in no way diluted his appetite for rebels and dissenters eyeing up a new world order. Los Angeles-born Candy, a rougher diamond with even bigger prejudices than Gaga to obliterate, presents a fresh challenge. Formerly a stripper, later specializing in hardcore rap imagery and lyrics (songs include 'I Wanna Fuck Right Now' and 'Don't Touch my Hair Hoe'), she is the fearless, hyper-sexualized cyberpunk to Gaga's asexual otherworldly vixen – a significantly harder sell. But her image in 2014 bears witness to a transitional period; where she was mostly recycling well-worn rap stereotypes in a bid to overturn the genre's massively misogynist tendencies, eventually she will shake off the hard-ass bling-and-bikini persona almost completely. Playing with gender is the next big shift – a metamorphosis the duo began with the video for 'Opulence' (2014), directed by Steven Klein. It is arguably one of the most spectacular and pleasingly disquieting video treatments of the last decade. The stripper shoes, cyber-goth cornrows and *Barbarella* body-con have morphed into a sci-fi-geisha vision of greased-back bleached-blonde *Gatsby* hair, gold grilles and an ornate skull-like face mask dripping with gemstones that conjures up the late great performance artist Leigh Bowery and, of course, Alexander McQueen.

11

12

12
Disrupting the mainstream: Brooke Candy in an advert for Diesel, for which Formichetti is the global artistic director. Photographed by Inez & Vinoodh.

> Maybe it's because I feel a bit like a misfit myself. I come from two different cultures and when I was young I always felt alone, but at the same time it's necessarily made me pretty good at [fitting in]. From the outside I may be very professional, but inside I've always had this kind of rage or feeling that I was different.
>
> Nicola Formichetti

Formichetti describes Candy's recalibration as a rebirth for an artist who, like Gaga, simply fascinated him at first (he initially spotted her in the Canadian electro-pop artist Grimes' video for the track 'Genesis'), far from being a commercial proposition. 'Opulence' was an experimental exercise in resetting an identity without losing the fierce visceral attraction that first sparked his attention: 'The idea was to make her almost so ugly that she wasn't even recognizable, in order to de-sexualize her and show the talent first, because the songs and the rapping are so beautiful. If you wear a leather bikini with high heels and blonde hair – it's essentially what Madonna created – it already exists. Therefore, while it's impossible to go wrong [with it] because it's so mainstream now, at the same time I feel a little uncomfortable with it. I want to just twist that, and in a way the "Opulence" video was the start of that journey.'

As always, Formichetti's role is both conduit and accomplice, a remit Candy acknowledges in describing Formichetti as 'an idol and mentor'. She credits his work with Gaga as the crux of their relationship: 'I used to obsess over what he was doing with her because I come from a punk rock and hardcore rap, tough and intense musical background, and through the visual imagery he carefully cultivated for her, I was drawn into her world and interested in why she existed. For me that's a near-impossible feat. I'm not impressed by pop stars and their gimmicks.' Formichetti's lesser-known skill as a musician (he is a classically trained pianist) has further cemented their bond. Candy says, 'Nicola is one of the only people who has access to the demo reel for my album because he also possesses insane musical gifts. He has a bit of a sixth sense for understanding the formula needed to make an amazing song that penetrates mass culture, and he isn't afraid to let me know.'

+ Lady Gaga, Brooke Candy, Color Code

It is a gift that has undoubtedly fuelled his divination of Color Code – the new Japanese girl band he is managing both creatively and musically – which presents another departure into uncharted territory. The project is rich with personal and professional significance: for the first time, he is pushing fully into his Japanese heritage by working with Japanese artists for, at least initially, the Asian market. While the trio was cast via an open *X Factor*-style competition, Formichetti's decision to override the standard 'karaoke-voice, model-looks' formula in favour of promoting their real singing and dancing talent is already nurturing an identity that cuts far beyond the cosmetic. Their first video, 'I Like Dat' (2014), is knowingly rich in the infectiously high-energy, Lolita-like world of regular J-pop, but bolstered with the tougher, street-smart edge true to both Gaga and Candy as well as the 'Harajuku-Harlem' styling of Formichetti's own fashion label, Nicopanda. Stretching from fluoro-talons and studded latex skull caps to dresses constructed from cuddly toys with the sci-fi asymmetry of Sadie Williams' gowns, in many ways Nicopanda is the ultimate confluence of the Formichetti manifesto: a multicultural mash-up of cute meets fucked up, or downtown *kawaii*. As he says of his creative process when working with Gaga: 'We always used to say "Fuck fashion" because we love it so much that it's almost unbearable, to the point where we want to destroy it. The idea is that we work so hard towards something – really studying to try and create something and then on the day of the event we turn it upside down. You have to be so confident to do that, and that's what generates the excitement.'

The path between West and East is notoriously slippery to master; as yet, even Japan's biggest J-pop star, Kyary Pamyu Pamyu, has not made the transition. Therefore, while the plan is to start slowly, if anyone can lead the crossover it is likely to be Formichetti, with his capricious cultural eye and form as a trendsetter. But why is he – the ultimate insider–outsider, now acknowledged as a key part of the fashion establishment without having had to absorb its elitist pretensions – so compelled to keep pushing boundaries? Heritage, apparently: 'Maybe it's because I feel a bit like a misfit myself. I come from two different cultures and when I was young I always felt alone, but at the same time it's necessarily made me pretty good at [fitting in]. From the outside I may be very professional, but inside I've always had this kind of rage or feeling that I was different.'

13

13, 14
The artwork and music video for the debut single of Formichetti's J-pop group Color Code, 'I Like Dat' (2014).

14

Jean-Paul Goude

+

Grace Jones

1

2

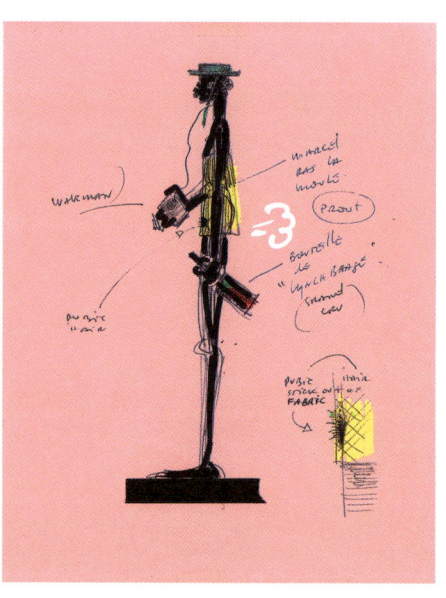

3

4

1
Goude's book *Jungle Fever* (1983), a controversial autobiographical retrospective documenting his obsession with black culture, immortalized his formidable ex-muse, Grace Jones.

2,3
Goude's sketches of Jones; extraordinarily, she epitomized drawings of the daydream.

4
Goude designed the artwork for Jones' single 'My Jamaican Guy' (1982) - a vivid manifestation of his singular vision to create a new breed of artist, and woman.

Perhaps nowhere in the rich historical co-mingling of music and fashion has the notion of 'becoming' been as vividly served up as by the Jamaican pop star Grace Jones. As the world's first new wave pop artist, Jones herself once attested, 'I wasn't born this way. One creates oneself.' But the story of Jones' creation is no solo show, for it was the irrepressible and exacting vision of Jean-Paul Goude - the legendary French art director, filmmaker and Jones' then lover - that drove her unforgettable visual legacy.

An icon in terms of both fashion and music, Jones collaborated with Goude to create performances, album art and music videos that propelled her semi-surreal image into the stratosphere. The pair met in New York in 1977, when Jones, then a model and aspiring singer, walked into his office at *Esquire* magazine. According to Goude, not only was she everything the other glossy models of the Farrah Fawcett-flick era were not, even more bizarrely she was the flesh-and-blood reality of his daydreamed sketches: 'It's a hot summer day and she's wearing a Miyake shirt to mid thigh, no skirt and there's no panties underneath, I swear, and flat shoes so it's almost like she's barefoot. She just has a little hat on the top of her head and, incredibly, things I've done in my own pictures – arm-warmer sleeves on her elbows and knees like colourful bandages. The contrast between the stark simplicity of the Miyake clothes and her wild look was amazing. And she was carrying a big bottle of wine – she was something else.'

5, 7
A deconstructed version of the cover for the album *Island Life* (1985), and the final version. The image (also known as 'The Impossible Arabesque') is central to Goude's mythology thanks to the 'French Correction' design technique: his graphic re-sculpting of the body to visualize physically unobtainable perfection.

6
The artwork for Jones' single 'Slave to the Rhythm' (1985). The video features clips from the pair's television ad for the car brand Citroën.

5

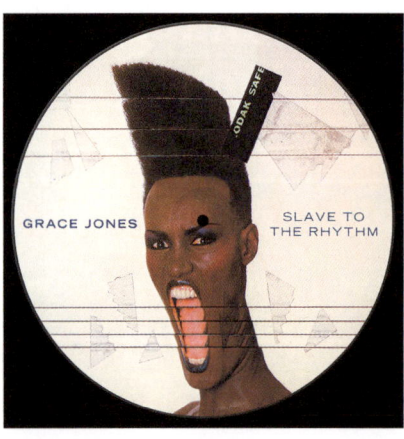

6

It was true lust, pre-love, compounded by the fact that Jones' extraordinary looks encapsulated Goude's well-documented fetishization of African and black culture (his first book is titled *Jungle Fever*) – a libidinous obsession born out of his childhood in Paris, where he lived close to both a former colonial museum and the zoo in Vincennes. The cocktail of exotic animals, alien landscapes and frescoes of half-naked African women constituted early but enduring visual prompts; Jones, a willing creative accomplice, lit the touchpaper. They partied hard, becoming permanent fixtures at New York's legendary club Studio 54. Goude says: 'The music–fashion fascination and my knack for entertainment comes from my upbringing: my mother was a dancer and had a little dance school. I was excited by it all – the costumes, the lights, the music, her screaming at the girls. But the first time it was all brought together, when I connected with the feelings I had had when I helped my mother at her dance recitals, was with Grace. I believe that you inherit your sensibility first of all, it's what orients you, and then your curiosity elevates you. With Grace I had not only an opportunity but also a very talented and extraordinary girl. I dropped everything.' The gesture was as grand as it was romantic. Goude was only 29, a prodigious talent ensconced at a prestigious magazine and a self-confessed playboy. 'But there's something devilish about Grace. Her wildness seduced me in a way I had never been seduced before.'

The relationship was cemented over a *New York* magazine shoot that produced the famous 'impossible arabesque' image that later became the record sleeve for *Island Life* (1985). The design is a piece of accidental iconography (in fact, all of Jones' seminal album covers were originally created as single portraits) that is regularly billed as one of the top 100 album artworks of all time. The image is critical to both Goude's mythology and the genesis of his partnership with Jones, thanks to the use of the 'French Correction' – a concept Goude coined at *Esquire* to denote on-page remodelling in the pursuit of superficial physical perfection. It was a precursor to the excessive retouching of the digital era; body parts were extended in a bid to correct what Goude, the ultimate inventor, saw as inherent weaknesses that offended his graphic-designer adoration of balance. Goude's sleeve design for *Slave to the Rhythm* (1985) and music video for the title song, which features clips of the duo's advert for the car brand Citroën, deploy similar extensions – stretching Jones' mouth and hair – but with arguable wit and approachability.

7

> # I take the truth and blow it up. I don't need reality, I just need to be exposed to it in order to come home to my studio and give you a synthetic version.
>
> Jean-Paul Goude

As canvases go, Jones was a dream come true – but Goude's vision ran faster, higher, bolder. Reality was a superfluous drag. 'I told her, "Your face is like a cubist character, I want to transform you into a minimal shape," and I gave her examples: Kandinsky, the Bauhaus, Russian constructivism,' says Goude. 'I tell good stories. I take the truth and blow it up. I don't need reality, I just need to be exposed to it in order to come home to my studio and give you a synthetic version of what I've lived through a drawing or a painting or a film. For me, to re-create reality is much better. As with Grace – I felt I was there to highlight the goods. In a lot of ways it was pure machismo, the oldest story in the world. I wanted my friends to know that I'd got the best girl and to understand why I found her interesting. In other words, I had to package it to show them.'

Jones' transformation was nascent, however, and Goude, as the ultimate architect of her new identity, had to persuade others of her latent stardom – including acclaimed musicians who had been asked to record with her, such as the Jamaican rhythm and reggae duo Sly & Robbie and Britain's Barry Reynolds. Goude launched a shock-and-awe visual campaign to set the tone and eradicate any unresolved issues of validity. Reynolds recalls, 'I'd listened to her albums and hated them. I thought they were clichéd like anything else coming out of Europe at the time – a tired disco beat with a bad string arrangement. But then I met Jean-Paul and I realized he was someone with a real vision that spanned music, style, everything. He has a groove that brought it all together and he really wanted us to cross a border. I'll always remember, they [Goude and producer Chris Blackwell] covered an entire wall in the studio with a huge poster of Grace with these huge shoulders and her legs apart – the image that was later used for the cover of the *Warm Leatherette* album, 1980, the first to display her new sound – staring down at all of us musicians. We were suitably shocked into understanding this was something different.'

9

Goude was killing off the more trite aspects of Jones' 1970s disco persona ('pulling her out of her disco rut') – rebirthing her via super sexually charged androgyny that would propel her into the pantheon of pop music's most illustrious gender-benders, including David Bowie and Annie Lennox. Her hair was cut and Goude had his own tailor create suits for her to cultivate a masculine sensibility. 'It was a total revolution. Diana Ross was her biggest competition. She [Ross] sold records but she was Broadway, she was Las Vegas – very glittery and glitzy in an American way, as opposed to Grace, who came from the art world. Grace was like a character out of a movie that didn't exist yet,' says Goude. Hollywood clearly took note: by the mid 1980s Jones had appeared in the Bond film *A View to a Kill* and in *Conan the Destroyer* – on both occasions capitalizing on her fearsome visual identity.

10

Even at the start I had the knock-'em-dead fantasy of presenting a new woman through her. I saw pictures of the [Claude] Montana shows and Thierry Mugler shows and everything I was seeing seemed weak next to what we were doing.

Jean-Paul Goude

8
The cover of the album *Nightclubbing* (1981) became a seminal image in pop-music history thanks to its hitherto unseen sexually charged androgyny.

9
The cover for Jones' album *Warm Leatherette* (1980) was created by Goude to shock even hardened industry doubters into understanding `that she was something totally different, crossing a border'.

10
Goude's artwork for *A One Man Show* (1982), a long-form music-video collection compiled from concert footage.

The cover for the album *Nightclubbing* (1981) boasts the image Goude believes most truthfully crystallizes his overall vision of her – a fearless modern heroine, outstripping all others with her extreme subversive beauty. Jones boasts a sharply structured flat-top hairline, a black square-shouldered Armani suit (later retouched to look more extreme) and a torso so sculpted that the décolletage-cum-breastbone could be male or female. Her skin is inky black (Goude painted it black himself then overlaid blue powder to deepen the look), her lips dark red – countered by the sleek stick of a white cigarette. 'I call it blue-black on black in black, as opposed to white on white in white – a typical black expression of the 1970s. It was about extremity, playing on her masculinity. Grace simplified to the maximum,' says Goude. For her A One Man Show tour in 1981, Goude reimagined the look with high-water trousers and a sharkskin jacket – even changing the lyrics of her songs to consummate fully the new identity. On 'Walking in the Rain', from the album *Nightclubbing* (1981), he changed the line 'feeling like a woman, looking like a man, making when I can' to 'feeling like a woman, looking like a man, mating when I can' for pure animalistic resonance. 'She was 8 feet tall and so skinny and so beautiful I could cry. I thought I was really touching her depth,' recalls Goude.

Jean-Paul Goude

11

11–13
Preparatory and final images for an elaborate mechanical maternity dress Goude conceived for Jones' 'baby shower performance' in 1979 at New York's Garage nightclub, an influential gay hub that was very receptive to her wildly uncategorizable, thrillingly larger-than-life persona.

14
Jones appeared on the cover of *The Face* magazine in 1987, in a classic example of the duo's deliberate assault on social etiquette in the form of taboos of gender and race.

Jones' performances, too, were critical in establishing her as a new breed of pop artist. 'I would try to bury all this disco music in lavish sets and presentations,' explains Goude, who got her to train at a boxing gym on New York's 23rd Street for one of her earliest club performances – so when she first arrived onstage in a hooded boxer's robe, she could shuffle and throw jabs with real presence. Inspired by his own short film about boxers, Goude employed Puerto Rican fighters to jump rope to the beat of Cuban drummers playing congas in the background. For the track 'La Vie en Rose', Jones mimicked playing the accordion before singing; while in a Halloween-night show at New York's Roseland Ballroom in 1978 (choreographed by Goude), she prowled on all fours, dressed like an alley cat, just inches away from a real caged Bengal tiger. When Jones was pregnant with their son Paulo, Goude created an elaborate mechanical maternity dress for her inspired by Japanese toys and constructivism, in collaboration with the 'Bauhaus-crazy' illustrator Antonio Lopez. It was worn at a 'baby shower' performance to 6,000 men at the Garage nightclub in New York, then reputed to be the city's wildest gay club. According to Goude, the influential gay clubbing community was critical to Jones' success: 'We needed the support of the gay community, whose eye was very sophisticated and who understood the ambiguity of the character and the imagery that I was proposing. As with Madonna or Gaga, it's the gay crowd that originally made them.'

Jones' fearsome identity has always been founded on the desire to craft a superstar. Says Goude, 'Even at the start I had the knock-'em-dead fantasy of presenting a new woman through her. I saw pictures of the [Claude] Montana shows and Thierry Mugler shows and everything I was seeing seemed weak next to what we were doing.' Nonetheless, Goude has faced criticism at regular intervals for his perceived objectification of Jones and her race. The cover of *The Face* in January 1986 features his photo of her with a white face, while her still visible shoulder blades remain black ('She always wanted to see what she would look like if she was white, and so did I,' says Goude, who later re-created the effect on himself, in reverse), while *Slave to the Rhythm* is rife with racial stereotyping, albeit deliberately daft.

12

13

+ Grace Jones

16

15-18
More sketches and montages for
portraits based on the notion of
extremity of identity - ideas that
later mutated into album covers, or
preparatory design work for them.

17

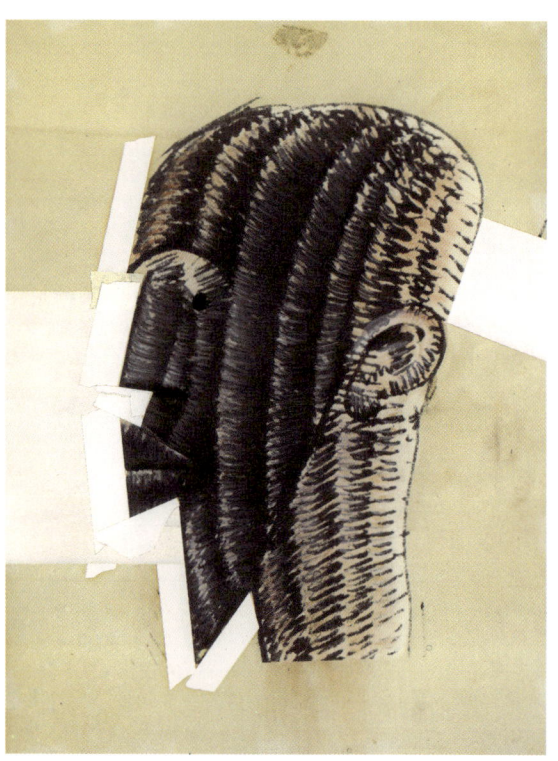

18

In truth I consider myself to be a sensualist, not an intellectual. Deep inside I'm afraid I'm much more fulfilled by watching or seeking beauty ... than I am [by] the content.

Jean-Paul Goude

Goude's ultimate riposte is the reminder of his aspect – that of an artist purely seeking to represent his own personal truth, not a man acting to defend political correctness. For Goude, life and art are inseparable follies: 'Imagine it, I was living across the road from Warhol's Factory, wanting to be an artist. I worked in magazines to make a living but I never lost the perspective or interest to be an artist, and I knew that you had to reach inside in order to bring out something original. I had to play on my own obsessions. Plus, I was quite the idealist, and therefore felt I was able to comment about my fascinations like anyone else could.'

Humour, in particular, has been key to communicating those obsessions with the warmth, charisma and almost childlike reverence that lie at their core. 'I do like to play with stereotypes. I guess that explains why I'm good at advertising, why I'm interested in parody, and why I have a lot of pictures that carry that sort of humour. Because I know that if people are not sensitive to the form of an image they might respond to its humour. In truth, I consider myself to be a sensualist, not an intellectual. Deep inside I'm afraid I'm much more fulfilled by watching or seeking beauty, looking at it for its shapes and form, than I am [by] the content.'

By the mid 1980s the often volatile affair – professionally and privately – was over. 'The day we broke up, the act broke up,' says Goude. But the legacy continues – as visible in the body-morphing silhouettes of Balmain and Céline, the stagecraft of current superstar Rihanna (never more so than her September 2009 cover of *Vogue Italia*, shot by Steven Klein) and almost every morsel of Lady Gaga's infamous performance fashion. Goude even reprised the now iconic *Island Life* artwork concept for an editorial shoot in 2007 with Marc Jacobs and Louis Vuitton for US *Harper's Bazaar*, while his *Paper* magazine cover of the reality TV star Kim Kardashian in 2014 was famously billed as ready to 'break the Internet'.

How, I ask, does he feel when he sees Grace now? 'I see a creature that's my ex-creature!' he says. 'It's as if I made a series of films with the same actress who eventually went on to work for other directors. There are new aspects of her but still those elements I recognize.'

19
Enduring influence: The fashion designer Marc Jacobs. Goude and the supermodel Naomi Campbell re-create `The Impossible Arabesque' for *Harper's Bazaar* magazine in September 2007.

20
Jones in a Goude-choreographed performance at the Roseland Ballroom, New York, 1978, just feet from a live Bengal tiger.

1

1
The sartorial urban magpie Gwen Stefani bearing her and Lieberman's stylistic signature: mixed cultural references underscored by a defiantly street-style edge. US *Elle* (2009), photographed by Carter Smith.

2,3
Lieberman's tribe: two of modern pop music's most important female powerhouses, Jennifer Lopez and Gwen Stefani - crossover stars whose visual identities Lieberman was integral to developing. From the videos for 'Jenny from the Block' (2002) and 'Let Me Blow Ya Mind' (2001).

Sliding from the gritty art and graft of grassroots New York hip-hop to the manicured extravaganzas of global pop, Andrea Lieberman - stylist, costumier and fashion designer - is a cross-genre creative tour de force who has elevated the identity of such megastars as Sean Combs (Puff Daddy), Jennifer Lopez, Mary J. Blige and Gwen Stefani.

Andrea Lieberman

+

Puff Daddy, Jennifer Lopez, Gwen Stefani,
Mary J. Blige

2

3

Lieberman has not only brought the worlds of music, high fashion and street style into exhilaratingly close proximity, but has also helped forward a modern, transculturally attuned vision of pop culture. It is a personal and professional journey for the native New Yorker that began with hip-hop etched into its very core. While her elder sister was listening to rock artists Deep Purple and Lynyrd Skynyrd, at just 10 years old she became hooked on the urban charisma of the Sugarhill Gang. Says Lieberman: 'Why hip-hop? Because it's so deeply embedded into the soul of New York. It is New York. And while I live in Los Angeles right now, I've always been a New Yorker.'

4

4
Lieberman's innate wandering eye and obsession with culturally disparate sartorial ephemera were cemented during an internship with the fashion designer Giorgio di Sant' Angelo, whose office walls featured images of the 1960s model Veruschka's iconic US *Vogue* desert shoot, photographed by Franco Rubartelli.

5
When two worlds collide: the epic couture shoot for US *Vogue* in October 1999, photographed by Annie Leibovitz, affirmed hip-hop's full transition into the pop-culture mainstream. Lieberman's client Sean Combs (aka Puff Daddy) was central to the new order.

Life as a teenager in the mid and late 1980s meant music, fashion (educated in Manhattan, Lieberman had an intimate window on to Madison Avenue fashion boutiques including Matsuda, Ralph Lauren and Kenzo) and clubbing. Area, Madame Rosa and Save the Robots were potent playgrounds of artistic self-expression, rooted in the authentic preoccupations of street culture that traversed race and gender. Lieberman, as so often, was at the nucleus of the action. 'It was such a magical time, so gritty and inspiring – hip-hop came from uptown to downtown, the Beastie Boys and Run DMC had just arrived on the scene and a lot of the now major streetwear labels like Stüssy had just started,' she says. 'Hip-hop had a profound influence on all things cultural; it really shifted the cultural landscape of New York in the 1980s.'

After high school, Lieberman was formally educated in fashion at New York's prestigious Parsons The New School of Design, but it was buying trips to England via a part-time job at the fashion boutique Style Council as well as an internship with the designer Giorgio di Sant' Angelo that nurtured both her nomadic eye and a taste for the kaleidoscopic wonderland of luxury fashion. Sant' Angelo's office was lavished with images from his famous US *Vogue* desert shoot in 1968 with the legendary 1960s model Veruschka ('it was colourful, it was sexy, it was inspiring'). A trip to Africa in her early 20s, which was supposed to last three months but spilled into two years, sealed Lieberman's voracious appetite for absorbing new social, cultural and visual languages ('the tribal culture, the city culture, the expat culture, the travelling culture'), incubating a career rooted in blending disparate vantage points. 'I'm obsessed with cultures, with rituals and adornment and the reasons why people wear what they wear. How these things manifest themselves is something I've always found amazing.' When she returned to New York in the early 1990s, she founded her own store, Culture and Reality, largely selling imported African accessories, but it was the raw energy of a club-land homecoming that took her career to the next level. A new era of alternative hip-hop had dawned, with groups De La Soul, A Tribe Called Quest and the ghetto-fabulous whirlwind that was rap megastar Sean 'Puff Daddy' Combs. After Lieberman dressed him and his production collective The Hitmen for *Vibe* magazine, they swiftly formed an unbreakable partnership.

+ Puff Daddy, Jennifer Lopez, Gwen Stefani, Mary J. Blige

The cross-pollination, culturally speaking, was epic.

Andrea Lieberman

Combs' self-styled image was already robust; Lieberman recalls a shoot with the photographer Annie Leibovitz for *Vanity Fair* magazine when he refused the role of a polo-playing horse rider, instead insisting on dressing like a 1920s Harlem gangster and being shot with his sons next to his Bentley. However, it was the nuanced cool of Lieberman's vision – recalibrating the hyped-up bravado of rapper bling for an aspirational but mainstream look – that elevated him fully into the eye of the luxury fashion storm. The most lucid example of the acceptance of hip-hop was a supersize endorsement via media behemoth US *Vogue*, whose embrace of the genre – via Combs, then the movement's figurehead – beamed its approval to the rest of pop culture at large. The vehicle was an epic, turn-of-the-millennium couture fashion shoot for US *Vogue*'s October 1999 issue – photographed by Leibovitz and starring both Combs (styled by Lieberman) and the supermodel Kate Moss (styled by *Vogue's* creative director, Grace Coddington). A mix of quintessential Parisian cityscapes of bridges and blue sky, a backstage hotel-room shot (hailing from Leibovitz's rock photography legacy) and lavish club scenes with models draped in the sexed-up apparel of Tom Ford-era Gucci, it was the confluence of new and old-school glamour. It even featured cameos from fashion design royalty: Jean Paul Gaultier, Karl Lagerfeld, Oscar de la Renta and John Galliano.

According to Lieberman, 'the cross-pollination, culturally speaking, was epic', confirming her ability to move others' narratives forward. 'With a lot of people I've worked with, I feel like I've helped them to evolve and elevate. As a stylist, it wasn't only about the collaboration and creating these images, but [also about] making people feel good – creating this world around them that would summon up some kind of mojo, allowing them to get up on stage and do their thing.' At times, whipping that persona into being became such a palpable emotional experience that it would bleed into her own demeanour: 'You're in such an intimate dressing-room scenario before they go out and evolve into this super-high-octane version of themselves that it would sometimes seep over to me. It would affect my mannerisms, the way I talked.'

5

Andrea Lieberman

6

Through Combs came Jennifer Lopez, his then girlfriend and an artist similarly on the periphery of a jumbo cultural crossover. Lopez, who concurrent to Ricky Martin became the first true global Hispanic superstar, dealt in Latin/R&B/hip-hop-inflected dance-pop anthems that built on rap/R&B's small but influential group of female players, which included Missy Elliott, Aaliyah, Mary J. Blige (Lieberman styled Blige's album covers *The Breakthrough* in 2005 and *Growing Pains* in 2007), SWV and Destiny's Child, who were slowly re-routing the genre's well-worn misogynistic tropes. While Lopez's persona was inarguably built on sexually charged charisma (notably it was Lieberman who put Lopez in the infamous plunge-front tropical-print Versace dress for the Grammy Awards in 2000), Lieberman says it was about reclaiming ownership over that sensuality and, as with Combs, blending the scent of stratospheric luxury with the grassroots authenticity of Lopez's Puerto Rican–Bronx heritage. The pair collaborated on numerous tours, public appearances and landmark videos – including those for the singles 'Play' (2001), 'Jenny from the Block' (2002) and 'Get Right' (2005) – each rich with such dual messaging. While the futuristically luxe, Pan Am setting of 'Play' is rife with traditional hip-hop swagger (plus a standout braided top by New Yorker Benjamin Cho), 'Get Right' is classic Lieberman/Lopez. The video is a vision of sports-luxury way before the term 'athleisure' was coined in 2014. In one scene, Lopez is dressed in gold Lurex cargo pants, high heels and a midriff-bearing dancer's T-shirt; another offers a cropped body-con roll-neck, low-rise leather trousers, fur-hooded micro puffer jacket, ghetto-fabulous hoop earrings and, channelling Lieberman herself, forearms stacked (tribal-style) with full-bling bangles.

Lieberman describes their partnership as an organic process of intensely intuitive fun in which Lopez, hungry for fashion insight, became her 'real-life doll'. Together they constructed an identity so popular that Lopez kick-started global trends in the blink of a video freeze-frame, such as the Juicy Couture velour tracksuit ('I'm Real', 2001) and the Manolo Blahnik, Timberland-style stiletto boots ('Jenny from the Block') – inspiring a host of emerging female hip-hop artists who, according to Lieberman (now deluged with requests), 'wanted to be who she [Lopez] portrayed: an in-control woman achieving her aspirations'.

6
Mary J. Blige, hip-hop's queen of soul and another of Lieberman's formidable female power players, photographed for her album *The Breakthrough* (2005) by Markus Klinko and Indrani.

7–9
Videos for Jennifer Lopez's singles 'Play' (2001), 'Jenny from the Block' (2002) and 'Get Right' (2005), micro-movies that melded the pride of unbound luxury with the grassroots authenticity of her Puerto Rican-Bronx heritage.

7

+ Puff Daddy, Jennifer Lopez, Gwen Stefani, Mary J. Blige

8

I'm obsessed with cultures, with rituals and adornment and the reasons why people wear what they wear. How these things manifest themselves is something I've always found amazing.

Andrea Lieberman

9

+ Puff Daddy, Jennifer Lopez, Gwen Stefani, Mary J. Blige

10
A still from Gwen Stefani's video for 'What You Waiting For?' (2004; top) and a behind-the-scenes shot. This *Alice in Wonderland*-themed visual epic steered Lieberman from intuitive stylist to the precision theatrics of costuming, and back again.

11
More from 'Let Me Blow Ya Mind', the beginning of the Lieberman-Stefani creative conspiracy.

However, of all Lieberman's collaborators, the most significant in terms of brokering a distinct and much-imitated style is the Californian singer-songwriter Gwen Stefani, the tomboy-beautiful, genre-defying pop rebel whom Lieberman helped transform from lead singer of noughties rock band No Doubt to solo superstar. In 2004 she even assisted with the launch of Stefani's own fashion label, L.A.M.B. – tellingly an acronym of the title of her debut solo album, *Love. Angel. Music. Baby.* from the same year. They were introduced during planning for the 2001 video 'Let Me Blow Ya Mind' (Lieberman had been commissioned to style the track's other artist, Eve), initiating a partnership stretching from No Doubt's *Rock Steady* album (2001) to Stefani's second solo album, *The Sweet Escape* (2006). While Stefani was no blank canvas (the video director Sophie Muller describes first meeting her as 'like seeing Marilyn Monroe's head on a punk body'), it was the overwhelmingly complementary collision of Stefani's Cali skater-chick and Lieberman's New York hip-hop home-girl, connected by their mutual love of music and subcultures, that drove Stefani's profile as an independent artist stratospheric and steered Lieberman from intuitive stylist to the precision-detailed world of fashion costuming. While Stefani had great instinct, Lieberman also had the fashion acumen. 'I didn't go to a fashion show until I was 30,' says Stefani. 'She [Lieberman] was everything cool that I wasn't – a party girl from New York who knew about fashion and who took my ideas to a different level. But ultimately it was as though she and I shared DNA, to the extent that I almost became addicted to her guidance.'

She [Lieberman] was everything cool that I wasn't - a party girl from New York who knew about fashion and who took my ideas to a different level. But ultimately it was as though she and I shared DNA, to the extent that I almost became addicted to her guidance.

Gwen Stefani, singer-songwriter and performer

Many collaborators also clocked the potency of the alliance from the start. Of the video for No Doubt's 'Underneath It All' in 2002, Muller (a long-time collaborator of Stefani) confesses, 'Until then I had always been a bit disparaging about stylists. I thought that if someone needed a stylist to provide ideas, it effectively meant they were slightly clueless; I thought it trivialized the artist. But then I met Andrea and I understood why she was so important – she built on a language that existed and elevated it. The woolly hat for "Underneath It All" made the stripping-it-back striptease idea [a response to criticism about Stefani's heavy use of make-up] less straightforward; it brought a reggae tip to the overdone aspect, funking it up. The styling she [Lieberman] introduced going forward meant the looks became more important, a bigger part of the art form, which I embraced. She took it somewhere that I couldn't, and I consciously let it happen.'

It is most evident in Stefani's 'What You Waiting For?' video (2004), the *Alice in Wonderland*-themed visual epic directed by Francis Lawrence, for which the pair devised an 'image bible' of references from colour palettes to hairstyles to the backing dancers' wardrobes. Lieberman, in charge of 'elevating and editing' the concept, indulged her own and Stefani's shared Anglophilia by travelling to London and plundering Alexander McQueen's archives (reference the headdresses worn by the caterpillar creature) as well as TV and film costumiers Angels – pulling Royal Ballet tutus that Comme des Garçons had used in a recent runway show. Every item, from the Prada bra to the Miu Miu ruffle shirt, became a painstakingly orchestrated piece of the theatrical fashion jigsaw.

11

12

13

We now live in a global multicultural world, in cities with multiple ethnicities within any 1-mile span. That inherently means blurred lines, with people from various pockets of behaviours having a profound influence on one another. It just needs to be done respectfully.

Andrea Lieberman

12
Evolution of a genre: a moodboard from Lieberman's own fashion brand A.L.C., launched in 2009, in which Stefani says she often sees subtle reflections of herself.

13
Gwen Stefani's album *Love. Angel. Music. Baby.* (2004), photographed by Nick Knight. The concept directly fuelled Stefani's own fashion label, as its name shows: L.A.M.B.

14
Stills from the video for 'Rich Girl' (2004), another demonstration of the Lieberman-Stefani capacity for mixed references, both cultural and historical.

Extended further, that jigsaw reveals one of the richest and most varied catalogues of transcultural references in pop history – from the chola culture cues at play in 'Luxurious' (2004) to the rockabilly gangster of 'The Sweet Escape' (2006) and, particularly visible, Lieberman's ongoing use of Japanese backing singers and dancers the Harajuku Girls. The references have been both lauded and criticized but are, according to Lieberman, wholly anchored in positive appreciation, far removed from accusations of thoughtless appropriation. 'Gwen grew up in Southern California, near Disneyland, where there's a huge Mexican influence, while I witnessed hip-hop shift across New York, fuelling everything about youth culture at that time. We now live in a global multicultural world, in cities with multiple ethnicities within any 1-mile span. That inherently means blurred lines, with people from various pockets of behaviours having a profound influence on one another. It just needs to be done respectfully.'

Trading on modern instincts is a default setting for both parties. The fact that the cultural mash-ups spawned by Lieberman and Stefani hit around the same time that microblogging platforms such as Tumblr kicked in has undoubtedly amplified their resonance; for an audience in the thrall of social media, accustomed to digitally devouring disparately sourced material in random succession (any era, any context), such cultural interchanges have rendered the work a vital sign of the times. Their playful, hybridized imagery arguably paved the way for later pop superstars such as Katy Perry, but while Perry represents the zenith of cartoon pop, Stefani and her more left-field references remain the hipper anime alternative. The cover art for the album *Love. Angel. Music. Baby.*, created by the iconic British image-maker Nick Knight, is a semi-surreal flashy reverie that mixes the candy-coloured world of Disney with a darker and more eroticized Harajuku underbelly – a lucid illustration of Lieberman and Stefani's idiosyncratic sensibility.

14

In any instance, Stefani's debut album and its suite of videos, including the memorable 'Hollaback Girl' and 'Rich Girl', are fully wedded to Lieberman's fashion intellect, which has rendered the performer a standout female pop persona who comfortably outwits casual stereotypes. It is an embodiment of strength that Lieberman continues to feed into her own fashion collection, A.L.C. (launched in 2009), within which Stefani says she often sees subtle reflections of herself. Says Lieberman, 'Gwen emerged on to the scene as a really strong female artist who represented that point in time – a moment that you can never remake, retrieve or re-create. But there are aspects of it in my collection because I constantly celebrate what I refer to as the women of my tribe. While I'm very classic in some ways, I also have a very rebellious spirit, and I think this whole generation of women who are growing up now with all these different cultural experiences and expectations have a similar spirit. Realistically, it [A.L.C.] must always have that mix because ultimately I'm a natural nomad – going everywhere but belonging nowhere.'

Anastasia Marano

+

M.I.A., Azealia Banks, Santigold

Must-have hot-lists and mainstream trends have little relevance to the artistic philosophy of the American stylist Anastasia Marano, who bills herself as the anti-fashion stylist. A key creative conspirator for a host of urban and rock music artists including M.I.A., Azealia Banks, Usher, Taylor Momsen and Santigold, Marano has created a breed of fashion that is a whirlwind of playfully rebellious pick-and-mix street couture and that shrugs off the standard diktats of good taste in the pursuit of crafting original identities.

1
The politically outspoken performer M.I.A. on the cover of *Spin* magazine in 2008, bearing Marano's trademark trend-phobic, genre-mashing, taste-challenging aesthetic. Photographed by Greg Kadel.

Marano has an innate sensibility that she says originated in her native New York. Her early experiences of fashion were steeped in the city's kaleidoscopic street culture – an already potent confluence of fashion and music, driven in no small part by its club scene. By 14 she was a regular at the Palladium (successor to the legendary club Studio 54) and subterranean rave space the Tunnel, devouring a meaty diet of anything-goes fashion and rapturously hedonistic rave ambience. 'It was a time when the club world in New York was at its peak, and it subsequently became a huge influence on me – full of insane, theatrical, fun fashion,' recalls Marano. 'I've always been thrilled by how people take fashion and mix it up. It's why I like to work with people who are serious about what they do but who don't necessarily take themselves too seriously.'

In 2000, after studying at the School of the Art Institute of Chicago, Marano returned to New York and reignited her appetite for provocative fashion with a course in costume design, while also interning at the SoHo showroom of the British designer Vivienne Westwood, one of her heroes. Already weaned on the kinetic-cartoonish sensibility that was the lifeblood of the clubs, Marano cemented her path with Westwood's world and its total disregard for convention. 'New York was still a thriving hub of entrepreneurial mavericks – communities of creatives mixing it up,' she remembers. Such mavericks included the stylists and showroom regulars Jane How and Katie Mossman, both of whom Marano later assisted. Shoots for magazines like *Vogue Italia* with How and the photography legend Steven Meisel fast-tracked her into the industry elite, but the experiences lacked the more visceral thrills and real-world bite with which the clubs had seduced her.

It was the American music magazine *Spin* – then a print publication, now an online webzine – that bridged that gap, offering a direct line to a host of musicians and 'affording me the ability to design, to create costumes, to style – to physically and conceptually create everything in one, experiencing more exhilaration than a standard fashion shoot where the blank canvas is just too controlled,' says Marano. A perfect storm of reality and artifice, it was an ideal playground for her to seek out the iconoclastic streak in her musician collaborators – giving licence to the boldest to be even bigger, using fashion to push their musical and personal agendas.

> **Anastasia came to *Spin* as this very unusual bridge between the worlds of urban and indie music ... Apple had redefined how we could mix and match music styles, which had a really major ripple effect ... All of a sudden we had all these subgenres that were near impossible to define. She would pull references that had very little to do with fashion in the conventional sense, nor music – really helping us not to get too hung up on ... those old boundaries.**
>
> Devin Pedzwater, creative director, Italian *Vanity Fair*

+ M.I.A., Azealia Banks, Santigold

Devin Pedzwater, former creative director of *Spin*, now creative director of Italian *Vanity Fair*, describes Marano's vision as the epitome of a wider cultural shift whereby music's traditional genres were dissipating in favour of a more varied, cross-fertilized outlook. He believes it made her crucial to both the evolution of the magazine and the artists with whom she worked: 'In many ways Anastasia came to *Spin* as this very unusual bridge between the worlds of urban and indie music. With the iPod, and significantly the iPod Shuffle, Apple had redefined how we could mix and match music styles, which had a really major ripple effect. For instance, *Spin* had been a distinctly indie title, as opposed to *Rolling Stone*, which was rock, but all of a sudden we had all these subgenres that were near impossible to define. She would pull references that had very little to do with fashion in the conventional sense, nor music – really helping us not to get too hung up on clinging to those old boundaries. By the end it was very much a case of "we're all indie now", where artists and readers were starting to completely reject movements that they'd always said they'd been a part of.'

2

3

One of the most significant of Marano's *Spin*-instigated relationships has been her partnership with the outspoken British Sri Lankan songwriter, rapper and general creative agitator M.I.A., with whom she worked during 2009–10, when the musician was most conspicuously in the public eye. Having initially collaborated on *Spin*'s celebrated 'Rebel Yell' cover shoot of November 2008 – which saw a fluoro-lipped M.I.A. in characteristically defiant club kid-meets-militant stance – the pair worked together on a series of stage shows and festival performances, including her infamous appearance at the 2009 Grammy Awards when nine months pregnant. Bearing poignant traces of the heavily pregnant pop star Neneh Cherry's controversial appearance on the British TV show *Top of the Pops* two decades earlier, it was a headline-grabbing moment, thanks to a body-con Henry Holland monochrome mesh minidress with strategically placed polka dots. Echoing Cherry, M.I.A. accessorized it with hot pants and beefed-up Reebok trainers, directly trading on her and Marano's street-style credibility, unapologetically subverting the conventional mother-to-be stereotype. Marano recalls it as a seminal juncture: 'It was a really special moment in her life – she had a major song ('Paper Planes'), an album, a baby. I felt it as it was happening, as opposed to the more usual sensation of experiencing the impact with hindsight. Fashion was key to that. That dress was actually a very sexy dress to start off with; she wanted it to look more like an art piece. My general rule is: the bigger the personality, the bigger the look they can handle, and M.I.A. is a very big personality.' Speaking about Marano and M.I.A.'s partnership, Pedzwater says, 'That was an incredibly important relationship because it was really the time that she [M.I.A.] found her identity.'

2,3
M.I.A. resplendent in pregnancy at the Grammy Awards in 2009 and for *Spin* (2008); the former performance echoed Neneh Cherry's controversial set on *Top of the Pops* two decades previously (see page 34).

4,5
M.I.A. performing at Coachella (2009) in rave-inspired light suits designed to spotlight grass-roots style. The outfits also constituted a subliminal comment on the cultural collisions that occur when decades-old clothing donated to charity resurfaces in other countries.

4

+ M.I.A., Azealia Banks, Santigold

While it's not exactly a political statement, it is typical of M.I.A.'s subliminal messaging techniques -

> **None of these women are trying to be one of the guys, despite being in a very male, machismo-oriented part of the music industry, nor are they doing what other women do and competing via over-sexualization. They don't shun it, they own it and because they're incredibly conscious of that fact, I am too.**
>
> Anastasia Marano

According to Michelle Egiziano, former photo editor at *Spin*, Marano's choice to run with a Holland piece for such a momentous occasion (similarly outré, club-kid designers Ashish and Jeremy Scott are also favourites of the stylist) is typical of her capacity to amplify the moment: 'She always had a deep understanding of the artists' strengths and vulnerabilities and would consequently pull in fashion to open their eyes to provocative ideas. She has a healthy irreverence for traditional paradigms of fashion and skews towards smart, playful designers that are dialled into youth culture with a sophisticated edge.'

The Coachella festival later that year reprised the duo's dissident approach to style and their desire to spotlight the grassroots energy of life beyond gilt-edged high fashion. Marano sourced a series of heavily rave-inspired light suits for M.I.A., her musicians and her dancers from the Californian designer Janet Cooke Hanson – aka Enlightened – who also creates stage looks for the French electro duo Daft Punk. M.IA.'s reference was the cultural collision that occurs when decades-old clothes from thrift shops end up on children in Africa: a displacement and recontextualization of resources that radically alter their original meaning. 'The aim was to craft a design derived in part from "real" clothes, beyond the showmanship,' explains Marano. 'While it's not exactly a political statement, it is typical of M.I.A.'s subliminal messaging techniques – there are very few things she does that don't have some kind of politically or socially significant meaning.'

Marano's work with M.I.A. has been bait for numerous worst-dressed 'filler' lists that circulate during awards season, a dishonour Marano almost relishes as certain proof of a job done with conviction. But her work has also not gone unrecognized; the duo's ballsy vision – an homage to the rougher and readier nature of true street style – can also be seen in a collaboration in late 2013 between M.I.A. and the Italian fashion giant Versace's diffusion line, Versus. The collection, ironically inspired by counterfeit product, resolutely affirms the power of the thinking pop star's voice.

While Marano has not worked exclusively with women, female stars self-assured enough to toy with their image, and their audiences, are the mainstay of her creative raison d'être. 'There is a common thread between all the artists I've worked with – Azealia Banks, M.I.A., Santigold, Lil' Kim. They're all powerful women who do their own thing. None of these women are trying to be one of the guys, despite being in a very male, machismo-oriented part of the music industry, nor are they doing what other women do and competing via over-sexualization. They don't shun it, they own it and because they're incredibly conscious of that fact, I am too.' In 2012, when she styled the then 21-year-old Harlem-born rapper/singer/songwriter Azealia Banks for *Spin*, the rave references surfaced once again, this time rebooted for a new, millennial generation seeking its own underground kicks. Dubbed 'Back-to-School Mermaid', the series referenced the Sea Punk movement – a social media-fuelled micro-trend spanning fashion, music and parties, of which Banks was deemed a forerunner. Conical iridescent seashell bras, aquamarine denim hot pants and a Bart Simpson sweatshirt constitute a look that is part rave-ready, part teenage beauty queen – a concerted effort of trashy cool.

6–8
Cult of youth: The rebellious Harlem rapper Azealia Banks styled by Marano for *Spin* (2012), bearing inflections of Marano's own New York club kid days, rebooted for a millennial mindset. Photographed by Jason Nocito.

+ M.I.A., Azealia Banks, Santigold

6

7

8

SPIN

FEATURING

TOP 40 ALBUMS OF THE YEAR
ADELE
YUCK
GIRLS
BEYONCÉ
KURT VILE
THE BLACK KEYS
LITURGY
WILD FLAG
DRAKE
BON IVER
THE WEEKND

+ OCCUPY WALL STREET, THE ARAB SPRING, AND THE COLLAPSE OF WESTERN CIVILIZATION AS WE KNOW IT

THE BEST OF 2011

ONE F**KED UP YEAR

DAMIAN ABRAHAM PHOTOGRAPHED BY LORENZO BRINGHELI

+ M.I.A., Azealia Banks, Santigold

Cool, says Marano, is a topic that is always at the front of her mind: 'In a world obsessed with trends, I think people have forgotten what "cool" is – the virtue of being unafraid to be yourself – which is why I work with artists who are truly individuals.' She cites the American photographer Amy Arbus' book *On the Street* (2006) – a decade's worth of edgy street portraiture, including shots of a young Madonna – as a constant companion, reflective of her own anarchic intuition: 'It [the book] is basically bad fashion, and I love it. I don't care about being tasteful, and I think that's an essential mentality for music. There's a lot of the same out there when it comes to fashion, a lot of people scared of not fitting the mould, which is why I go for complete individuality.' She recalls a favourite shoot, with the photographer Lorenzo Bringheli, of Damian Abraham from the Toronto-based hardcore punk band Fucked Up: 'I brought nothing for him in terms of clothing – it was all about these pieces we made that were entirely beyond fashion in normal terms. There was a wire top hat and an Elizabethan-style collar made out of baby doll heads. A lot of pop punk bands are entirely missing the point – the fact they want to look like everyone else in that genre is really the antithesis of the punk ideology, which is about ripping it all up and starting again.'

10

I don't care about being tasteful, and I think that's an essential mentality for music.

Anastasia Marano

9
Damian Abraham of the punk band Fucked Up, styled by Marano for *Spin* magazine in 2012. Marano created the look on spec, a fact that is indicative of their joint predilection for anarchic intuition.

10
The singer-songwriter Santigold – an artist just as genre-blurring as Marano – photographed for *Spin* magazine in 2012.

While Marano is certainly not the first stylist to be influenced by a club scene, nor the punk movement, her signature remains distinctive thanks to an additional wider fascination with Americana, including its more pedestrian, less cinematic threads. Where New York was once her prime hunting ground, she is now focused on travelling beyond the country's metropolitan epicentres (her husband is a musician from Nashville) to places where the lines blur. 'I love seeing how certain areas of America can be reflected in people's clothing choices. I'm not poking fun at these choices, but celebrating it. I grew up in Staten Island [a borough of New York City] with an appreciation of a stereotypical style that some would call gaudy, mixed with a really urban undertone – casual streetwear mixed with athletic clothing. Down South you get this real American pride thing – rockers and bikers and country folk – a whole different world of denim, boots, leather and American flags. I love having both the outer-borough New York and Nashville influences in my life. The interesting stuff to me is just outside those cities.'

With rebels and dissidents clearly high on her collaborative agenda, who is next on her hit list? The answer is Mykki Blanco: an American rapper and a performance artist who performs in drag – no mean feat in the still machismo-driven world of rap and R&B. 'I'm fascinated by how he does his own thing,' says Marano. 'Not just what he's doing now, but how he got to be doing that in the first place; how he made it there and how he doesn't give a shit about what anyone else thinks.'

Jordan Mooney

+

Sex Pistols, Adam and the Ants

1

2

3

1
Subversive workwear: Jordan tending the shop floor of Vivienne Westwood and Malcolm McLaren's Sex – a space she unofficially governed – wearing a latex fetish bodysuit. Photographed by Sheila Rock.

2
Jordan in her influential early tenure as manager of the cult post-punk group Adam and the Ants in the Marquee Club dressing room, 1978. Photographed by Ray Stevenson. Ant credits Jordan with having 'created punk rock ... literally selling it on the frontline'.

3
Johnny Rotten and Sid Vicious of the Sex Pistols pictured at Heathrow airport in 1977. Jordan had a significant bearing on the style of this group of infamous punk legend.

True visionaries – those genuinely unimpeded by a need for adulation, fully content to risk ridicule in pursuit of their own personal truths – are few, far between and like precious oxygen to the fashion-music fraternity, for whom originality is life. One such figure is the punk queen Jordan Mooney, whose pivotal role at the nexus of Vivienne Westwood and Malcolm McLaren's riotous (Sex and Seditionaries-era) world was vital to the looks of bands such as the Sex Pistols and Adam and the Ants.

+ Sex Pistols, Adam and the Ants

4
An iconic image of Jordan in formidable repose at Sex, a hub of Britain's punk activity, in 1976.

5
The legendary English ballerina Margot Fonteyn was an enduring influence for Jordan, who had herself been a competition-standard ballet dancer. Jordan's infamously sexed-up 1950s silhouette was derived directly from ballet, as were her signature leotards – covert clues to her disciplined nature and integral to the near-myth of punk's appropriation of the safety pin.

Jordan emerged as one of punk's standout poster women. Often immortalized in grainy black-and-white photography as a severe vision of bleached-blonde-beehived, Cleopatra-eyed, latex-sheathed, fuck-you defiance, she inspired creative iconoclast musicians for whom stylistic attitude was as critical as music. Yet there is far more to her influence than straightforward anarchic provocation. Rebellion was actually something of a by-product. Art ('I often described myself as a living work of art'), personal expression and a militant desire to champion the underdog, including the unusual, were all at the real crux of her infectious perspective.

Born in Sussex, in southern England, Jordan (née Pamela Rooke) is something of a living fable: a still-fetishized punk icon whose unique and highly developed sense of identity, coupled with her quiet but total withdrawal from the scene after a decade of immersion, has made her a near-mythical figure. According to her, that uncompromising sense of self, an understanding that she was different and happily so, was in place from early childhood. It started (at 6 or 7 years old in the early 1960s) with the extravagance of a bright-pink velvet cape, transferring through her teenage years into an extreme, vampy twist on 1950s styling: cinched waists and prom skirts, sexed-up stilettos and the beginning of the famous bleached-blonde, moulded bouffant hair. Her blonde/punk semi-mohican at the time was styled at the Smile Salon in Knightsbridge, London, by Keith Wainwright, who also worked with the band Roxy Music – and it caused the then prefect to be suspended from school for fear of a rush of copycats. She returned, wearing a headscarf, but would stand at the school gates at the end of the day, proudly inviting everyone to absorb her look. 'I was amazed they thought anyone else would copy it. In truth, back then, everyone was laughing at me,' recalls Jordan, whose compulsive individualism manifested as an entirely solo activity until the Westwood/McLaren 'family' transpired several years later.

Details from Jordan's early life, just as in the maelstrom of punk and later the New Romantic period, were essential to the 'becoming'. Her famous racoon-esque striped eye make-up was partly inspired by a story directed by the French make-up artist and image-maker Serge Lutens in *Vogue* magazine; the retro footwear (exquisite and/or vertiginous, from wild Perspex heels to coquettish mules) was uncovered in thrift stores and a vintage shop in Brighton's lanes; while the 1950s silhouette was derived directly from her (competition-standard) passion for ballet. The legendary British ballerina Margot Fonteyn remains one of her biggest inspirations. Notably, at 14, she also (unofficially) changed her name to the traditionally male moniker 'Jordan' – borrowed from a character in *The Great Gatsby* – sealing her subversive self-styled genesis. 'I truly felt I'd been labelled the wrong thing, like a kind of name dysmorphia,' she laughs. Others branded the change either insane or courageous, although she states emphatically that it was neither: 'It's not courageous if you feel entirely comfortable with it. The way I dressed wasn't an act of rebellion per se, it was about feeling comfortable in my own skin.'

5

6
The sociopolitical fashion souvenirs of Sex. Only those who subscribed to the shop's anarchic manifesto were allowed to buy the clothes, and Jordan was head gatekeeper.

7
Jordan surveys her domain as chief whip of Sex, the emotional heartland of punk.

When Jordan left school, London beckoned, firstly with a job in Harrods department store, then another at Westwood and McLaren's shop on King's Road. The shop, named Sex (renamed Seditionaries in 1976, then World's End in 1980), was an established beacon for young dissenters who, disenfranchised by Britain's depressed economic climate, were itching for social revolution. For Jordan, Westwood and McLaren (then a couple) represented kindred spirits. Their new-generation Teddy Boy designs for the shop's earlier incarnations (named Let It Rock in 1971, it had been renamed Too Fast to Live, Too Young to Die in 1973) had not only gauged the power of fashion as a visual mouthpiece for youth's insurgency, but also mirrored Jordan's stylistic obsessions with 1950s culture. For a long-term loner like Jordan ('I've always been very happy in my own company, I've never needed a diversion of any sort'), the burgeoning world of punk that they were seeding – pop culture's eternal anti-tribe tribe – felt 'like home'.

The wrong person wearing it would bastardize the message, so the clothes couldn't go to just anybody. Some people railed at the price because of the [deconstructed] nature of the pieces, but beauty and style and originality shouldn't just be given away.

Jordan Mooney

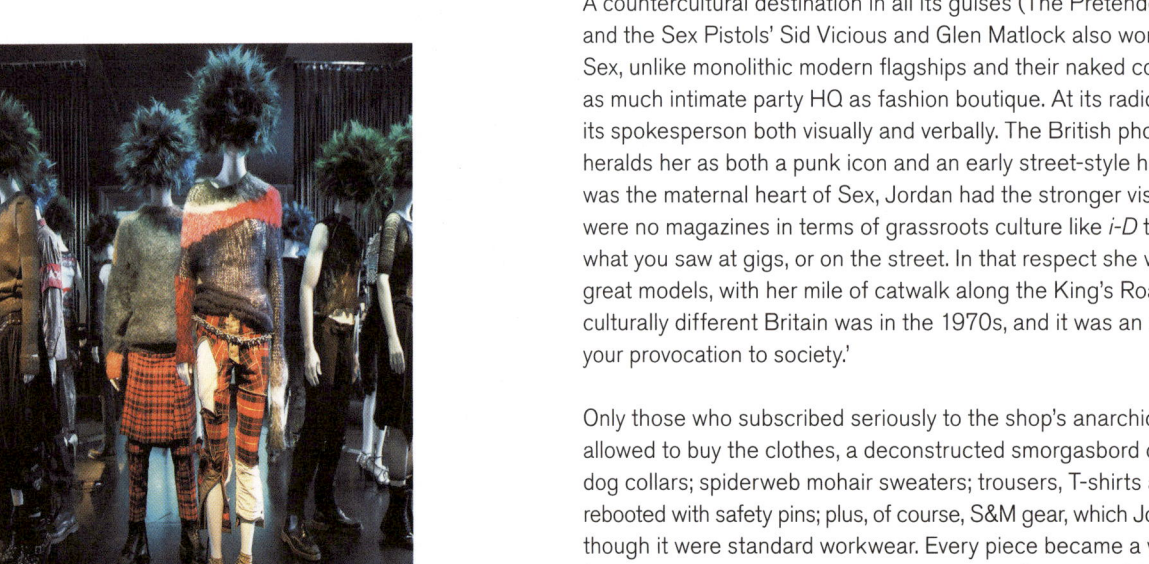

6

A countercultural destination in all its guises (The Pretenders' Chrissie Hynde and the Sex Pistols' Sid Vicious and Glen Matlock also worked there at times), Sex, unlike monolithic modern flagships and their naked commercialism, promised as much intimate party HQ as fashion boutique. At its radical heart was Jordan, its spokesperson both visually and verbally. The British photographer Nick Knight heralds her as both a punk icon and an early street-style hero: 'While Vivienne was the maternal heart of Sex, Jordan had the stronger visual presence. There were no magazines in terms of grassroots culture like *i-D* then: fashion was what you saw at gigs, or on the street. In that respect she was one of the first great models, with her mile of catwalk along the King's Road. People forget how culturally different Britain was in the 1970s, and it was an amazing way to display your provocation to society.'

Only those who subscribed seriously to the shop's anarchic manifesto were allowed to buy the clothes, a deconstructed smorgasbord of Scottish tartan and dog collars; spiderweb mohair sweaters; trousers, T-shirts and shirts ripped and rebooted with safety pins; plus, of course, S&M gear, which Jordan famously wore as though it were standard workwear. Every piece became a wearable sociopolitical fashion souvenir. Having by now transitioned from her 1950s bias to pneumatic, rubber-clad, fetish-wear punk vixen ('I'm actually quite a shy person as far as sexuality goes – it was purely about the look, it wasn't a sexual thing'), she recalls how she and Westwood would effectively interview those who dared to make the pilgrimage. A level of sartorial alienation was absolutely essential. 'The wrong person wearing it would bastardize the message, so the clothes couldn't go to just anybody. Some people railed at the price because of the [deconstructed] nature of the pieces, but beauty and style and originality shouldn't just be given away.'

8

The album artwork for *Never Mind the Bollocks, Here's the Sex Pistols* (1977), designed by Jamie Reid, was an enduring part of the band's critical visual mythology.

9,10

Johnny Rotten (John Lydon) in signature `cobweb' sweater, a look borrowed from Jordan (seen here with Bertie `Berlin' Marshall). Photographed by Ray Stevenson (9) and Simon (Six) Barker (10).

11

A still from the video for `Buffalo Gals' (1982) by the US hip-hop group the World's Famous Supreme Team (managed by McLaren). The thick mud stripes on the girl's face echo the face packs Jordan wore while working at Sex.

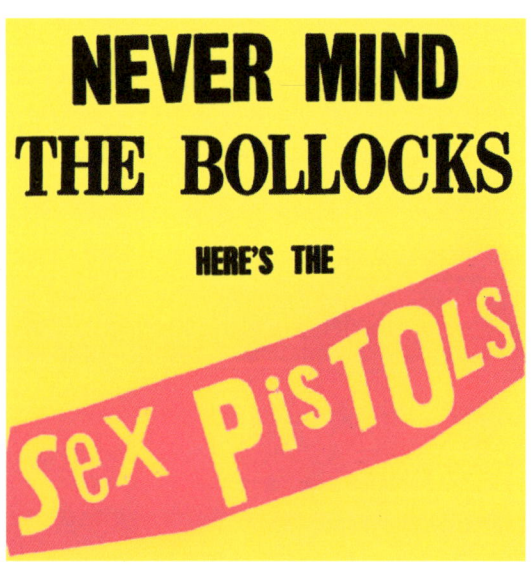

8

That wider message, according to Jordan, truly climaxed only when music, specifically the Sex Pistols (the band McLaren was managing), became a significant part of the picture. 'Sometimes things come together, and the machinations of how they happen aren't clear, but they forge something amazing. The Sex Pistols, and also Jamie Reid [the British graphic artist whose single and album artworks were critical in defining punk's visual thread], brought that scene and that attitude to life,' says Jordan. Steered by the hyper-commercially astute McLaren and powered by Sex's ambience of rebellion, Westwood's designs as stage wear and Reid's graphic communications, the Sex Pistols were the first great example of visual-sonic-attitudinal alignment: a full package borne of entrepreneurial marketing genius, created with the help of willing accomplices.

Often described as the fifth Sex Pistol, always visible at their gigs, Jordan was instrumental – not only as a linchpin muse to the movement, but more practically as a kind of surrogate, unofficial stylist. On many occasions, her core sartorial traits at the time slipped directly into their looks, most notably the unravelling cobweb sweaters ('they wouldn't last an entire day'), cigarette-burnt garments and the most iconic of all: safety pins. The pins came directly from an instance when she had worn to the shop a bright-blue leotard (one of many dancing references, subtly symbolic of her disciplined nature) that she had pinned together after over-slicing a rip across the chest. Other artists in a quest to stand out visually also scavenged significant details: Pete Burns, flamboyant frontman of the early 1980s band Dead or Alive, lifted her one-time penchant for wearing *Nosferatu*-style red contact lenses. McLaren's later collaboration on the track 'Buffalo Gals' with the US hip-hop group The World's Famous Supreme Team was accompanied by a video in which the women bore thick mud stripes across their faces, resembling the face-packs Jordan would wear on the shop floor. Even David Bowie once asked her for the homemade starling's-feather earring she wore to one of his gigs (then still at school, she said no; as a sign of how far she's come since, the pair would later share a stage at the Cannes film festival). The British music journalist Caroline Coon – who coined the term the 'Bromley Contingent', a tag for the Sex Pistols' core punk conspirators including Jordan, Siouxsie Sioux, Philip Salon, Simon Barker (aka Six) and Steven Severin – has even suggested that Madonna's infamous conical bra devised by Jean Paul Gaultier was an idea bounced from Jordan, who would wear 1950s-style pointy satin bras in the shop.

Although not a stylist in the traditional sense, Jordan was certainly someone with a capacity to wield fashion as an exhilaratingly disruptive force (as long as it tallied with her own perspective). She remained a pivotal figure in the fashion–music crucible at the dawn of the 1980s, when the nihilism of punk slid into the brighter, more theatrical epoch of new wave/New Romantics. While aesthetically disparate at first glance, the movements shared a core parity based on increasingly fluid gender roles. 'During the punk period, fashion and sexuality became one,' she says. 'For the first time, men wanted to dress up as much as their girlfriends, meaning there was a certain type of equality playing out. In many ways punk was actually a new form of dandyism, and that carried on.'

At the centre of that shift, grounded fully in the riches of such dandified visual gameplay, was the cult pop group Adam and the Ants. McLaren had signed the group, then cannibalized it, taking all but Adam (Stuart Goddard) to form Bow Wow Wow, ostensibly as a platform for Westwood's New Romantic collections. Having learned McLaren's mastery of media spin by osmosis, Jordan became an early manager for the reincarnated version of Adam and the Ants. She was involved in every part of strategizing the creative process, stretching from listening to demo tapes and plotting videos to, of course, the fashion.

+ Sex Pistols, Adam and the Ants

During the punk period, fashion and sexuality became one. For the first time, men wanted to dress up as much as their girlfriends, meaning there was a certain type of equality playing out. In many ways punk was actually a new form of dandyism, and that carried on.

Jordan Mooney

> **Jordan created punk rock. She was literally selling it on the frontline. She was living it on public transport when other people were just dressing up. There is fashion and there is style, and she is the epitome of style. It was an extremely auspicious start to have someone looking that good managing us.**
>
> Adam Ant, musician and singer-songwriter

Playing to the pirate theme already established before the break-up by McLaren ('Malcolm and Adam initiated it, I elevated it,' says Jordan), they extended the maverick stance of the punk era but embellished it with the more theatrical sensibility (the highwayman look) that distinguished them from their harder, more aggressive punk predecessors, not to mention a glossier edge primed to seduce a more mainstream global audience. She recalls their televised Royal Variety Performance at the London Palladium, in which she styled the bassist Kevin Mooney 'to look like a palomino pony in white culottes, his face painted in all kinds of colour, and big leather pirate boots'. She also recalls the seminal album cover for *Kings of the Wild Frontier* (1980). Its tribalism theme, echoing the African 'Burundi Beat' that underscored the album's sound, is epitomized by Adam's own 'half Clint Eastwood, half Geromino plus white Apache war stripe (symbolic of my declaration against the music business)', as he put it. Other visual tics reverberated with her handiwork: ribboned ringlets – directly borrowed from her own look – and an ever-so-slightly unhinged blur that recalls the frenzy of punk's original, most feral phase. 'Jordan created punk rock,' says Adam Ant. 'She was literally selling it on the frontline. She was living it on public transport when other people were just dressing up. There is fashion and there is style, and she is the epitome of style. It was an extremely auspicious start to have someone looking that good managing us.'

Jordan was now so famous (before the seventies expired, she had enjoyed a private audience with Andy Warhol, had played the lead role of Amyl Nitrate in Derek Jarman's feature film *Jubilee* and was regularly receiving fan mail) that people in the street or at gigs would accuse her of imitating herself, amazed that the real Jordan would be grafting with the band. As the audiences got bigger and the styling for tracks such as 'Prince Charming' became more pantomime ('I was never into creating characters; I always veered towards it being more realistic'), she bowed out. 'It was essentially self-preservation. I have never done anything I haven't totally wanted to commit to,' she says, inadvertently observing her own legend. Ultimately it is Jordan's unflinching capacity to remain entirely individual that has ensured her a place in one of the twentieth century's most influential periods in pop culture. 'There are some people in this world who need to be reinforced by others, and there are some who never need that assurance. Ultimately it's about not being precious with your identity, or vain, which is the common misconception concerning people who dressed like me. It's about the opposite – simply knowing who you are.'

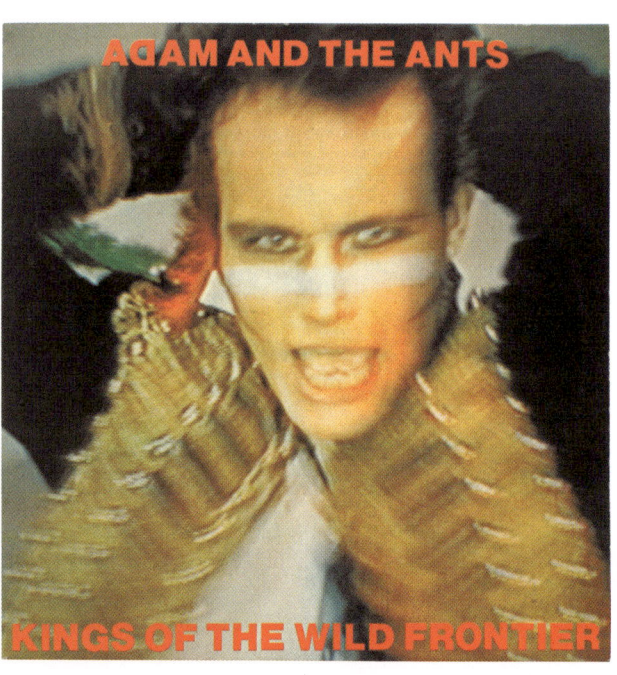

12

Arianne Phillips

+

Madonna, Lenny Kravitz, Courtney Love

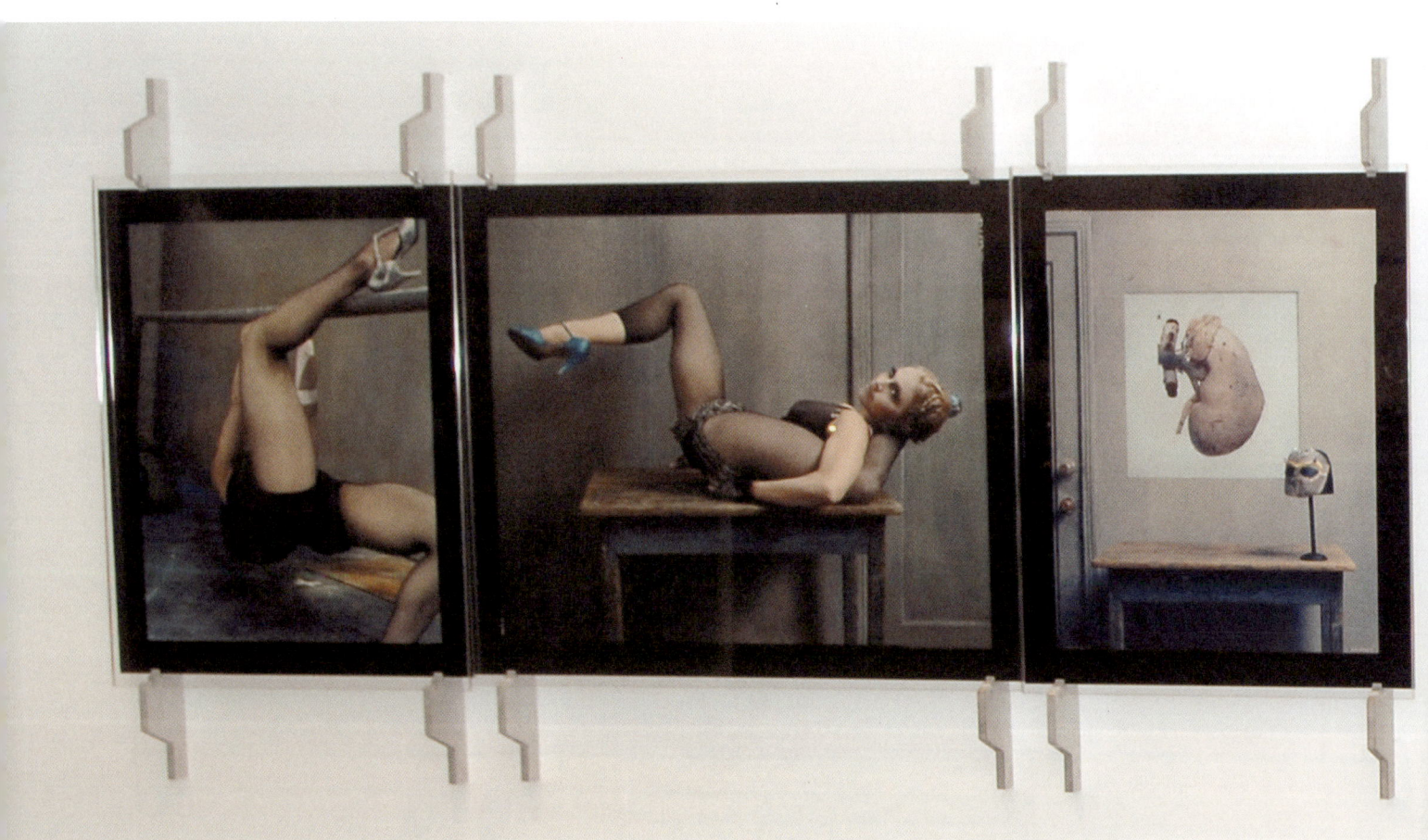

1

Great storytelling is always seductive and frequently challenging, but it is never more powerful or provocative than when the stage is primed for a global audience, as Arianne Phillips - multiple-Oscar-nominated costume designer, fashion stylist and Madonna's most enduring creative collaborator - can attest. Her fashion acumen and calm revolutionary spirit have made her one of the most influential visual raconteurs in the world.

2

3

1
Images from `X-STaTIC PRO=CeSS', a seminal 30-page shoot for W magazine (2001) that exemplifies Madonna and Phillips' epic odysseys of artistic storytelling. Photographed by Steven Klein.

2
Madonna's music video `Nothing Really Matters' (1999) was inspired by Arthur Golden's book *Memoirs of a Geisha*.

3
Lenny Kravitz in the video `Are You Gonna Go My Way?' (1993), for which Kravitz credits Phillips with creating an identity that `helped me to become myself'.

Phillips' unique creative drive – which has left its mark on stadium tours, music videos, catwalk shows and Hollywood movies (*W.E.*, *Walk the Line*, *The Crow*, *Tank Girl*, *A Single Man* and *The People vs. Larry Flynt*) – reaches back, in its essence, to 1960s California. As the child of liberal academic parents ensconced in the heart of America's Youth Movement – a sociopolitical storm defined by civil protest and experimental practice (in teaching, parenting, religion, sexuality) – she grew up with rock concerts and peace rallies running hand-in-hand, both cloaked aesthetically in psychedelic flamboyance. 'The rock and roll that influenced me had a sense of the peacock about it. It was colourful, provocative, shiny and glittery, and it was dependent on you to create something very expressive visually. You were encouraged to let your freak flag fly, which meant it was dangerous but not particularly dark. All of which I loved,' recalls Phillips, who describes herself as a 'cultural anthropologist'.

4

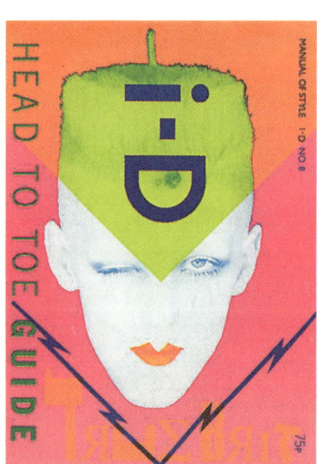
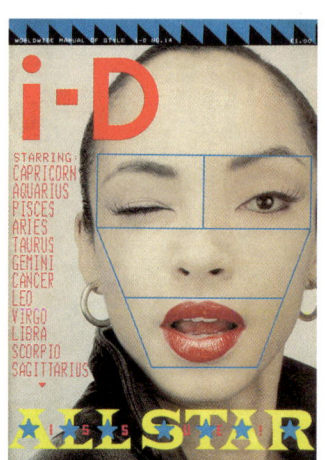

5

It was also an early life defined by spontaneity – Phillips' parents moved often – which instilled an inescapable sense of voyeurism fundamental to her professional success. Always the interloper, she used adaptation and transformation as a survivalist toolkit: 'As a kid constantly moving around to different schools, it was all about fitting in. I was very self-aware and hyper-sensitive of my surroundings, which transformed me into an expert observer. It informed my ability to read a situation, then mentally organize it, which ultimately became like a kind of muscle I could use in my work as a storyteller. As a teen, however, it was the opposite – I crafted an identity as a mode of rebellion.'

Integral to that rebellion was the cult musical comedy *The Rocky Horror Picture Show* (1975) and its raucous affirmation of the power of the rebel outsider. A brilliantly demented story of a gender-bending cosmos of misfits and outsiders wrapped up in an exhilarating visual tableau, it was, according to Phillips, an attitudinal 'game-changer' (the song 'Don't Dream It, Be It!' remains her personal mantra) that has positively ricocheted throughout her career. Fashion was not the point, but it was vital to the story's message. Potent echoes of that homage to alternative lifestyles were also to be found in London's late 1970s/early 1980s club scene – another hotspot fuelling Phillips' fashion–music fire. The city was alight with a subcultural tribe of hedonistic party people, helmed by the iconic performance artist Leigh Bowery, who was challenging the status quo with extravagant shows of costumed self-expression. An irresistible bunch of urban libertines competing to stand out aesthetically, worlds apart from the casual sun-soaked vibe of California, they prompted Phillips to wear her own difference like a badge of honour. Fed by British magazines such as *Blitz* and *i-D* and album covers from bands including Depeche Mode, Spandau Ballet, This Mortal Coil and The Slits, Phillips says, 'British street culture fired my motivation for everything… [it] influenced my entire career.'

+ Madonna, Lenny Kravitz, Courtney Love

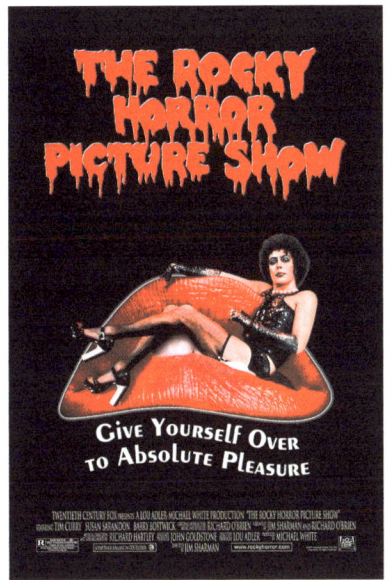

6

4,5
Blitz and *i-D* – two key British magazines offering creatively experimental windows on street style and grassroots culture that were seminal early influences for Phillips.

6
Poster for the cult musical film *The Rocky Horror Picture Show* (1975), a visionary tale of otherworldly rebel misfits that fired Phillips' creative motivation.

7
More stills from Kravitz's music video for `Are You Gonna Go My Way?' (1993).

At 20 Phillips moved to New York, echoing Madonna ('we were both incredibly influenced by music as a tool for self-definition, and New York was a key part of that'). She was cast almost immediately in a catwalk show by the seminal London club-kid fashion designers BodyMap – Stevie Stewart and David Holah – who were renowned for their radical stance on inclusivity and predilection for mixing fashion, music and dance. An agent followed, as did stints working for fashion magazines and a spot assisting on the short-lived TV show *Fashion America* (created by Sandy Hill, the then wife of MTV founder Bob Pittman), all of which confirmed Phillips' rejection of 'pure' fashion. 'Fashion was about making things look pretty or sexy, whereas music was something to be inspired by,' she says. 'There was always a reason for the clothes – a story, an image and a point of view – and I felt that had much more gravitas. It gave me motivation and a thoughtful context.' Her first shoot with musicians, titled 'Rock Star Fashion Trips', was for *Details* magazine and featured Iggy Pop and Chrissie Hynde.

Phillips' first full collaboration was with the then little-known American funk-rock musician Lenny Kravitz, a lifelong friend whom she met shortly after arriving in New York. For the cover art of both his debut album *Let Love Rule* (1989) and *Mama Said* (1991), Phillips mined their shared love of 1970s rock-and-roll bohemia to develop a neo-hippie style that spotlighted the soulful aspect of his already visible rock edge. She also styled the Mark Romanek-directed video to Kravitz's 'Are You Gonna Go my Way?' (1993) – a project she believes was a career-defining moment. In the video, Kravitz – holding court in a golden amphitheatre that is part stadium, part disco – is resplendent in a tight red jumpsuit, platform boots and signature dreadlocks. Kravitz perceives it as a similarly galvanizing experience: 'When I played her my music, she saw images. Her creation of the red suede suit propelled me to somewhere I hadn't been. It had a real sense of ceremony, of the tribal – a kind of minister of rock-and-roll vibe that completely set the tone. It was the centrepiece that commanded everything. My first two albums were based on thrift-store looks that were very vibrant at the time, but this video signalled the beginning of custom pieces – an identity that didn't follow existing fashion but was original to me. Ari effectively helped me to become myself, and together we changed things.'

7

It had a real sense of ceremony, of the tribal – a kind of minister of rock-and-roll vibe that completely set the tone ... Ari effectively helped me to become myself, and together we changed things.

Lenny Kravitz, musician and singer-songwriter

8
A scene from the 2014 version of the stage show *Hedwig and the Angry Inch*, a pioneering story of brilliant social outliers, costumed by Phillips.

9
On Madonna's video for 'Frozen' (1998), Phillips collaborated with 'kindred spirit' Jean Paul Gaultier to produce pieces that evoked a sense of spectral transformation.

10

11

10
For *Rolling Stone*'s 30th anniversary issue, 'Women of Rock' (1997), Phillips styled both Courtney Love and Madonna, the latter for the very first time. Photographed by Peggy Sirota.

11
Madonna's album *Rebel Heart* (2015), styled by Phillips, photographed by Mert and Marcus. Typical of Phillips' work with Madonna, and directly echoing the Che Guevara-referencing *American Life* (2003), the image is rife with themes of romance, rebellion and the iconography of freedom fighters.

Madonna, whom Phillips refers to as a 'true creative athlete', presented the next seismic shift in her fashion–music continuum. Having been formally introduced by Courtney Love, the pair first worked together to shoot the cover of *Rolling Stone* magazine's 30th anniversary Women of Rock issue in November 1997 (Phillips styled both women for the cover, which also featured Tina Turner). Their first video collaboration was 'Frozen' (1998), directed by Chris Cunningham. Jean Paul Gaultier's spring–summer 1998 'Tribute to Frida Kahlo' collection – a gothic homage to the transgressive Mexican painter – had inspired Madonna, who appears in the spartan darkness of the Californian desert as an ethereal shape-shifting spectre, and it was Phillips' job to reimagine his designs for film. The trio met, with Gaultier and Phillips collaboratively sketching reworked versions of his original pieces while listening to the track – an exercise that led to the addition of a sweeping hood shielding Madonna's face in the video as a series of mystical transformations transpires. Phillips describes the video as another landmark moment, courtesy of Gaultier's extraordinarily passionate track record (partly built in tandem with Madonna) for pushing atypical ideals of beauty, identity and gender: 'It was an incredible moment because [like Madonna] he was also an artist of rock-star proportions, and a huge inspiration in terms of his gender-bending and the barriers that he's broken between womenswear and menswear.' Phillips and Gaultier are kindred creative spirits, and his legacy remains close to her heart – clearly visible in her *Rocky Horror*-recalling costuming of both the film and Broadway versions of *Hedwig and the Angry Inch*, the fictional story of a 1970s glam rock band fronted by a transgender singer.

'Ray of Light' (1998) followed, by which time Phillips had become comfortable enough with Madonna to truly co-steer the newest chameleonic reinvention ('until then I'd been absorbing her'). Just after Madonna's starring role in the film *Evita*, her infamous *Sex* book and the ultra-conceptual visualization of 'Frozen', Phillips cultivated a look that would translate Madonna's introspective search for personal enlightenment (the singer had begun practising yoga, had converted to Kabbalah and had also given birth to her first child) into a straightforwardly joyous sense of celebration. The resulting imagery – anchored by subtly reimagined, simple but iconic clothing including a white vest, grey wool trousers and a denim jacket atypical of her former, aggressively sexualized sensibility – served to humanize the pop queen, who had hitherto been inscrutable. The naturalized styling in 'Ray of Light' also mirrored the song's lyrical ode to freedom and the album's clubby electro-pop sound; it additionally attuned Madonna to a near-noughties, pre-millennial audience similarly hungry for change. 'I wanted it to be very simple, quite anti-fashion in a way. "Ray of Light" was all about joyousness and dancing and abandoned movement – it was the right time to do something less high concept, more street,' says Phillips.

It is a more accessible stance visible in several of Madonna's other Phillips-guided videos and album artworks: the dancer's leotard of 'Hung Up' (2005), the cowgirl denim and plaid of 'Don't Tell Me' (2009) and the sports-luxe look of 'Girl Gone Wild' (2012). But every shift in look, says Phillips, is ultimately an organic process, a combination of the artist's own life and both women's devotion to characterization in order to amplify message: 'She [Madonna] is very into storytelling and narrative to give a purpose and a context to a conceptual idea. What may surprise a lot of people is that she's actually a very private person and probably most comfortable when she's channelling a character. She's a perpetual student with a huge appetite for art and culture, which is an integral part of her dialogue, informing the look, but there is always a truth to the reinventions – a conversation connected to her preoccupations. It's probably the reason for our long relationship – because we both militantly believe in self-expression and creativity, and the need to be who you really are in order to express yourself.' Madonna affirms this in her praise of Phillips, whom she describes as having an utterly 'unique and clever' vision: 'All of her choices are character driven. She works from the inside out when it comes to styling or fashion design, which is why we work with as much attention to detail on a photoshoot as we do on a film and why I cannot imagine making any film without her.'

12

There is always a truth to the reinventions - a conversation connected to [Madonna's] preoccupations. It's probably the reason for our long relationship - because we both militantly believe in self-expression and creativity, and the need to be who you really are in order to express yourself.

Arianne Phillips

The video for 'Nothing Really Matters' (1999) also recounts that drip-feed of personal obsessions. Madonna and Phillips were inspired by Arthur Golden's novel *Memoirs of a Geisha* (1997); the video's centrepiece is a silken red Jean Paul Gaultier kimono with a latex obi belt that Gaultier had personally crafted from bandages. The cowboy-esque styling and classic American suburban backdrop of the *Music* album cover (2000) are direct reflections of the fact that Madonna had been learning to play the acoustic guitar – an emblem of Americana-led curiosity. A customized hat inspired by the fashion editor and photographer Lisa Eisner's gritty-but-glitzy photo-journal *Rodeo Girls* of the all-American pastime compounded the visual theme.

Fashion applied to music is, according to Phillips, best served not only in terms of crafting compelling characters to flesh out concepts but also as immortalized snapshots of our social history. 'I've done quite a few covers of *Rolling Stone* over the years and I've always seen that as quite an echo of our times,' says Phillips. 'I did the cover many years ago with [US rapper] Ice T when he released his *Cop Killer* album [a major protest record challenging police brutality], and he was wearing a police uniform. It was all about what was happening in that artist's career at the moment. Madonna is a similarly of-the-moment and forward-thinking artist. She doesn't like to look back or repeat herself, unless it's poking fun at something – like the tongue-in-cheek twenty-fifth anniversary performance of 'Like a Virgin' that we conceived for the MTV awards with Britney Spears and Christina Aguilera [all three were dressed in 1980s bridal wear].'

13

+ Madonna, Lenny Kravitz, Courtney Love

12
Madonna performing `Nothing Else Matters', wearing the Phillips/Gaultier interpretation of a kimono.

13–15
Lisa Eisner's photo-diary *Rodeo Girl* (2000) was an authentic study of a strand of Americana that fed directly into Phillips' styling of Madonna for the album *Music* (also 2000).

16

17

[Arianne] works from the inside out when it comes to styling or fashion design, which is why we work with as much attention to detail on a photoshoot as we do on a film and why I cannot imagine making any film without her.

Madonna, pop icon

+ Madonna, Lenny Kravitz, Courtney Love

18

16
Another image from the seminal
`X-STaTIC PRO=CeSS' series of 2001.

17
Madonna on stage during her
Confessions tour of 2006, which
Phillips partly costumed.

Another seminal moment for Phillips includes 'X-STaTIC PRO=CeSS' – an epic, 30-page super shoot that she created with Madonna and the photographer Steven Klein in 2001 for *W* magazine. Phillips believes the shoot epitomizes her and Madonna's symbiotic vision. An homage to transformation and to the value of art as an agent of change, the images are based on Madonna's own metamorphosis as an artist – tracing a line from her professional origins as a dancer in fishnet tights and a leotard to her current status as world-dominating pop Queen, represented by an extraordinarily extravagant body-encasing Christian Lacroix gown. Later, in 2003, Klein translated the imagery into a book and video installation for the New York gallery Deitch Projects. The shoot also spawned Klein's subsequent moving imagery for Madonna's Reinvention tour in 2004 and the sensational equestrian imagery of the Confessions tour in 2006. Other tours on which the pair have collaborated include Drowned World (2001), Sticky & Sweet (2008) and MDNA (2012), for which Phillips directed the costumes for every segment. Her union with Madonna has also extended into a cinematic alliance. For Madonna's directorial debut on *W.E.* (2001), Phillips was head costume designer. She says: 'I love being on the same side of the camera to her because she doesn't have to insert her physicality into the equation, allowing her a different perspective. And she has great taste. Most directors don't have the vernacular to talk about clothes or costumes.'

Sexual ambiguity, transformation, justice and the fight for freedom of self-expression run deep throughout the careers of both Phillips and Madonna – past, present, conjoined and solo. As their gender-bending shoot for the May/June 2014 issue of *L'Uomo Vogue* shot by Tom Munro affirms, old habits die hard, and true global pop superstars (and their collaborators) never renounce their ability to stimulate or push buttons.

19

18
The controversial *Rolling Stone*
cover featuring rapper Ice-T and
styled by Phillips bears references
to the rapper's topical protest
record `Cop Killer' (1992), a
key snapshot of social history.
Photographed by Mark Seliger.

19
Madonna and Phillips refocus on
their enduring preoccupations –
sexual ambiguity, transformation
and the right to self-expression
– in the shoot `Art for Freedom',
photographed by Tom Munro for
L'Uomo Vogue (2014).

Antony Price

+

Roxy Music, Duran Duran

Possibly one of Britain's greatest under-celebrated couturiers, Antony Price was using fashion to make music heard before fashion had any affection, genuine or mercenary, for the pop stars it now feverishly cherishes like demi-gods. His vision, largely centred on the 1970s/1980s British art-rock pop stars Roxy Music and later post-punk New Romantic pop sensation Duran Duran, has left an indelible, enduring influence.

Several decades too early to bask in the full glow of fame that the twenty-first century's super-stylists now revel in, Price was undoubtedly the prototype for the modern definition of creative director – layering art direction, photography, set design, lighting and styling on to his highly accomplished core skill set as a Royal College of Art-trained fashion designer in order to deify his pop star cohorts. Price's future-retro vision of hardened Hollywood glamour and impenetrable yet romanticized beauty (bubbling with a potent sense of sexual confusion) both defined the media presence of the bands he worked with and spawned a new male aesthetic. Oozing a camp theatricality mixed with the exaggerated bravado of a generation acutely aware of the sexual spoils and commercial rewards of being a pop star, he was involved in the bands' clothes, album art and music videos and was, in fact, the first 'stylist' to be officially credited on a music album.

2
Creative polymath: Price's illustration of the fictional retail vixen Zonda, from his shop, Plaza. The character pre-empted the now iconic pantheon of Roxy Women whom Price codirected into being.

Price grew up in the Yorkshire Dales in northern England, within an inspirational idyll of nature, animals and a coterie of curvy sisters whom he adored entertaining; 'I had no desire to be a woman but I loved to dress them,' he says. It was at the Royal College of Art in London that he became a master of precision cutting ('I modelled my career on Balenciaga and Givenchy – brands that required architectural cutting skills'). Addicted to the power of sartorial illusion, after graduating in 1968 he found a role with the British fashion label Stirling Cooper, at the heart of London's thriving West End fashion scene. Fuelled by fantasies including Travis Banton's costumes for Marlene Dietrich in films by Josef von Sternberg, Price began crafting highly structural pieces with a fetish-meets-1930s influence. His bridge-crutch trousers – 'like an underpant over trousers but with a ziggurat seam', as he puts it – enticed Mick Jagger and the Rolling Stones as well as David Bowie, who adopted the signature trousers.

+ Roxy Music, Duran Duran

Price was also building his own reputation in the early 1980s with shows that he dubbed 'Fashion Extravaganzas'. A love–hate activity for him, the shows pre-empted the late-nineties/early-noughties catwalk spectacles-cum-media events whipped into being by the icons Alexander McQueen and John Galliano, both of whom were in Price's audiences, not yet even fledgling designers. Flamboyant in the extreme, Price's shows featured omnipresent entertainment: Nick Kamen walked while singing John Leyton's 'Wild Wind', and the DJ Jeremy Healy looked like 'Barbie meets Action Man', recalls Price. Unfortunately, he was too far ahead of the curve. 'I loved the showmanship of doing fashion shows, even as they trembled towards their incredibly hard-to-control, glossy climax,' says Price. 'But unlike my successors, we didn't have the support of the big French or Italian brands, which would have been the equivalent of landing a major record deal. It was just me, my assistant, my business partner Rick Cunningham and a few machinists.' While the shows proved too exhausting on every level to continue, the requisite stagecraft found a kindred spirit in pop music; Price's innate perception of fashion as an art form to be witnessed in the glorious silkiness of cinematic motion would even go on to influence other seminal music–fashion stylists including Judy Blame (see page 30), who cites him as 'one of the people who inspired me to find my own visual language, sealing my direction'.

For straight guys I was the acceptable face of fashion. I was glamorous but not mincy, and the clothes were avant–garde, things that look good on stage. Plus the 'manly' rural skills I'd picked up in Yorkshire helped with the bonding process.

Antony Price

Between the shows and the shops (first Stirling Cooper, featuring an interior of extravagant black pagodas designed with fellow RCA graduate Jane Whiteside, then Price's own store, Plaza), musicians gravitated towards Price's showy signature style; Roxy Music, which was working on its first, self-titled album, was followed by Duran Duran and David Bowie, among others. The shops in particular became beacons for musicians who were seeking sartorial salvation and were happy to sacrifice rock's anti-fashion stance to achieve it. Plaza 'had mirrored changing rooms, to which clothes would be brought to you in your size. People didn't know if it was a massage parlour or a betting shop,' recalls Price, who even illustrated its advertisements featuring a fictional vixen, Zonda – a spiky caricature of the seductresses to come. The gatekeeper of telegenic sex appeal, Price offered a bridge – accessible but outré enough to be inspiring – between the gay and straight communities: 'For straight guys I was the acceptable face of fashion. I was glamorous but not mincy, and the clothes were avant-garde, things that look good on stage. Plus the "manly" rural skills I'd picked up in Yorkshire helped with the bonding process. I could make a dry-stone wall; I could build and fix things. I was highly technical.'

Key to the connection was Price himself. Just as Freddie Burretti (Bowie's first serious fashion accomplice and author of Bowie's famous boxy suits and many of the early Ziggy Stardust costumes) had been a template for the sharp styling of Bowie's nascent career, Price, too, was a flesh-and-blood aesthetic blueprint for the Roxy Music look. 'They basically said: "Do to us what you do to yourself." Bryan [Ferry, Roxy Music's lead vocalist and songwriter,] was more Savile Row in his private life, classically English, but he needed a sharper edge for the stage. I made well-proportioned suits in fabrics that worked under the lights – Hollywood tailoring rather than Savile Row. But then Hollywood tailoring was actually borrowed from Savile Row in any case.'

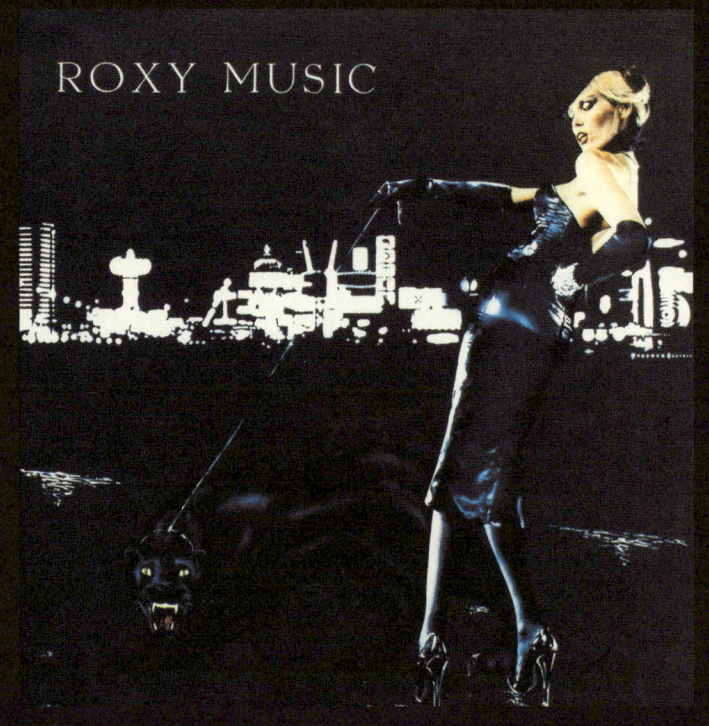

3

4

5

6

3–6
Roxy Women – the army of still-fetishized cover artwork muse-goddess-vamps that became a signature of the band and a benchmark for rock glamour: *For Your Pleasure* (3; 1973) featuring Amanda Lear, photographed by Karl Stoecker; *Country Life* (4; 1974), shot by Eric Boman (an image initially considered so pornographic that it was banned in the US); *Roxy Music* (5; 1972), featuring Kari-Ann Muller, also shot by Stoecker; and *Flesh + Blood* (6; 1980), by Price, photographer Neil Kirk and graphic designer Peter Saville.

7
Album artwork for Bryan Ferry's single 'Slave to Love' (1985), which Price photographed himself.

Having redefined the suit in the suavest, slinkiest form for public appearances, Price next worked on the group's first artwork collaboration, for the cover of *Roxy Music* (1972), shot by Karl Stoecker and featuring Kari-Ann Muller sprawled showgirl-esque across a kitsch 1950s pastel bedspread. The project was the first to showcase one of the now iconic Roxy Women: a still-fetishized pantheon of semi-predatory model–muse–goddesses. While putting women on the album covers was Ferry's idea (Roxy Music was also the first band to have backing dancers, all of whom Price dressed, because 'Bryan likes to have as many women in his entourage as possible to boost the glamour factor'), it was Price's styling and shrewd codirection that helped to render them immortal. While they are sometimes criticized for bordering on chauvinistic, the images of the women reflect a Guy Bourdin-esque 'sexy over sexist stance' that – bolstered by a coincidence with the first true wave of all-conquering female supermodels, a breed of glamazonian women with heavenly bodies, formidable characters and the critical aura of a stratospherically unattainable lifestyle – cemented their legacy. Sky-high aspirations and faster/sexier/sunnier fantasies were essential ingredients of the perfectly packaged charm.

I loved the idea of the art of the makeover, the transformation. Most fashion people share a sense of dissatisfaction with themselves, which is what leads them to fashion in the first place.

Antony Price

One of the most notable Roxy Music album covers is *For Your Pleasure* (1973), featuring Amanda Lear, stalwart of the 1970s club scene, model–muse to Salvador Dalí and friend of Ferry. Sheathed in black latex and holding a panther on a leash, Lear poses in film noir-meets-Allen Jones style. The enigmatic Lear, an unconfirmed transsexual who happily traded on rumours of her own fictionalized backstory, was as fitting a symbol as possible for a band toying with carving out a niche as pop's perfect artefact. The cover of the album *Country Life* (1974), shot by Eric Boman and featuring the German models Constanze Caroli and Eveline Grunwald wearing next to nothing against a verdant backdrop, was considered so close to soft porn at the time of its release that the American cover art featured only trees; while *Stranded* (1973) boasts a gatefold cover emblazoned with Marilyn Cole, one of the first major *Playboy* models. *Siren* (1975) remains Price's favourite album cover. Featuring the legendary Texan supermodel Jerry Hall crawling across a rocky shoreline like a mythical blue mermaid, it was an all-hands-on-deck DIY endeavour; Price selected Hall's waterproof make-up, spray-painted her costume and even pre-sketched the scene for the photographer, Graham Hughes. *Flesh + Blood* (1980) – co-attributed to Price, photographer Neil Kirk and acclaimed graphic designer Peter Saville – again replaced the band with models, in this case angelic girls in simple white vest-dresses.

7

8

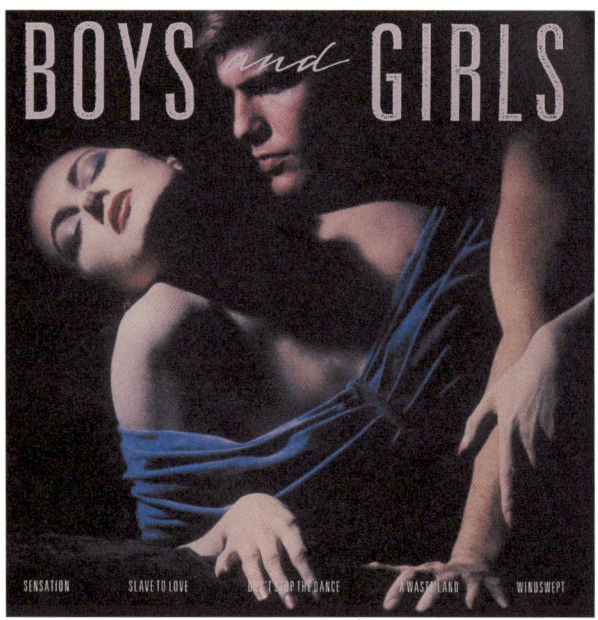

9

I was thinking of MTV years before it happened, as was Bryan [Ferry]. We always wanted visuals to go with the music.

Antony Price

10

Ferry's solo work continued the legacy; *Olympia* (2010) features an ultra-glossy vision of the twenty-first century's arguably most iconic model, Kate Moss, reclining on white silk sheets. Price too has taken the concept elsewhere. The back cover of Lou Reed's *Transformer* album (1972) features another of Price's favourite models, the former ballerina Gayla Mitchell, in a black basque-like leotard with chiffon sleeves; she poses opposite an ultra-masculine figure in blue jeans and white T-shirt, reminiscent of a camp Tom of Finland illustration – another of Price's core artistic references. It's classic Price: exaggerated visions of both masculinity and femininity – pulled to the point of almost doubling back on themselves like adult-only versions of Barbie and Ken.

So significant was Price's contribution to Roxy Music that in several instances – including Ferry's album *Boys and Girls* and its single 'Slave to Love' (both 1985) – he even photographed the cover artwork. Videos, too, fell under his creative stewardship, with Roxy Music's 'Angel Eyes' (1979) and Ferry's 'Let's Stick Together' (1976) and 'Slave to Love' combining fashion and set design duties. 'I was thinking of MTV years before it happened, as was Bryan. We always wanted visuals to go with the music,' says Price.

8
Transferred aesthetic: the back cover of Lou Reed's album *Transformers* (1972), styled by Price, has the same hallmarks of exaggerated sexuality that Price deployed for Roxy Music.

9
Bryan Ferry's solo album *Boys and Girls* (1985) was styled and photographed by Price.

10,12
Price produced both the fashion and the set design for Roxy Music's music videos 'Slave to Love' (10; 1975) and 'Let's Stick Together' (12; 1976).

11
Price's collection for the UK fashion giant Topman (2009-10) affirmed the continuing influence and appeal of the Roxy Music look, in particular Price's famous suits.

11

12

> **Ultimately, fashion makes trends then distances itself from them when they become popular, whereas in music a number one is a number one. I'm completely comfortable with the idea of mass adoration.**
>
> Antony Price

Although Roxy Music and its experimental art-school approach to making music have been lauded as an influence on artists as disparate as the cult indie group The Smiths, grunge gods Nirvana and overlords of stage-camp Scissor Sisters (all for different reasons), it is arguably the decadence of the band's carefully cultivated peacock-ery that propelled it to superstardom, prophesying with a wink the sleekly manufactured pop that dominated the 1980s. Artifice itself was pitched as worthy of aspiration, not solely as a superficial diversion. 'I loved the idea of the art of the makeover, the transformation. Most fashion people share a sense of dissatisfaction with themselves, which is what leads them to fashion in the first place,' says Price. But while the Roxy look filtered through into the mainstream, almost inexplicably Price has remained on the outskirts of the fashion industry's appreciated inner sanctum – aside from a collaboration in 2009–10, Priceless, for the British high-street giant Topman, which momentarily pumped Price's vision back into the public consciousness. He attributes his exclusion to the industry's largely female hierarchy and ongoing distaste for populism: 'In the fashion world, men's taste doesn't really exist because there is no true male equivalent in terms of a tastemaker to someone like Anna Wintour. Women dress in such a way as to impress each other, whereas music is far more "baked beans" – it's about men and women and sex and popularity. Fashion's artistic snobbery wouldn't accept someone with blue satin trousers that you could see their religion through and a black curly mullet. Ultimately, fashion makes trends then distances itself from them when they become popular, whereas in music a number one is a number one. I'm completely comfortable with the idea of mass adoration.'

13

> I once spent my entire EMI [record label] budget on one Antony Price suit; John [Taylor] did the same on a black leather jacket – both worn in the 'Planet Earth' video [1981].
>
> Nick Rhodes, musician

14

13
Pop megastars Duran Duran, another of Price's key creative collaborators, in their seminal music video `Rio' (1982), wearing the now iconic `electric silk tonic suits'.

14
Another look from Price's collection for Topman (2009-10).

While Roxy Music used fashion to amplify its initial sonic ambitions, Duran Duran was, says Price, wholly invested in the pure power of fashion as its route to superstardom. Price dressed the band in citrus-coloured Caribbean-attuned suits (aka the 'electric silk tonic suits') for its now iconic yacht-based video 'Rio' (1982). Fleshing out a template of glamour entirely fit for purpose, he has subsequently collaborated with the band on stage outfits for numerous tours and performances. According to the group's keyboardist, Nick Rhodes, Price has been 'an asset throughout our entire career. We didn't use stylists much until the nineties and were left to our own devices. I once spent my entire EMI [record label] budget on one Antony Price suit; John [Taylor] did the same on a black leather jacket – both worn in the "Planet Earth" video [1981]. We've worked with a lot of designers but he's the cleverest – an inventor and an innovator. A true artist.'

In another universe, Price might indeed have followed a career as a costume designer for film. He cites the designers Charles Knode (who codesigned the looks for *Blade Runner*), Janty Yates (*Gladiator*, *Prometheus*) and Eiko Ishioka (the late Oscar winner behind Francis Ford Coppola's *Dracula* and Tarsem Singh's *The Cell*) as creative heroes, in acknowledgement of a methodology rooted first and foremost in fantasy. Interiors, too, still hold an allure; he would, he says, be interested in designing another fashion store. At present, he continues to design for a roster of private clients, including actresses and models, seduced by his capacity to frame, guide and redefine the human body. He recalls the moment he dressed pop star Kylie Minogue for an appearance on the British version of TV show *The X Factor* (2012) in a Hollywood-esque pleated gold lamé dress that married style and structure so snugly that it literally informed her performance: 'It basically just took over her; it made her behave in a certain way that was so visible that the presenter was inadvertently practically mimicking her moves.'

In any instance it is the rich theatre of the ebb and flow of life, in all its grandeur and drama, that keeps Price's provocative instincts tethered to the pursuit of perfection, summarized by his unswerving love of gardening: 'There is no greater set of designs than nature, and nothing more natural than sexuality,' he says.

1
The NY punk/drag club Squeezebox!, which Schmidt cofounded in the 1990s, was an incubator for unorthodox, original personal style and became a beacon for cultural innovators.

2,4
Jeremy Scott's autumn-winter collections in 2011 (2) and 2012 (4) featured printed metal mesh pieces by Schmidt. Scott and Schmidt collaborate regularly.

3
Tina Turner, the archetype of Schmidt's female 'warriors', wearing a Schmidt-designed minidress engineered using thousands of crystals on body-skimming mesh. Photographed by Herb Ritts for her album *Foreign Affair* (1989).

Michael Schmidt is a rebel innovator whose 'voracious need for the new', extreme levels of craftsmanship (his iconic stage wear is as much armour as clothing) and seductively elegant rock aesthetic have entranced, and enhanced, a formidable list of collaborators over the course of the last three decades, including Cher, Aerosmith, Debbie Harry, Tina Turner, Madonna, Rihanna, Britney Spears and Lady Gaga.

Michael Schmidt

+

Cher, Debbie Harry, Tina Turner,
Britney Spears, Rihanna, Lady Gaga,
Madonna, Aerosmith

Michael Schmidt

A fashion designer renowned for operating far beyond traditional parameters – a paragon of rock-and-roll-style creativity – Schmidt was born and raised in Kansas City, Missouri, an epic stretch (literally and metaphorically) from the bright lights of America's hot pop-culture epicentres. Schmidt describes music and the wider entertainment industry as vital escape routes from relative isolation – thrilling connective hooks dangling hand in glove with fashion. 'From a young age I had a very visceral connection to clothing: I realized that the way one presents oneself is vital in communicating your intentions and your perceived place in the world, and entertainers – singers, performers, concerts – were my outlet, my way of experiencing what I felt was out there.'

Schmidt, who is now based in Los Angeles, has effectively been substantiating that connection by offering fashion creations to his idols ever since. His introduction to the music industry was, inadvertently, colossal: a baptism of fire via a serendipitous meeting with Cher (already a global superstar), who had spotted a tattered chain-mail mesh dress he had created hanging in the window of a small boutique in SoHo, New York. It was 1984; he was just 19 years old and had been creating one-off pieces of jewellery and fashion in his tiny apartment from remnants of metal and found objects scavenged from the streets. For Schmidt, who had been obsessed with Sonny & Cher's TV show in the late 1970s, it was 'no small miracle'. He describes the female star as 'the greatest example of pop-culture fantasy and glamazon beauty that a kid like me in the Midwest could have'.

As their partnership blossomed, Schmidt countered Cher's ritzy showgirl-esque personae, created with the costume designer Bob Mackie, with a more fashion, feral, street-influenced look – a stylistic redirection so enduring that the original tattered chain-mail dress was recycled two decades later to promote her residency in Las Vegas. Cher began giving Schmidt's pieces to other artists fully grounded in the rock sensibility, including Jon Bon Jovi and Tina Turner. The small trophies fed Schmidt's burgeoning reputation as an original designer with performance-ready edge, and spurred requests for stage wear from bands including Skid Row, Aerosmith and Bon Jovi.

The gifted pieces, effectively mementoes of support and admiration, solidified Schmidt's design methodology, which focuses on amplifying personae already in play rather than reinventing or building from scratch. Nonetheless, every creation of his boasts his inimitable creative handwriting, because artists who commission Schmidt do so in full knowledge of his capacity to respond to an exhilarating vocal presence with a corresponding visual spectacular. 'I'm not interested in dictating far-out fantastic ideas. I'm interested in the constraints of their public persona, the persona to whom they have a responsibility to the public, and how I can embellish that beast,' says Schmidt. 'While I love the concept of these powerful beings writ large on a stage, it's ultimately about delving into the core of their being to reveal who they are, even if it's pushing into the strange or unknown to create an iconic moment that will help them live on in the eyes of the people who love them. And yes, in many ways I probably am living vicariously through them, but it's important to me not to be just an interpreter of someone else's vision. It's imperative that I create my own distinctive material set, because that's how I distinguish my work. I grew up admiring Kansai [Yamamoto; see page 192] and later Issey Miyake and Rei Kawakubo because of their interest in pushing boundaries. Their work is based on making revolutionary silhouettes that have never been seen before, and I can relate to that desire.'

The enduring motivation of stepping into the unknown has rendered Schmidt an agent of change in more ways than one: in addition to an acclaimed history of material manipulations that border on science fiction – the sculptural 3D-printed dress he created for Dita Von Teese in 2013 arguably remains the most impressive sartorial use of the technique to date – he is also a cultural engineer of sorts. During a hiatus from design in the 1990s, disillusioned by the spectre of grunge ('it became less desirable to have a look – grunge was really the original normcore, which killed off rock style for while'), he cofounded the legendary New York punk/drag club SqueezeBox! The now defunct cult venue brought together New York's gay and straight scenes for the first time, with a stream of fans who revelled in the opportunity to deviate from the city's alternative but still segregated nightlife. Drag queens performed live alongside a

+ Cher, Debbie Harry, Tina Turner, Britney Spears, Rihanna, Lady Gaga, Madonna, Aerosmith

5
Cher, Schmidt's first music-industry client, in one of his signature chain-mail designs – re-routing the pop icon's identity from schmaltzy showgirl to rock diva.

6
Burlesque star Dita Von Teese in a pioneering 3D-printed dress (2013) that exemplifies Schmidt's capacity for genre-busting materials innovation.

> I'm not interested in dictating far-out fantastic ideas. I'm interested in the constraints of their public persona, the persona to whom they have a responsibility to the public, and how I can embellish that beast.
>
> Michael Schmidt

7

> While I love the concept of these powerful beings writ large on a stage, it's ultimately about delving into the core of their being to reveal who they are, even if it's pushing into the strange or unknown to create an iconic moment that will help them live on in the eyes of the people who love them.
>
> Michael Schmidt

7,8
The cover and dramatic gatefold design of Tina Turner's album *Foreign Affair* (1989). Photographed by Herb Ritts.

9
Rihanna on the cover of *Rolling Stone* magazine in April 2011, wearing metal mesh shorts made by Schmidt using previously unexplored design and tooling techniques.

8

+ Cher, Debbie Harry, Tina Turner, Britney Spears, Rihanna, Lady Gaga, Madonna, Aerosmith

house rock band, drawing a disparate crowd including the musicians Debbie Harry, Joan Jett, Marilyn Manson and Marc Almond; the film director John Waters, who referred to it as 'the greatest club in America'; and political heir John F. Kennedy Jr, among others. The transgender-focused play *Hedwig and the Angry Inch* (later a film) was even workshopped there by its creator, John Cameron Mitchell. 'That club really sated a lot of people's need to express themselves,' says Schmidt. 'You never knew who would be there and nobody cared, which was the whole point. There was no bottle service, no VIP area and no press, so it was a very private experience – very freeing and fun. Because of my background in theatrical rock and roll, it was a perfect confluence of people, and it became a magnet for designers and stylists tapping into fresh, influential personal style. A good nightclub is really an incubator for ideas and style, but those ideas need to be explored over time, something which the Internet and the highly pressurized quick-change culture it's built up has largely stifled.' While Schmidt believes stylists 'do an incredible job of mitigating some of that pressure', he suggests that the incessant hunger for newness driven by the relentless churn of social media can actually kill creativity in young stars. 'A smart artist will put themself out there in a very controlled way, and then they'll go away – allowing the public time to heal. By lying low you're cleansing the palette and building suspense for the next thing you do.'

Schmidt's recuperative interlude at SqueezeBox! reinvigorated his passion for progressive fashion design: 'telling a story, creating a character, emoting a narrative – it brought me back to a place where I thought I had something to say.' He returned to a world of garments momentous enough not only to seduce an audience for one night but also to enthral them for decades to come. He recalls designing a now iconic dress for Tina Turner for her 1989 *Foreign Affair* album cover, photographed by Herb Ritts. The minidress, an idea initially rejected by Turner, was made from thousands of red Swarovski crystals linked into a supple, body-skimming mesh. The dress was hugely labour-intensive to produce; Ritts, giving Schmidt free rein over the design, had simply requested something to define a 'great Tina moment'. When it arrived she loved it, as did Ritts, whose shot of her in it became the centrefold of the album sleeve and the focus of a supersize pull-out poster. 'It was an interpretation of the best of Tina Turner but in a new, modernized way,' says Schmidt.

For Rihanna's *Rolling Stone* cover in April 2011, styled by the Swedish dynamo B. Åkerlund (see page 11), Schmidt referenced a classic icon of American fashion – the Daisy Duke cut-off denim shorts (an icon for an icon) – but with a characteristically Schmidt-esque twist. The shorts were created in a hitherto unprecedented adaptation of printed metal mesh, requiring him to devise unique tooling equipment in order to inkjet the print on to a hard surface. The shorts were deconstructed, photographed, printed on to the mesh and then re-linked back into shorts to retain the exact proportions of the classic garment. The technique has since filtered into the catwalk collections of fellow Kansas City native Jeremy Scott, with whom Schmidt regularly collaborates. Says Schmidt: 'We're all visually stimulated, regardless of whether we consider ourselves creative. The original rock stars were religious icons and saints. We all need something to believe in and these stars, with these looks, are essentially rendering themselves immortal. It's very special to be able to contribute to that.'

9

> **A good nightclub is really an incubator for ideas and style, but those ideas need to be explored over time, something which the Internet and the highly pressurized quick-change culture it's built up has largely stifled.**
>
> Michael Schmidt

+ Cher, Debbie Harry, Tina Turner, Britney Spears, Rihanna, Lady Gaga, Madonna, Aerosmith

10
On the cover of *Rolling Stone* in June 2009, Lady Gaga wore a `dress' created by Schmidt in 15 minutes, after the initial concept for the shoot collapsed. Photographed by David LaChapelle.

11
Debbie Harry in Schmidt's infamous razorblade dress, made in 1993 – a garment symbolic of Harry's unattainable, dangerous beauty and typical of Schmidt's skill for creating powerful tension.

11

It's a very intimidating piece but simultaneously inviting ... You want to have that tactile experience with it, but you know you literally mustn't, so it creates a conflict in the viewer which is intriguing. It's also ... very Debbie Harry: the unapproachable goddess. She's the most beautiful woman of all time but you can't touch her, you can't have her.

Michael Schmidt

Not all iconic moments have been so carefully premeditated. Another enduring *Rolling Stone* cover underpinned by Schmidt's handiwork is the issue of June 2009 featuring Lady Gaga in a 'bubble dress', photographed by the infamous visual agitator David LaChapelle. Gaga's press team positioned the cover as a rebuttal of stereotypical visions of pop star sexiness, but it was, in truth, a far more spontaneous rejection of the initial concept. When the first (paparazzi-inspired) idea dissipated, within just 15 minutes Schmidt had commandeered a series of small plastic spheres from the set, drilled and sewn them, and Scotch-taped them to Gaga's body.

The majority of Schmidt's most momentous looks have involved an intense physicality to enable the wearer's sense of 'becoming'. One of the most famous is Debbie Harry's razor-blade dress – an opulent, columnar, floor-length sheath dress comprised of approximately 3,500 actual razor blades. Similar to Cher's tattered chain-mail dress, it is testament to Schmidt's preference for longevity over seasonal glory: Harry wore the dress – originally made for a show in 1993 – several times, including to the Q magazine awards in London in 1998. While wearing it for a New Year's Eve performance in Montreal, Harry recalls feeling as though she was being possessed by a warrior-esque snake-like being – a notion that helped her transform on stage into the ultimate siren Medusa. She says, 'I felt a great admiration for the creatures who wear these layered skins, and [Michael's] inventiveness regarding bringing armaments to fashion.' According to Schmidt, the garment's inherent contradictions are essential to its allure: 'It's a very intimidating piece but simultaneously inviting. The silhouette it creates is highly desirable, but it's also standoffish. You want to have that tactile experience with it, but you know you literally mustn't, so it creates a conflict in the viewer which is intriguing. It's also something that's very Debbie Harry: the unapproachable goddess. She's the most beautiful woman of all

Michael Schmidt

12

13

+ Cher, Debbie Harry, Tina Turner, Britney Spears, Rihanna, Lady Gaga, Madonna, Aerosmith

> **I go back to this idea of adapting materials that you wouldn't normally associate with the body because it really is about clothing the body in an indestructible manner - in very real terms sheathing the body, albeit in a sexy way. Because these are all women who are warriors, women who are standing up and exposing themselves to the world.**
>
> Michael Schmidt

12
Madonna performing on her MDNA tour (2013) in an exceptionally heavy monastic-style crystal mesh tunic (co-created by Schmidt with Arianne Phillips; see page 122) emblematic of the correlation between art and pain.

13
Bespoke metal talons for Coldplay's 'Princess of China' video (2011), in which Rihanna plays an erotic yet fierce female warlord.

time but you can't touch her, you can't have her.' Such contrasts are core components in Schmidt's bid to create images that elicit a truly visceral reaction. 'I've always strived to have a punk rock elegance with everything I do, because it's the sense of tension that's exciting to me,' he says. 'The great moment of stasis when you take these weird materials and you create something that shouldn't be but actually works is very satisfying.' For the finale of Madonna's MDNA tour (2013), Schmidt worked in collaboration with her long-term stylist, Arianne Phillips (see page 122), to create a similarly intense piece – a gown based on the directive of Joan of Arc meets Shaolin monks. Their response was an extraordinarily heavy monastic-style floor-length skirt and tunic made from metal mesh, accompanied by a huge crystal chain-mail collar and an armoured sleeve and gauntlet (also in crystal). Schmidt describes it as nearly impossible to wear under the pressure of Madonna's elaborate, strenuous choreography – making the garment itself a lavish yet formidable symbol of professional martyrdom: art is pain.

Like Phillips, Schmidt is a serious exponent of liberation through self-expression. At the heart of many of his collaborations are female champions – either outright survivors or those visibly in the process of triumphing over adversity. In Coldplay's 'Princess of China' video (2011), featuring Rihanna, she is cast as a female warlord, both fierce and erotic, with Schmidt's bespoke golden talons producing the greatest visual resonance. More significant still are the tattered motorcycle capelet and metal mesh hot pants that Britney Spears wears in the opening scenes of the video for 'Work Bitch' (2013). It is an epic moment that is bristling with strength and control – underscoring its wider relevance as one of Spears' key comeback tracks following a rollercoaster half-decade of relative turmoil since her original blistering success.

'I go back to this idea of adapting materials that you wouldn't normally associate with the body because it really is about clothing the body in an indestructible manner – in very real terms sheathing the body, albeit in a sexy way,' says Schmidt. 'Because these are all women who are warriors, women who are standing up and exposing themselves to the world. They quite literally go into battle when they go on stage, which is a very vulnerable place to be. The artists I work with have taken their lives to a crazy level, and that can inspire us all. I'm essentially helping them to shield a side of themselves while projecting power and magnificence.'

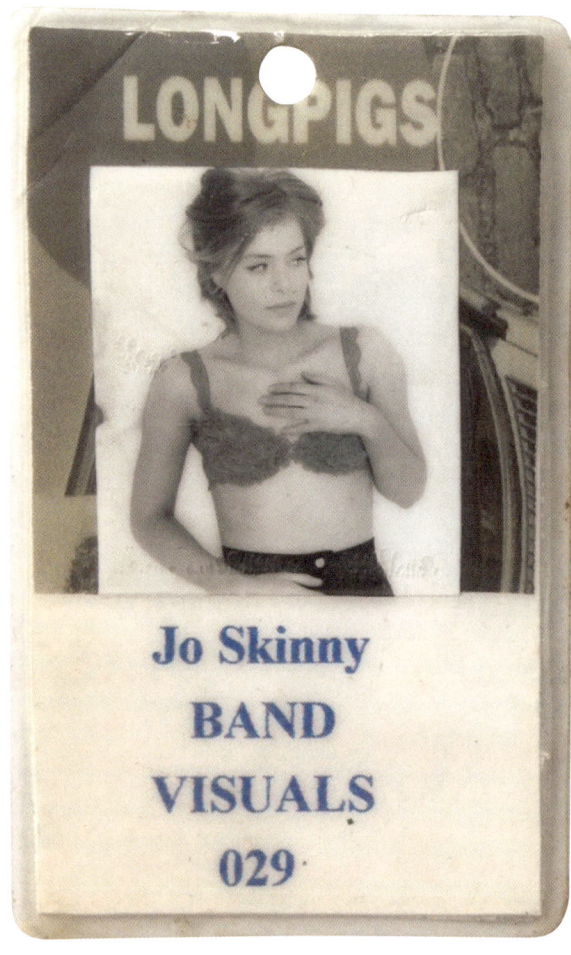 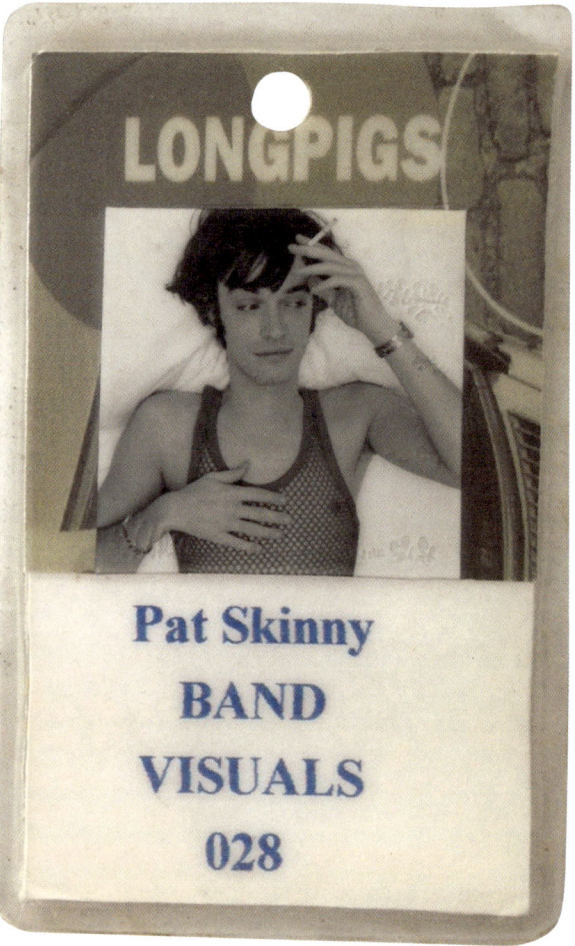

1

Jo and Pat Skinny

+

```
Pulp, Blur, Suede,
Republica, The Longpigs
```

2

1
Always with the band: the Skinnys' backstage passes for 1990s group and key Britpop fringe players the Longpigs, featuring images of the duo's own appearance in Pulp's seminal track 'Disco 2000' (1995).

2
The cover of 'Disco 2000', the video of which Jo and Pat Skinny styled, co-art-directed and appeared in.

Partners Jo Gollings and Patrick Holley (aka Jo and Pat Skinny) are the so-called anti-stylists whose light touch, eclectic art-school eye and perfectly honed appetite for louche, alternative glamour stealthily fuelled the look and attitude of the 1990s Britpop era. From styling album covers to art-directing music videos, the Skinnys were responsible for synthesizing the aesthetic of bands such as Blur, Pulp, Suede, Republica and the Longpigs – producing a legacy that continues to inspire.

Jo and Pat Skinny

So integral to the Britpop scene were the Skinnys that they became its self-elected poster couple, immortalized on screen courtesy of Jarvis Cocker. They are, however, a couple of epically unsung heroism beyond the inner circle of the era in which they dominated. The pair first met as teenagers (they are now married) while studying on an art foundation course in Grimsby in northern England, but it was London and Central Saint Martins school of art that initiated their passage towards Britpop. It was the early 1990s and London, in a counter-movement to the unkempt angst of grunge, was fast becoming consumed by house music megaclubs such as Ministry of Sound and Shoom ('Ibiza gone global and commercial', recalls Pat). According to Jo, for all those not subscribed to the synthetic charms of house/rave music, it fostered a genuine fear of deprivation: 'We identified quite early on that we were going to miss out on our youth in terms of having a really good gang to follow and be part of in London. We'd dallied with Shoom but didn't really like the music, and the fashion was so practical – baggy clothes for getting hot and staying hydrated. On the back end of that disappointment came a sense of creating the very scene we wanted.'

3

Where rave culture set up home in the guerrilla takeover of anonymous warehouses and multi-storey car parks, the Skinnys' scene conversely claimed two decadent central London club spaces as its spiritual epicentre: Blow Up, a beacon for mods, and Smashing, a partial resurrection of the flamboyance of the Blitz club, which traded on a glamorous, cabaret-inflected Roxy Music vibe. 'It was essentially a regrouping in which we found these nooks and crannies around Regent Street to reinhabit, to grow that type of West End swagger,' says Pat, who also pinpoints that a sense of eclecticism, now seen as the bedrock for the Britpop/indie manifesto, was essential. 'London had been smashed apart by the megaclubs, generating a scene with no room for the cooler, more sensitive art type, something which directly influenced the look of [our] clubs. Men, at least in the art-school half of Britpop we sided with, became peacocks again, after a lapse of eight or nine years, and the look of both genders began to converge to form a mutual mod look. At one point, Justine Frischmann [Elastica], Brett Anderson [Suede] and Damon Albarn [Blur] dressed almost identically. Even the music, shifting between fifties, sixties, seventies and eighties, was an unbarred convergence. Smashing's main DJ, Martin Green, would mix up early David Bowie with Sammy Davis Jr as well as playing music from people who were actually in bands that were in nightclubs, so we'd all be dancing to Blur, with Blur.'

+ Pulp, Blur, Suede, Republica, The Longpigs

The clubs became a secondary education – a vital social community that provided all the talent the Skinnys, as burgeoning stylists (when styling was an informal, professionally fluid tag), needed. 'Everybody was very creative, and most of them were art-school kids, so everybody had an opinion about every part of the industry and process. We wore our badge of belonging to those clubs with pride and thrived off each other,' says Jo. Now-acclaimed image-makers including Elaine Constantine, Donald Milne and Ralph Perou were all fellow club-goers whom the industrious Skinnys would commandeer 'for half a day here and there, on the basis of giving them portfolio pieces and the bands great imagery'.

4

> **London had been smashed apart by the megaclubs ... Men, at least in the art-school half of Britpop we sided with, became peacocks again ... and the look of both genders began to converge to form a mutual mod look.**
>
> Pat Skinny

5

3–5
Single artworks for the Longpigs' 'She Said' (1995) and 'Lost Myself' (1996), devised by the Skinnys. Heavily inspired by the aesthetic of the creative agency Hipgnosis, who had designed album art for bands including Roxy Music, Pink Floyd and 10cc, the look propagated a visual charisma that railed against the other, more laddish strand of Britpop.

The first group to seriously receive the Skinnys' stylistic curation was Flowered Up, a north London echo of the Madchester scene. The pair art-directed and styled the cover of Flowered Up's album *A Life with Brian* (1991), photographed by the 1970s rock photographer Dennis Morris, as well as the group's initial videos. Other bands swiftly followed, including The Verve, for which they re-crafted a logo for the band's introduction to the US market. For the Longpigs, the Skinnys art-directed a host of singles covers, including 'She Said' (1995) and 'Lost Myself' (1996), that were heavily inspired by the dramatic aesthetic of London creative agency Hipgnosis – a collective responsible for the album art of several visually heavyweight bands including Roxy Music, Pink Floyd and 10cc. Tapping into a growing desire for a breed of stylistic charisma that transcended the more laddish side of Britpop, the cover art for 'Lost Myself' tells the story of an extravagant suicide involving a Mercedes, a wig, a beautiful designer dress, a pair of shoes and a highly stylized Roxy-esque model – part predator, part victim. Consciously conceived to amplify the band's mythology, the back and front covers were split: one shot in London, the other in Paris. 'Even mentioning the fact that the photography was shot in different cities was really important to the band and to us and to the glamour of it, even though it was slightly faked,' recalls Pat. The concept for 'She Said' exudes a similarly rich retro-modern merger of glamour and pathos, ordinary scenarios with extraordinary aspirations, reflective of a unique time in modern British history. Dubbed 'Cool Britannia' by the mainstream media, the 1990s in the UK heralded a freshly patriotic, ultra-productive, cross-pollinated cultural vortex spanning art, music, literature and comedy (the Skinnys also styled Eddie Izzard). Britpop mirrored Britart – specifically the Young British Artists (YBAs), including Tracey Emin and Damien Hirst, all of whom then prime minister Tony Blair's New Labour government was embracing feverishly at every possible press opportunity. 'We'd be hanging out with people like Damien Hirst, The Auteurs, Rankin and Jarvis [Cocker] at a house party somewhere, all sharing ideas as if planning the next move,' says Pat.

Jo and Pat Skinny

6

We'd buy a lot of stuff from pay-by-weight warehouses in New York, then visit Quentin Crisp for lunch on the way back.

Pat Skinny

6,7
The Skinnys became so emblematic of 1990s pop-cultural cool that in 1996 they appeared on the revamped cover of Dr Alex Comfort's cult 'sex manual' *The Joy of Sex* (first published in 1972). Photographed by Deirdre O'Callaghan, art-directed by Rankin.

8
The seminal comic-strip video for Pulp's 'Disco 2000', a perfect example of the Skinnys' holistic creative impact. The duo worked on the aesthetic treatment, orchestrated the wardrobe and even played the central characters – a pair of lovers.

7

The Skinnys and Cocker and his band Pulp formed a critical alliance for both parties. The union directly coincided with the blossoming of the Internet, which had spurred a host of additional viewing channels and mass-access music platforms, in turn creating a voracious demand for more music videos. At the beating heart of a scene that was now considered a major commodity, the Skinnys became indispensable creative conduits employed to replicate their essence for a wider audience – particularly on projects where multi-tiered creative symbiosis was a critical factor. The video for 'Help the Aged' (1997), which oozes a brooding sense of 1970s melancholy, was directed by Hammer & Tongs, a duo who went on to direct the films *Son of Rambow* (2007) and *The Hitchhiker's Guide to the Galaxy* (2005). It features art direction and images by the American painter John Currin, who is renowned for sexually provocative, exaggerated erotica (Currin also co-art-directed the cover for Pulp's album *This Is Hardcore*). It was the Skinnys' role, says Pat, to 'create an idea that happened somewhere between those four heads'. However, it is the creative campaign for Pulp's 'Disco 2000' (1995), a love story set entirely within the 'scene', that remains the standout example of their full-spectrum creative touch, as well as a very personal homage to their place in the history of pop culture. Depicting a cartoon-esque version of the club scene they were immersed in, the video (shot in the real venue for Smashing, complete with iconic jewel-coloured light-up dance floor) is filmed as animated frames of a comic book. The Skinnys directed the wardrobe, codeveloped the aesthetic treatment (including assisting in devising its distinctive lush, retro colour palette) and also played the main characters. The additional cast were their fellow club-dwellers – all styled in the fundamentally slippery 'loungey, louche' style that the pair had exalted into a full-blown trend. 'It was an ethos rather than a look but definitely had seventies New York Studio 54 thrown in there, a bit of eighties CBGB. It was ever shifting: T-shirts one week, shoulder pads the next. We'd buy a lot of stuff from pay-by-weight warehouses in New York, then visit Quentin Crisp for lunch on the way back – he was also a big influence on us,' says Pat. Two years earlier, the Skinnys had been considered so emblematic of the epoch as to be chosen as the cover stars of the relaunch of the legendary sex manual *The Joy of Sex* in 1996 (photographed by Deirdre O'Callaghan, art-directed by Rankin); testifying to the continued allure of their celebrity, the reception to the 'Disco 2000' video was so positive that, in the week of its release, the Skinnys – now officially the telegenic poster couple for the entire movement – were offered both a record deal and the opportunity to present a TV film review programme. They accepted neither.

+ Pulp, Blur, Suede, Republica, The Longpigs

9

10

> **In the 1990s, if Pat and Jo hadn't dressed bands like Pulp and Suede, then it might not have crossed the collective mind of the British public to embrace a previously unexplored shabby-chic, junk-shop, street-clothing aesthetic. It's entirely feasible that their magnetism rubbed off on many other significant players of the era.**
>
> Phill Savidge, PR agent and writer

While louche glamour was key, the trailing influence of grunge's deconstructed, no-gloss, imperfect/perfect sensibility propagated by photographers such as Corinne Day meant that subtlety and the perception of effortlessness were also essential to the art-angst demeanour of Britpop, even for bands such as Suede who fell towards the more sexually ambiguous, libertine end of the spectrum. Grunge's influence necessitated a deceptively difficult, uncontrived approach to styling that the Skinnys possessed in a way magazine-based fashion directors did not. 'The brief would be as simple as "we just want a leather jacket", but to get the perfect jacket is probably the most difficult thing to do – like putting on make-up to achieve a natural look. We'd be trawling Portobello market, not calling in big brands,' says Jo. According to Alan Parks, former creative director of London Records, it was a matter of attunement and intuition: 'The bands trusted them. They looked great and they saw them at Smashing, at gigs and at people's flats at the end of the night. They were "faces" – as much a part of the scene as the bands were. They knew what bands would want to wear, what would work for them, their personalities and their music.' Phill Savidge, codirector of one of Britpop's most influential PR agencies, Savidge & Best, suggests that their input informed the wider pop-culture zeitgeist: 'In the 1990s, if Pat and Jo hadn't dressed bands like Pulp and Suede, then it might not have crossed the collective mind of the British public to embrace a previously unexplored shabby-chic, junk-shop, street-clothing aesthetic. It's entirely feasible that their magnetism rubbed off on many other significant players of the era.' Jo describes their remit as a support mechanism of sorts, based

9
Stills from Blur's video for 'Coffee and TV' (1999), styled by the Skinnys. Jo describes their work with the Britpop kings as largely 'about procuring special pieces that joined the [band's] identity', ensuring they weren't seen as just 'playing at being pop stars'.

10
The cover of Pulp's 'Help the Aged' (1997) directed by Hammer & Tongs (Garth Jennings and Nick Goldsmith), featuring art direction by the American painter John Currin. The Skinnys' role was to 'create an idea that happened somewhere between those four [the group's] heads'.

11
Stills from the video for 'Help the Aged' (released 1998).

11

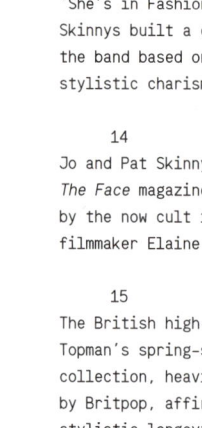

12, 13
Stills from the video for Suede's 'She's in Fashion' (1999). The Skinnys built a cohesive look for the band based on Brett Anderson's stylistic charisma.

14
Jo and Pat Skinny photographed for *The Face* magazine in the mid-1990s by the now cult image-maker and filmmaker Elaine Constantine.

15
The British high-street giant Topman's spring-summer 2015 collection, heavily influenced by Britpop, affirmed the era's stylistic longevity.

12

> **We were often employed from the beginning to build the band. With some bands, such as Suede, whose lead singer [Brett Anderson] had a relatively fully formed look, it would be a case of creating a cohesive image around him.**
>
> Jo Skinny

13

on rolling out an aesthetic language attuned (usually) to a lead singer – spanning tours, videos, interviews and press shots. 'We were often employed from the beginning to build the band. With some bands, such as Suede, whose lead singer [Brett Anderson] had a relatively fully formed look, it would be a case of creating a cohesive image around him – pushing his style out across the band. With Suede we were going out and buying clothes. With Blur there was also a need for cohesion; it was more about procuring special pieces that joined the identity. We developed looks that the artists were very much "encouraged" to wear because it was very important that they were seen as being "on" at all times and not just playing at being pop stars,' says Jo. The looks they built or refined became so established that 'in collaboration with the bands, we'd essentially help develop a style guide for the artists … and other creatives to follow,' says Pat. Beyond the band's clothing, the Skinnys would advise about 'a specific kind of lighting, a very particular kind of girl for the love interest in the video. Everything connected to generating an aesthetic mood.'

+ Pulp, Blur, Suede, Republica, The Longpigs

As both the faces on the poster and the people behind the scenes, the Skinnys were integral to defining an era which, as with all the best examples of authentic grassroots pop culture, remains a resilient aesthetic continually plundered by new generations of creatives. Definitive proof of the potency of that legacy is the British high-street giant Topman's almost wholesale revival of the look for its spring–summer 2015 catwalk collection. Topman's design director, Gordon Richardson, described the mood board for the collection as encompassing 'Britpop at one end and Woodstock at another', with the former clearly invoked via lean Cocker-esque silhouettes, flares in cord and pinstriped wool, a Liam Gallagher-style jumbo parka, canary-yellow mod T-shirts and Adidas Gazelle trainers. Blur even featured on the soundtrack. 'Everyone could be part of this cultural moment as it almost eschewed trends, rooted as it was in classic iconic perennial clothing,' says Richardson. 'The subsequent attitude continues to inspire designers looking for authentic fashion references and inspiration.'

Parks agrees that it is the aura of authenticity that continues to magnetize young pretenders: 'That weird mix of suburban seventies, sportswear and Regency mod was very much them [Jo and Pat] and was probably one of, if not the last, proper youth look that came from a combination of bands and the street. That authenticity is why it keeps bubbling up every so often; it was real, it had weight and it had meaning. If you look at someone like Christopher Shannon [a British menswear designer with a preference for Northern Soul-inflected street-ready sportswear], you can see how he's used it as an inspiration, and without Pat and Jo that wouldn't be happening.'

14

> **That authenticity is why [Britpop style] keeps bubbling up every so often; it was real, it had weight and it had meaning.**
>
> Alan Parks, creative director

15

Stevie Stewart

+

Kylie Minogue, Britney Spears,
Girls Aloud

1
Kylie Minogue during her Aphrodite tour (2011), a theatrical extravaganza of ingenuity that was heavily costumed by Stewart in collaboration with William Baker (see page 26).

Stevie Stewart has entertainment in her blood. Raised in a family immersed in the glitziest theatrics of old-world show business, nurtured by the heady creative crucible of London's 1980s club scene and cemented as cofounder of the iconic fashion label BodyMap, the palpable pull of performance-led visuals - including collaborations with Kylie Minogue, Britney Spears and the acclaimed choreographers Russell Maliphant and Michael Clark - has made her one of the entertainment industry's most sought-after maker-creatives.

Stewart's story is a fascinating tale of nature, nurture, business acumen and cultural intuition, spawned from a rarely documented upbringing that was aptly larger than life from the beginning. Her paternal grandparents were high-flying trapeze artists in Barnum & Bailey's circus in Canada; her father, Wally Stewart, was a famous tap dancer during World War II, later cofounding the clownish comedy collective The Nitwits; while her mother was a sometime model and member of the dance troupe The Valentine Lovelies. Home life was a capricious shuffle thanks to a biannual geographical quantum leap from a bedrock of British suburbia – Totteridge in north London – to the bright lights of Sin City: Las Vegas. Although the two places were worlds apart in pace and style, the aura of showmanship was an omnipresent influence; self-expression was inextricably tethered to flamboyance, diversity and a celebration of the unorthodox. Family friends included the British comic legends Spike Milligan and Peter Sellers alongside an extended suite of theatre 'family' – a sure precursor to the avant-garde club-clan that later constituted Stewart's own BodyMap collective. Her childhood favourite was Christina, a Vegas trapeze artist who hung from her hair: 'I was completely intrigued by what she did, and completely enamoured with the skimpy, sequinned and crystal-embellished leotards she wore,' recalls Stewart. 'My father was also quite bohemian and loved dressing up to the extent that he'd sometimes collect me from school looking like a cowboy or something similarly wild. I imagine I am genetically predisposed towards entertainment.'

After her father's death, Stewart temporarily resettled into life in the London suburbs, against the backdrop of Thatcherite Britain. A potentially devastating sweep of spending cuts across arts education inadvertently served to galvanize an entire generation of dissenting creatives, including Stewart, into oppositional DIY action. Via a stall in Camden Market that would later host BodyMap's early design experiments, she self-funded a degree in fashion at Middlesex University – where she met BodyMap cofounder David Holah. While the pair created separate graduate collections (later combining and remaking them with a commercial edge so fierce that they secured an offer from the prestigious London boutique Browns), the crux of their partnership was inexorably incubated within the hedonistic hothouse of London's infamous 1980s club scene – a throbbing source of visual inspiration and joyful rebellion epitomized by outré characters and deliriously excessive flamboyance.

BodyMap's avant-garde yet unusually wearable designs evinced a brave new world of possibilities. Dynamic, graphic overtures to fashionable athleticism, driven by directional fabrics and innovative pattern-cutting techniques, they were a reflection of the high-energy, anything-goes vibe of the club scene, but with a hitherto unseen populist manifesto in mind. Quite unlike the often slim-fetishizing, contortionist proportions of their design predecessors, BodyMap's clothes offered stretch (the duo even pioneered Lycra), allowing them to be worn by anyone, of any age or size. Conceptually liberating and physically crafted to be viewed in motion, the designs united costume and fashion – inseparable tools in the fun-fuelled game of generating identity.

+ Kylie Minogue, Britney Spears, Girls Aloud

The film and TV producer Helen Terry, a former singer with Boy George's band Culture Club, recalls the clothes as a hugely valuable reaction to the more tightly orchestrated, consciously put-together message of fashion designers such as Antony Price (see page 132) – the man behind Bryan Ferry's Roxy Music look and many of Duran Duran's signature styles – whose glossiness consciously championed stylistic elitism. Says Terry: 'Their [BodyMap's] ethos was inclusivity, which set them apart from their contemporaries because the majority of new designers were making clothes for an idealized clientele: their friends, the relentless fashion victim or the wealthy. In the early eighties, the stylist played almost no part in the image projected by the artist. When I made videos or had to do a photoshoot, I used my own clothes. I'd go and see them [BodyMap] and they'd miraculously produce exactly the right thing for me, so it is certainly true to say that, at the time, BodyMap shaped my public persona as well as my private one. Someone like me, who was a size 18 at the time, became empowered through wearing their designs. I cannot stress enough just how important this was. BodyMap articulated an attitude that had yet to find favour – Stevie's philosophy was ahead of the cultural curve.' That sense of inclusivity, solidarity and community was also instrumental in an era when the spectre of AIDS publicly emerged. According to David Yarritu, one-time member of English band ABC and BodyMap client: 'BodyMap also expressed a "sex-positive" attitude which was something that was desperately needed in the early eighties at the advent of the AIDS crisis. It was saying, "Sexiness is fun, having sex is great, it's nothing to be ashamed or scared of. Your body is something to love, to flaunt, whatever your weight or height or age."'

5

> **Their [BodyMap's] ethos was inclusivity, which set them apart from their contemporaries because the majority of new designers were making clothes for an idealized clientele: their friends, the relentless fashion victim or the wealthy.**
>
> Helen Terry, singer and TV producer

2–4
Stewart's parents were performers whose extended circle of theatrical cohorts created a deep appreciation of the value of wider, unorthodox and creative families that fed into Stewart's later life inside London's vibrant 1980s club scene.

5
A promotional image for BodyMap, the seminal 1980s fashion label that Stewart founded with David Holah, and which dressed numerous pop stars.

The synergy between fashion, music and image-making that had been building amid the club scene's increasingly incestuous mix of artists, designers, musicians and designers hit tipping point with BodyMap's first catwalk shows. Celebrated pieces of stagecraft that mesmerized the fashion elite and the popular press alike, they demonstrated a perfect symbiosis of the two industries essential to the long-term evolution of the fashion–music communion. Significantly preceding the twenty-first century's televised music–fashion mega-events observed by corporate monoliths such as Victoria's Secret and more recently the Italian megabrand Versace, BodyMap's shows confirmed that combined concepts hold an infinitely greater power to seduce. Exploding the then relatively sedate, linear parade of traditional catwalk presentations, the shows echoed the collectives of Stewart's youth.

Stevie Stewart

BODY MAP

+ Kylie Minogue, Britney Spears, Girls Aloud

> **BodyMap also expressed a 'sex-positive' attitude which was something that was desperately needed in the early eighties at the advent of the AIDS crisis. It was saying, 'Sexiness is fun, having sex is great, it's nothing to be ashamed or scared of. Your body is something to love, to flaunt, whatever your weight or height or age.'**
>
> David Yarritu, musician

7

6
Affirmation of the continued influence of BodyMap was provided by a shoot for V magazine in 2008 that used archived pieces, styled by Tabitha Simmons and photographed by Craig McDean.

7
The pop-fashion continuum: Stewart's costumes for the British choreographer Michael Clark's ballet *Who's Zoo* (2012), set to music by the pop-rock star Jarvis Cocker.

The extended BodyMap family – including the singers Terry and Karen Kinky (another Culture Club star), pop musicians such as Boy George and dancers such as Michael Clark – would perform, alongside the duo's own families. DJs Jeremy Healy and Jeffrey Hinton (also a filmmaker) would add layers of music and soundbites to help illustrate the often surreal, always theatrical show narratives. Titles included 'The Cat in the Hat Takes a Rumble with the Techno Fish' and 'Barbie Takes a Trip Around Nature's Cosmic Curves' (autumn–winter 1984 and 1985 respectively). The latter show, which featured cross-dressing models of numerous shapes and sizes, latex wigs and exposed flesh, is famed for leaving American buyers in shock, adding invaluable fuel to the promotional fire. Says Stewart: 'I do have an anarchic spirit. David and I always wanted to make a difference, which extends into my work on film, music and even set design now. To an extent, everything I do is subversive costume design, but always with a modern sensibility. I never reference the work of other designers.'

Inclusivity aside, BodyMap was also allied to the wilder cartoon fantasies that many burgeoning pop stars were absorbing into their stage personas. Leigh Bowery – the legendary performance artist, costume maker and doyen of the club world, with whom Stewart and Holah also collaborated – heralded a conscious rejection of feted fashion orthodoxy and the legibility of the human body in favour of humour and fun. Other artists who wore BodyMap included Bananarama, Tears for Fears, Amazulu, Neneh Cherry, Thompson Twins, Depeche Mode, Deee-Lite's Lady Miss Kier and Kylie Minogue. 'Our look had an awareness of the artificiality of pop style if anything, making it anti-ego,' Yarritu remembers. 'We allowed ourselves to become cartoons. We were in on the pretentiousness of thinking your style equalled your identity, which isn't to say that the whole look was a critique, it was actually celebratory of all those things that we loved. Our outfits were vivid and unapologetically camp and showbiz-y: a bit of Soul Train via Walt Disney – mismatched patterns, brightly coloured prints, shiny satins, patent vinyls and cartoonish proportions.'

8

To an extent, everything I do is subversive costume design, but always with a modern sensibility. I never reference the work of other designers.

Stevie Stewart

8
Kylie Minogue's Aphrodite tour (2011), for which her creative director, William Baker (see page 20), commissioned Stewart to craft both the fashion and much of the surrounding stage ephemera.

9
A dancer encased in a tunic designed to drape and move during extreme movement, created by Stewart for the choreographer Russell Maliphant's ballet *The Rodin Project* (2012). The design echoed revolutionary early BodyMap Lycra pieces, conceived to support but also free the body.

Until the brand ran into production problems in the 1990s, it was a resounding success – with considerable commercial achievement to match its column inches. Continual whispers of product reissues remain a constant reminder of the brand's hold over the fashion industry's collective imagination. Indeed, BodyMap clothes were even resurrected in a full fashion story in *V* magazine in spring 2004 – shot and styled by fashion heavyweights Craig McDean and Tabitha Simmons, respectively – wholeheartedly championing their continued relevance.

Post-BodyMap, following stints guest-styling for MTV, past UK TV music show *Top of the Pops*, TV commercials, films and ad campaigns with the film director John Maybury and production designer Alan MacDonald, Stewart's innate understanding of the reciprocal love affair between fashion and music has continued to make her a critical, if less publicly visible, member of the music industry fraternity. Invaluable, too, is the level of her fabric innovation/engineering know-how, which enables her to produce illusory silhouettes, rich in stage presence *and* freedom of movement for a non-model body (reference Russell Maliphant's production *The Rodin Project* (2012), for which she created a series of apparently simple, drapey silk jersey dresses, deceptively engineered for rigorous dance movement).

+ Kylie Minogue, Britney Spears, Girls Aloud

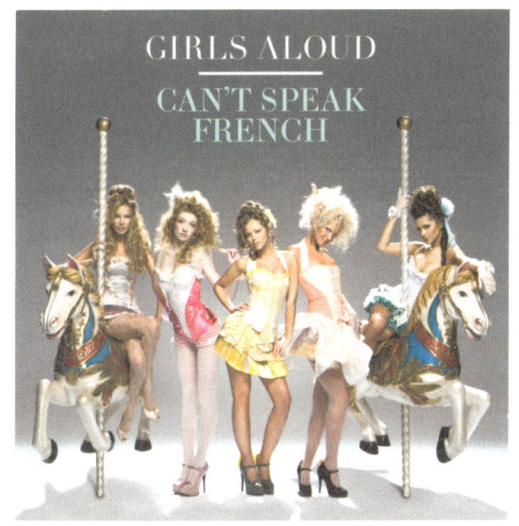

11

Consequently now a go-to designer for creative directors orchestrating stadium tours, Stewart has a list of key credits that include costumes for Britney Spears' Circus tour in 2009 ('we created a "tattoo" bodysuit that was a direct call back to my BodyMap days') and Kylie Minogue's KylieX2008 and 2011 Aphrodite tours in collaboration with the British creative director William Baker (see page 20). Minogue's Aphrodite tour was, Stewart says, a perfect vehicle for her own wider preoccupation with crafting not only garments but also the worlds beyond them – a joyous escapism rooted in the hyperbole that is so specific to music videos and stage concepts. The role required her to create everything from Minogue's intricately bejewelled Grecian goddess-style corsetry and stylized togas to a huge set of articulated wings. 'In Aphrodite there were boys pulling chariots in scary S&M gear, princesses, Roman soldiers. The dancers are just as important for me because they're essentially a visual framework for telling the story. In any instance it's quite extreme, and not without some kind of super-camp variety of Vaudeville performance that again probably ties back to my Dad in some way,' she laughs. 'Ultimately, [for me] as a designer, [Minogue's tour is] everything: it's fashion, it's costume, it's styling, it's set pieces – it encompasses all my worlds.'

A video for the British pop star Will Young's cover of the Doors' 'Light My Fire' in 2002, for which Stewart did everything from the prop styling to the fashion, similarly demonstrates her full-spectrum vision. She and Baker are currently in the process of orchestrating video concepts for the young British singer Sam Way. Now very far from the hyper-constructed playgrounds of club-land culture that kick-started her own career, Stewart is still crafting make-believe. Will fabricating fantasy worlds always enthral her? 'I will always be interested in the sense of creating an alter ego,' she says, 'of creating the facade, the armour.'

10
The pop icon Britney Spears performing in a Stewart-designed `tattoo bodysuit'.

11
The pop group Girls Aloud's single `Can't Speak French' (2012), styled by Stewart, which she describes as `subversive costume design'.

12
The video for Will Young's cover of `Light My Fire' (2002); Stewart undertook both the spatial concept and the fashion design.

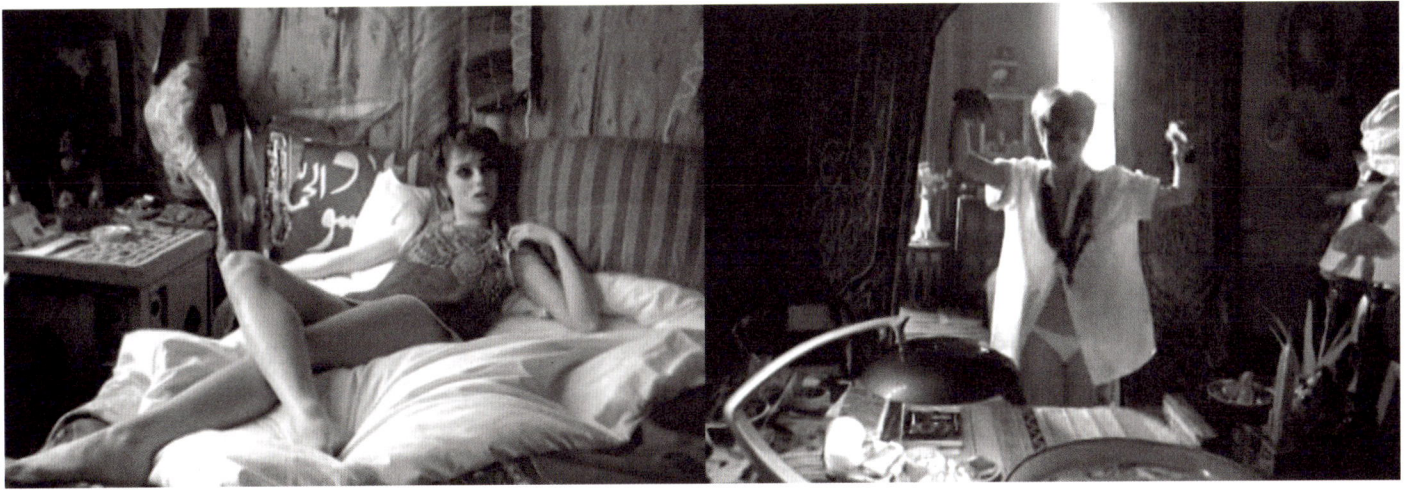

12

Jenke-Ahmed Tailly

+

Beyoncé

Transmitting a twenty-first-century rallying cry for ambitious self-reliance wrapped in an unapologetically glamorous package, Beyoncé was a timely emergent counterpoint to the machismo-fuelled world of R&B music. But a key influence in her evolution, as well as a factor in her much-scrutinized credibility as a feminist role model, has been her former creative director Jenke-Ahmed Tailly. His own preoccupations with African heritage, his encyclopedic list of literary, philosophical and cinematic references and his hugely female-influenced upbringing have provided an overwhelmingly nurturing symbiosis.

1

2

3

1
Beyoncé in the controversial story for *L'Officiel* magazine's 90th anniversary in 2011; it marked the birth of a key period of exploring her visual identity, steered symbiotically with Tailly. Photographed by Mark Pillai.

2
Beyoncé's debut *Dazed & Confused* cover was part of a wider strategy to subvert R&B's standard beauty-pageant glitz, megawatt smiles and clichéd chanteuse stereotype, taking her into new territory and earning her countercultural credibility.

3
A shot from Beyoncé's album *4* (2011), which was conceived as a visual compendium of reignited creativity, each track with its own visual story – more fashion mag than traditional music. Image by Greg Gex.

Many of the most inspirational periods in the fashion–pop-music continuum are bound to an almost supernatural serendipity: a perfect storm of right time, right cultural backdrop and right people. When Beyoncé, with her girl group Destiny's Child, brought out the track 'Independent Women' in 2000, pop culture at large was ripe for an audacious new poster girl for female empowerment (the song also headlined the female action movie *Charlie's Angels*). But a decade in the spotlight is a long time, and even the biggest artists, bolstered by the most ardent fans, must face the spectre of evolution to maintain legitimate dominance. Jenke-Ahmed Tailly, born on the Ivory Coast to a Senegalese mother but based in Paris, has been a principal player in the team driving Beyoncé's enduring success.

Tailly entered the fashion industry as a model; he was subsidizing a degree in business by working on the sales floor of New York department stores Barneys and Bergdorf Goodman when his striking looks and stylistic charm were noted by the stylist June Ambrose (fashion advisor to rap and R&B stars including Jay Z, Pharrell Williams and Mary J. Blige). Shoots with photographic greats including Annie Leibovitz beckoned, but it was ultimately a life less satisfying, dogged by the fashion industry's lack of racial diversity – a still contentious factor that has proved a substantial source of career motivation. 'I'd be requested to go on a casting and people would say, "Oh, we love your look but we've already booked a black person," even though the campaign would be for 12 people. But how do you change that? So it wasn't exactly that I'd lost touch with my heritage, but I started doing shoots to really reveal my culture. I became a creative director because I wanted to have control of all aspects of the creative process to inform people.'

Beyoncé, simultaneously, was an artist on the cusp of introspection after years riding fame's punishing treadmill. She and Tailly met in 2011 via a special story for the French fashion magazine *L'Officiel*'s historic 90th anniversary issue. In its entire canon, the magazine, which states that it targets 'upper-income, educated women', had featured only two black cover stars – despite France having the highest proportion of black citizens in Europe. Tailly agreed to do the anniversary issue on the basis that it would begin to redress the balance with a third cover: Beyoncé. The pair, in their first collaboration, embarked on a shoot that pays very literal visual homage to African queens, such as Egypt's Nefertiti, and ceremonial activities, pulled from the Senegalese Wolof, Mauritanian Tuareg and Nigerian Yoruba tribes – themes that resurfaced repeatedly throughout their partnership. The styling stretched from African-inspired fashion by designers including Gucci, Azzedine Alaïa, Fendi, Pucci, Chanel, Louis Vuitton, Rodarte, Dolce & Gabbana and Lanvin to make-up based on tribal face paintings, created by the Italian artist Francesca Tolot. Hair was by the revered Senegalese stylist Astou Toure, using head wraps bound with African fabrics, conceptualized with Tailly.

Unsurprisingly, the shoot was not without controversy. Detractors – and there were many, from blogs to broadsheets – suggested that the facial paint constituted 'blacking up', lazily reducing an entire continent to a damagingly basic 'exotic' stereotype. Tailly saw it differently: as a mass-circulation exhibition of rituals and customs designed to educate a digitally obsessed generation for whom, he believes, the details of their ancestry and cultural heritage are at risk of being buried under the weight of fast facts and blurred visual chronologies. 'The Internet and its exchanges of information are fantastic but it's important for older people, those beyond digital natives, to provide a sense of substance; it's our role through creativity, more than ever as artists, to inspire people to educate themselves and learn about cultures beyond just travelling to the places that are trendy.'

4

5

4,5
The contentious *L'Officiel* shoot in 2011 placed Beyoncé and Tailly at the centre of a row over the representation of race and cultural heritage.

Pop and fashion go hand in hand; all the best stars understand that. But it has to come from somewhere genuine and they have to have something worth saying. If they don't have that, they don't last.

Rod Stanley, former editor-in-chief, *Dazed & Confused*

> **I was lucky to be in [Beyoncé's] life at the time when she was growing differently as an artist and a person; she was about to become a mother and she wanted to move that girl-power narrative forward. Our relationship was built on trust and passion, enabling me to introduce her to new designers and new horizons, and I'm sure me being from Paris with my African background had an added value in terms of my take on the world.**
>
> Jenke-Ahmed Tailly

Whether the *L'Officiel* shoot (photographed by Mark Pillai) was misjudged or not, just a few weeks later Beyoncé proposed to Tailly that he become her first in-house creative director. Journeying into African history was not his only appeal. Strong women, too, have long been a driving force in Tailly's world. From the battered 1940s photographs of his regal grandmother that became a core reference for the video to the overtly feminist anthem 'Run the World (Girls)' of 2011, to the influence of reading a hidden copy of French philosopher Simone de Beauvoir's feminist manifesto *Le Deuxième Sexe* (1949) as a child, Tailly's innate reverence for women was the final piece of the jigsaw puzzle for Team Beyoncé. A seminal, nearly four-year working relationship ensued; a meeting of minds characterized by a new creative vision. 'I was lucky to be in her life at the time when she was growing differently as an artist and a person,' he says. 'She was about to become a mother and she wanted to move that girl-power narrative forward. Our relationship was built on trust and passion, enabling me to introduce her to new designers and new horizons, and I'm sure me being from Paris with my African background had an added value in terms of my take on the world.'

Testament to his influence, on arrival he immediately killed a fragrance campaign shot by a revered photographer (and one of Tailly's own heroes), recommissioning imagery by a lesser-known photographer, Lionel Gasparini. It was the genesis of a bigger plan to shake up the standard production line of glossy smiley or sultry covers with a strategically mapped roster of mainstream publications interspersed with cooler, more countercultural projects capable of outpacing Beyoncé's earlier incarnations with real credibility. When she headlined the Glastonbury Festival in 2011 – the first woman ever to do so in its 25-year history – she wore a sequinned gold minidress by then unknown French couturier Alexandre Vauthier for the entire two-hour set. Vauthier's work reappeared – this time a fox-fur stole dripping with strands of Swarovski crystals painstakingly interlaced by the prestigious Lesage embroidery house – as part of the associated artwork for her album *4* (also 2011) alongside a stream of pieces by barely nascent, sub-30-year-old designers. Key pieces included vertiginous footwear by Holland's Jan Taminiau, a figure-sheathing bodysuit by student Lleah Rae (only recently graduated from Parsons The New School for Design in New York) and a purple-and-black beaded dress by France's Maxime Simoëns, which adorned the cover of the album's deluxe version.

6
Beyoncé performing at Glastonbury Festival in 2011 in a dress by the then unknown couturier Alexandre Vauthier, the first of many new-generation, under-30 designers whom Tailly brought to her arsenal.

7,8
Additional imagery from the format-breaking sonic-visual partnership that constituted Beyoncé's album *4*.

7

8

Conceived as a series of stories each with its own narrative, the visuals for *4* deferred to the chaptered arrangement of fashion magazines, rather than the symbiotic track-to-track flow of music albums. Essentially a kaleidoscopic hit list of Beyoncé's visual obsessions ('a kind of gumbo of everything she liked'), the artwork even featured a gleaming fold-out cover, emulating fashion's supersize September issues. The structurally unorthodox concept and heavy emphasis on visuals blazed an important artistic trail for the fifth, self-titled album (2013). Developed as a concurrent audio–visual project, the entire work – 14 tracks, each accompanied by a music video/mini-movie realized by different directors, stylists and producers – arrived completely unannounced in its entirety via iTunes. Three bonus videos further affirmed a belief in the necessity of the visual within Beyoncé's creative manifesto. Tailly did not work on *Beyoncé* directly (bar the video for the single 'Grown Woman'), but he did supply 'a book of 21 ideas regarding moving girl power forward' that influenced the project.

Jenke-Ahmed Tailly

9

9
Tailly describes the the *Dazed & Confused* editorial of 2011 as being `about celebrating beauty in a different way, with a different power and a different sense of sufficiency'.

10
The cover of *L'Officiel*'s controversy-stirring 90th-anniversary edition, 2011.

> This was ... about a less overt and uncomplicated materialism. It was two or three years into the economic crisis, so there was a desire to move away from the more gratuitous bling .... Plus, [*Dazed & Confused*] was a magazine that always liked to subvert expectations, strive for the unexpected and play with convention.
>
> Rod Stanley

The conceptual seeds sown with the album *4* are also visible in another editorial showpiece, in 2011, for the British style bible *Dazed & Confused*. The shoot was part of the album's promotional plan as well as of Tailly's relentless push to drop both the standard beauty-pageant glitz of the then R&B uniform and the hackneyed stereotypes of the ball-busting chanteuse. The original shoot concept, which posited Beyoncé on a New York rooftop to symbolize her chart-topping domination, was supplanted by a trailer-trash theme based, according to Tailly, 'on projecting a feminist idea of strength – another way of being fabulous synonymous with the notion that wealth is not always the key element to happiness. It was about celebrating beauty in a different way, with a different power and a different sense of sufficiency.' According to Rod Stanley, *Dazed & Confused*'s editor-in-chief at the time, the reimagining of wealth connected to a wider cultural note: 'This was, in part, certainly about a less overt and uncomplicated materialism. It was two or three years into the economic crisis, so there was a desire to move away from the more gratuitous bling of the earlier part of the decade. Plus, it was a magazine that always liked to subvert expectations, strive for the unexpected and play with convention. We can shoot a global pop icon? Great, let's do it in a rusting naval dockyard with some grilled meat.'

For anyone other than the self-made superstar, the sentiment might have appeared trite, the bleached-blonde hair and maximalist leopard print meets fluoro-floral crop top a disingenuous folly. For Beyoncé – an artist reconciling the myriad roles of entertainer, mother, wife and businesswoman while experiencing fame, financial riches and incomparable media attention – it was a fantasy grounded in very genuine preoccupations; a compelling riff on an identity in real flux. Styled by Tailly and *Dazed & Confused*'s fashion editor Karen Langley, the shoot included a number of bespoke pieces including items from Riccardo Tisci, the creative director of Givenchy – a megabrand certainly, but one willing to tailor for a specific 'performance' to relay an original message. 'Pop and fashion go hand in hand; all the best stars understand that,' says Stanley. 'But it has to come from somewhere genuine and they have to have something worth saying. If they don't have that, they don't last.' Tailly cites the cover of the 1970s soul/R&B singer Minnie Riperton's album *Adventures in Paradise* as an invisible metaphorical reference. Riperton is depicted sitting in a blue living room, next to an enormous lion; a sassy, soulful, regal-looking woman teetering close to the gaping maw of danger. The same lion appears again, literally this time, in the forefront of the 'Run the World (Girls)' video. Power, it suggests, does not come without risk.

10

11

11
The cover of 1970s soul/R&B singer Minnie Riperton's album *Adventures in Paradise* (1975), one of Tailly's covert metaphorical references for power underscored by risk.

12
Tailly's legion of potent female influences loom large on planet Beyoncé, never less than in the video for 'Run the World (Girls)' (2011), her most militant feminist anthem.

13
Cover of the March 2012 edition of *The Gentlewoman*, a seminal point in Beyoncé's transition from all-American pop star to all-round female icon. Photography by Alasdair McLellan, styling by Jonathan Kaye and creative direction by Jop Van Bennekom.

A story in March 2012 for the British biannual *The Gentlewoman* – a magazine pitched at 'modern women of style and purpose', revered for its erudite but empathetic ethos, wider cultural bite and 'anti-fantasy' policy – provided another opportunity to present an entirely different persona, and further evidence of Tailly's strategic, linchpin contribution within transitional brand Beyoncé. Photographed by Alasdair McLellan and styled by Jonathan Kaye, with creative direction by Jop Van Bennekom (the exacting Dutch publishing revolutionary also responsible, with Gert Jonkers, for the cult magazine *Fantastic Man*), Beyoncé was cast in natural make-up and semi-architectural yet superbly ladylike pieces from the avant-garde Belgian fashion designer Raf Simons' first couture collection for Dior. According to Tailly, there are whispers of the US photographer Bert Stern's now-iconic Marilyn Monroe shoot of 1962, 'The Last Sitting', and later eponymous book – one of the last and most intimate series of images of the icon before her death. In any case, the arrestingly curtailed glamour and the stripped-back but warmly inviting ambience of fragility (unprecedented at that stage in Beyoncé's visual repertoire) are palpable, and fascinating.

From Riperton to Monroe, Tailly's female influences loom large, some more visible than others. 'Run the World (Girls)' – a militant feminist anthem constructed from an eclectic musical melange of African drumbeats, pop, hip-hop, R&B and dancehall – is an homage to alpha-female pop pioneers the industry over. In the video, Beyoncé's bespoke crown, created by the jewellery designers Erickson Beamon, is conceived not only as her own spoils but also as an appreciation of the entire oeuvre in which she sits: female frontrunners past, present and future. 'I was looking for a powerful woman,' says Tailly, 'but with an almost priestess-like, voodoo-esque mysticism, some kind of metaphysical aspect; saluting the power of giving life but also the ability to stand beyond convention.' Odes to the legendary African American entertainer Josephine Baker are expected, while tributes to characters in French cinema are far subtler but equally revealing, specifically Jean Seberg's character in Jean-Luc Godard's influential new-wave film *À bout de souffle* (*Breathless*; 1960), which depicts a woman struggling to reconcile being in love with respecting her own morality. The conflict and pressure and the fight to stay on top are all neatly manifest in 'Run the World (Girls)'. Ultimately, says Tailly,

12

13

14

14
Tailly's post-Beyoncé oeuvre continues to build a legacy bound to his African heritage, including the multi-artist project – uniting international visual artists, musicians and writers with emerging African fashion designers, artists, writers and musicians – all as part of his own platform, Taste Atelier.

observing a truth with artifice, no matter how much that truth may be creatively embellished, is imperative to maintaining genuine traction: 'Something really fantastic cannot be entirely fabricated. The thing that touches people is being allowed to really enter the realm of that artist and pull something out of it.'

Tailly's post-Beyoncé projects (their creative relationship is now on hold, although they still communicate) continue to build on a compulsion to craft a legacy bound to his African heritage. They include an ambitious multi-artist plan (involving visual artists, musicians and writers) in connection with the acclaimed octogenarian African photographer Malick Sidibé, among others. Part of Taste Atelier – Tailly's own creative platform, devised to support young African talent within fashion, art, literature and music – the inaugural project will be a compilation album expressed as dialogues between internationally famous and emerging or underground African musicians. Each pairing must work in response to a Sidibé image and each will have an accompanying video-cum-documentary, three of which Tailly plans to direct himself. The profits will be used to help build an art school on the Senegali–Mali border in West Africa. The mutable muse-and-master relationship he enjoyed with Beyoncé clearly lingers, offering plenty of creative fuel: 'I don't want to be a role model, absolutely not, but I do want to provide inspiration,' he asserts. 'Something I've learned from Beyoncé? It's not necessarily [about] focusing on what people think you should be or do but rather about competing with yourself.'

Johnny Wujek

+

Katy Perry, Shakira, Nicki Minaj

1

2

3

1
Katy Perry showcasing the Wujek-designed cupcake bra in her video for 'California Gurls' (2010). A typically saucy, slapstick-esque symbol of their capacity to create cult visuals with populist appeal, it has been commercialized as a fancy-dress outfit and has also found fans among the drag queens of West Hollywood.

2
Perry performing on her California Dreams tour (2011) in semi-mechanical fantasy stage wear.

3
Accessible sexuality: the whipped-cream-dispensing bralet that cemented Perry and Wujek's naughtily erotica-inflected, Americana-drenched humour as a pop-industry staple.

For those who revel in pop music's role as an ultra-connective, kaleidoscopic carnival of televisual entertainment, Johnny Wujek is a princely figure. A key player in the realm of heartfelt cartoon pop, he is the stylist and creative director behind the sartorial fantasy worlds of artists including Katy Perry, Shakira and Nicki Minaj.

Wujek's desire to talk to an audience beyond the rarefied elite of the fashion industry with genuine warmth and humour has made his stylistic 'curatorship' an ongoing source of media gold. It is an endearingly unpretentious attitude drawn from showbiz aspirations that are rooted firmly in Wujek's Midwest American family life. Inspired by the punk/skater style of his four older siblings and by a grandmother to whom he refers as 'an incredibly chic woman, always perfectly dressed', Wujek, grounded though he was, was unlikely to be professionally sated in Detroit, a city built on the concerns of industrial car manufacturing. Fashion beckoned early, prophetically via the wider lens of mass-media publishing and entertainment.

4

5

'We do tend to push things, any ideas, to their limits, and it would probably be fair to say that I do get off on chaos.

Johnny Wujek

At 20, just before finishing art college, Wujek decamped to San Francisco to work on the start-up website Kibu – an online forum targeting the *Teen Vogue* market (13- to 18-year-old girls) that was born in the original turn-of-the-millennium dotcom boom. In a lucid portent of his later remit as creative consultant and photoshoot guide on the reality TV show *America's Next Top Model*, Wujek's job entailed writing a weekly column dubbed 'Dear John', which supplied relationship and dating advice in response to audience requests. After eight months of preparation, miles ahead of the curve that has since brought content and e-commerce together as near-inseparable entities, the start-up imploded within just two weeks. But it had given Wujek a ravenous appetite for the fashion-fuelled limelight, which prompted a trip to Los Angeles and a three-year stint switching between castings as a model and actor and duties as an agent's assistant. However, the compulsion to create, in any capacity connected to fashion, proved most powerful, leading to internships, first with the super-stylist Maryam Malakpour on the Hollywood film *Wonderland* (2003), then with Maryam's sister Marjan Malakpour – also a stylist – on heavyweight pop videos and commercials for bands and brands such as Blink-182 and Budweiser. It was a baptism of fire, although for Wujek the demands of creative ingenuity mixed with mass-market relevance were an easy marriage; he flourished, expediting his path into industry recognition.

+ Katy Perry, Shakira, Nicki Minaj

6

While commercials and pop videos both fed a need for large-scale creativity, nothing hit the professional spot for Wujek quite like the unique experience of collaborating with pop stars whose everyday existences require a village-sized feast of multifarious visual theatrics. It is a sweet spot that has transported him to the very pinnacle of the pop scene, across a host of high-production odysseys for artists like Nicki Minaj – including her appearance at the American Music Awards in 2011, in which she channelled a robotic dominatrix complete with light-up metallic bodice (a mechanical feat that is now a Wujek signature) – and the video for Shakira's 2010 football World Cup anthem 'Waka Waka'. But the most definitive proof of his skill at whipping an irrepressibly alluring pop package into being is his decade-long-and-counting union with the California-born megastar Katy Perry. As 'cartoon pop' stars go, they do not come much bigger, more colourful or more entertaining than Perry. Since cannonballing into the charts in 2007, she has consistently racked up number-one singles across the globe as well as extraordinary Youtube/Vimeo play for her videos (at the time of writing, the video of her single 'Dark Horse' of 2013 had alone racked up more than 1 billion views, and it was the most watched video of 2014).

How the pair met is now a well-documented story, but one that poignantly underscores the cheeky, straight-up nature of their inextricably intertwined personal and professional dialogue. While attending the same Hollywood party (long pre-fame), having seen him at the bar with a man, Perry asked Wujek whose team he was on. When he confirmed it was not hers, she informed the entire party, loudly, that he was gay. 'That's Katy,' says Wujek. 'Anything but subtle. We do tend to push things, any ideas, to their limits, and it would probably be fair to say that I do get off on chaos.' And so the almost mythical relationship began, on zero budget and utter faith. Their first project was shooting the cover for Perry's debut album with the photographer Terry Richardson. The album was never released (Perry was famously dropped by her first label), but the process initiated a methodology that had serious traction. Raiding the costume department of Universal Studios, they had collated an army of outfits from Joan Jett rocker to 1920s baton-twirling majorette – classic Americana embodied in multiple brilliantly overblown guises. Costume and role-play had headlined their agenda – a default creative setting that has become the lifeblood of Perry's ultra-physical, bordering-on-slapstick, chameleonic character shifts and has allowed Wujek to play curator to a host of the world's most ingenious specialist 'makers'. With every performance dictating fresh problem-solving, often including technological or mechanical innovation, their list of collaborators is constantly growing. Standouts include LA-based ShowFX, for the cartoon-erotic Cool Whip bra worn in 'California Gurls'; Todd Thomas, former Victoria's Secret collection designer and original 1980s New York club kid, for the costumes on the California Dreams tour; New York design duo The Blondes for the glitzy Carmen Miranda-style 'fruit jubilee' dress worn at the 2014 Grammys and for the infamously hazardous rotating peppermint-wheel bra, also worn on the California Dreams tour; and London-based wearable tech experts CuteCircuit for the 2010 Met Ball gown bearing 3,000 colour-changing LEDs.

7

4
At the American Music Video Awards in 2011 Nicki Minaj wore a light-up, robo-dominatrix bodice, more evidence of Wujek's appetite for buzzworthy theatrics.

5
Shakira, another of Wujek's fantasy-inducing female pop icons, performing during the closing ceremony of the FIFA World Cup in 2010.

6
Perry's Carmen Miranda-style 'fruit jubilee' dress for the Grammy Awards in 2014. Beneath the flirty sass, the costume acknowledges the power of female superstardom; by 1945 Miranda was the highest-paid woman in the United States.

7
Wujek worked with wearable tech experts CuteCircuit on Perry's colour-changing Met Ball gown in 2010.

> I'll never forget when the song 'California Gurls' came out. I went out on Halloween and saw both little girls and drag queens in West Hollywood dressed in the cupcake bra outfit ... The idea that these things have filtered down at such different levels, that sense of reach is extraordinary and very pleasing.
>
> Johnny Wujek

Such pumped-up fantasy garments have become both extensions and reflections of the hyper-fictionalized tour concepts and also video environments that are now emblematic of Perry's world – including the part-CGI scenes embraced by Motion Theory, the US production company that has handled videos including 'Roar' (2013) and 'Dark Horse'. But beyond the frothy, tongue-in-cheek surface of Wujek's substantial costume parade – never illustrated better than on the cover of the first two albums, *One of the Boys* and *Teenage Dream*, photographed by Michael Elins and Will Cotton respectively – such sartorial mischief has also indulged Wujek and Perry's joint belief in mass appeal over critical acclaim in order to build a legacy with real longevity. 'While Katy can clearly handle a sophisticated red carpet moment, it's usually not about being on the best-dressed list, it's about making an outrageous costume for a performance that will really resonate,' says Wujek. 'I'll never forget when the song "California Gurls" came out. I went out on Halloween and saw both little girls and drag queens in West Hollywood dressed in the cupcake bra outfit. The jungle costume from "Roar" has now been licensed as an official Halloween outfit, and some of these pieces are even in museums [the "fruit jubilee" dress resides in The Grammy Museum in Los Angeles]. The idea that these things have filtered down at such different levels, that sense of reach is extraordinary and very pleasing.'

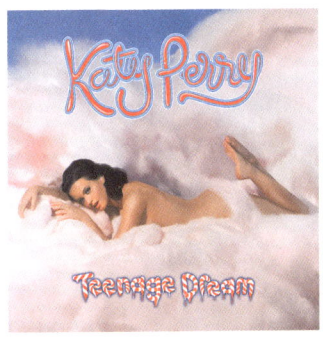

9

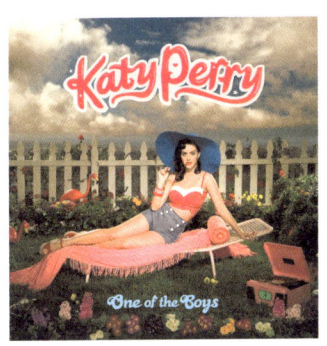

10

11

8
Classic Perry-Wujek: the music video `California Gurls' (2010), grounded in playfully accessible, tongue-in-cheek erotica.

9,10
Album artwork for Perry's *Teenage Dream* (2010) and *One of the Boys* (2008), both of which established her unique brand of pop kitsch.

11
Perry's video `Roar' (2013), a cartoon-influenced ode to personal empowerment.

Such broad reach is testament to the fact that Perry's appeal, co-mastered with Wujek, is actually underscored by authenticity. Contradictory as it first appears, the rampant artifice is far from impenetrable; the gloss is always a Willy Wonka-esque ode to the more bizarre, lighter side of life and is often attached to an autobiographical underbelly. One of the most self-deprecating pop princesses in the global mix, for Halloween 2014 she outshone Los Angeles' sex-bomb set and drew huge applause via social media by attending a star-packed Hollywood soiree dressed as a Cheetos corn snack. The Wujek–Perry manifesto means making entertainment that strikes a chord with the fan on the street, not the charmed inner sanctum of the fashion-industry elite. While her pop peers such as Rihanna and Miley Cyrus play on outright sex appeal and/or provocation, Perry pairs sensuality with what Wujek describes as 'accessibility or relatability. Ultimately she's a real girl, and real girls are attracted to that.' While the videos for the singles 'Thinking of You' (2009) and 'Teenage Dream' (2010) and the cover for the album *Prism* (2013; photographed by Ryan McGinley, an artist renowned for beautiful, pathos-laden imagery) are the most stylistically naturalistic presentations of Perry to date, Wujek also cites the video for the electro-hip-hop track 'E.T.' (2011; featuring Kanye West) – in which Perry is barely recognizable – as indicative of their push to stay genuine. 'It's part of that desire to say, this is who I am, I'm not perfect, accept me for that,' says Wujek. 'As she says in her movie [the documentary *Part of Me*, 2012], "Thank you for believing in my weirdness." She's always owned herself and that's incredibly important to the work we do.'

12
Perry's album *Prism* (2013) featured notably softer art direction – an acknowledgement of the autobiographical nature of Perry's oeuvre that Wujek says is central to their work, however cartoonish. Photographed by Ryan McGinley.

13,14
The epic, hyper-stylized staging of Perry's Egyptian-themed 'Dark House' video (2014) and her geisha-referencing MTV performance in 2013 called out the pop industry's relationship with cultural appropriation.

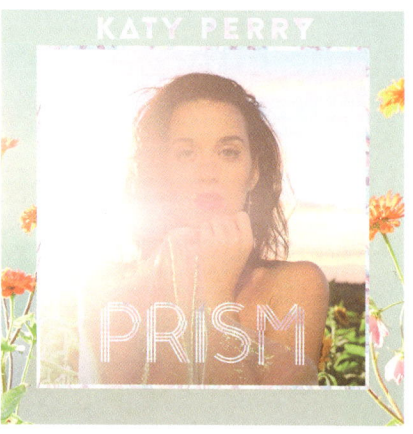

12

13

14

Ownership aside, it would be remiss not to mention that Perry and by proxy Wujek have been lampooned for heavy-handed cultural appropriation while in the pursuit of cartoon messaging. Videos including 'This Is How We Do' (2014), in which Perry sports cornrows; the Egyptian-themed 'Dark Horse', which features extras styled by the acclaimed costume designer and 1980s iconoclast Kim Bowen; and Perry's geisha-based performance of 'Unconditionally' at the MTV Video Music Awards in 2013 have all come under fire. Wujek suggests that such examples reflect an uncomplicated, homage-driven sentiment propelled by the search for either exceptional beauty ('Unconditionally' at the AMAs) or near-comedic daftness ('Dark Horse'); themed fascinations are plundered with genuine sincerity in appreciation of their sheer visual impact. Subtle it is not, but then neither is the bedrock of the Perry–Wujek partnership, which takes overt visual emblems over esoteric or trend-led references every time. Additionally, pop artists have, of course, been borrowing potentially contentious visual jewels from other cultures for decades: David Bowie's rich association with the Japanese fashion-design visionary Kansai Yamamoto (see page 192) was a cultural curiosity that fired an entire persona; Madonna also adopted a geisha stance, via Jean Paul Gaultier, for the acclaimed video 'Nothing Really Matters' in 1999; Rihanna's character in the video for the track 'China Princess' (with Coldplay) in 2011 embraced stylistic cues of mixed Asian origins, which many Chinese commentators on social media took to be a sign of Asian influences pushing positively forward into Western media; while the pop icon Beyoncé was the subject of a (white-trash) trailer-park cover story for the British style bible *Dazed & Confused* in June 2011 – a story that loosely originated in her reassessment of wealth and fame. The topic is complex, far from resolution and ultimately indicative of a new era of slippery cultural plurality.

15

> It's part of that desire to say, this is who I am, I'm not perfect, accept me for that ... As [Katy Perry] says in her movie ..., 'Thank you for believing in my weirdness.' She's always owned herself and that's incredibly important to the work we do.
>
> Johnny Wujek

15
The video for Katy Perry's single 'E.T.' (2011) was driven, says Wujek, by a wider desire to celebrate weirdness, imperfection and, ultimately, individuality.

17

16
Stills from Perry's 'This Is How We Do' (2014), another red rag to those who complained of cultural appropriation. Many failed to grasp the video's premise: a self-aware stroll through social media-fuelled youth culture, built on chaotically spliced, jumbled visual references.

17
Tapping the trickle-down: Katy Perry Eylure false eyelashes. Perry's depiction as a cartoon character is a potent metaphor for the success of the Wujek-Perry brand: larger-than-life fantasies presented for popular consumption.

18
Perry in typically high-energy form for *Rolling Stone* in July 2011, photographed by Terry Richardson.

19
The *Wheel of Fortune* TV host Vanna White, one of Wujek's earliest inspirations, symbolized his creative raison d'être: melding fantasy glamour with the warmth of prime-time accessibility.

Where the visual styling for the video of 'This Is How We Do' succeeds is in upholding Perry in one of her most honest guises: the comedic modern pin-up. Rife with the unapologetic self-awareness that typifies the Wujek–Perry alliance, the video portrays her as a cartoon-esque, decade-hopping pop star strolling from scene to scene within a flattened landscape based entirely on Tumblr. A layered mosaic of animation, film and collaged graphics, the video is an affectionate ode to youth culture circa 2014. It crystallizes the role of pop stars and the incessant (social media-necessitated) reinventions that maintain their visual equity. Brands worn include Opening Ceremony and Kenzo, emblematic of Tumblr-influenced, social media-fuelled fashionista tribes as well as indicative, says Wujek, of Perry's overriding personal preference for hipster alternatives over luxury megabrands. While the breakneck speed of such sartorial reinventions may prove eye-watering for some, Wujek states that his oeuvre has actually benefited from the pace: 'I'm not feeling pressure – it's more of a motivating force. I'm more inspired to think next-level, to think outside the box – to think about what people aren't doing, what haven't we done and what could we do better, bigger.'

For Wujek, when it comes to creating exuberant costumed fantasies, bigger and better is always likely to be derived from his enthusiastic embrace of the fun, trashy or simply most visually resilient parts of pop culture. Wujek's own creative heroes include the visionary French art director Jean-Paul Goude (see page 80), the British fashion photographer Tim Walker and the film director Tim Burton's long-time costume designer, Colleen Atwood. And it is little surprise that the US photographer David LaChapelle, an artist famous for images built on a lasciviously over-saturated mix of high-gloss, kitschy pop-culture references, is one of Wujek's favourite collaborators for commercial advertising projects (it was LaChapelle who shot the hairstyling brand GHD's ads featuring Perry in 2011). Tellingly, however, it is a far more populist, comparatively lowbrow, TV-related fantasy that remains a key source of motivation: 'Growing up I remember watching *Wheel of Fortune* and looking at Vanna White who pushed the letters – imagining how fantastic it would be to style her in the most fabulous couture. It may seem weird but I feel like I am that. I grew up in the middle of America and I know how I was when I was a kid and what fascinated me. It's glamour and fantasy but also things simultaneously embedded with the reality of attainability.'

18

19

Kansai Yamamoto

+

David Bowie, Lady Gaga

1

1
Yamamoto with Lady Gaga, a latter-day superstar highly attuned to David Bowie's vast sartorial legacy, created in league with the Japanese designer.

2
David Bowie in the now iconic 'Tokyo Pop' PVC kabuki bodysuit devised by Yamamoto. Prophetically, considering Bowie's legendary gender-fluidity, the design was originally created for a woman. Photographed by Masayoshi Sukita.

Kansai Yamamoto – designer, director and one of David Bowie's linchpin early collaborators – is a creative so dynamic that, according to Victoria Broackes, head of performance and theatre exhibitions at the Victoria and Albert Museum in London, 'in many ways regular fashion simply cannot contain him.' Since his debut in the 1970s, he has been an unparalleled magnet for those with an appetite for the extraordinary.

The first Japanese fashion designer ever to show in London, Yamamoto arrived explosively on the city's already fever-pitch fashion scene in 1971, generating a hurricane of activity. It was a spectacle prophesyed by *Harper's & Queen* magazine (which devoted a six-page editorial plus cover to the story) as an industry game-changer: 'The room is almost pitch black, lit by a few spotlights; it's very crowded, very hot and very late. Suddenly, at 11.23 p.m. precisely, the house lights go down and a tremendous discord of wild, upbeat Japanese music heralds the start of the Show of the Year. A spectacular coup de theatre – Kansai's models came on moving. They leapt, ran, whirled like dervishes, danced, flung out their arms so that the brilliant clothes meshed and merged into a kaleidoscopic cartoon of colour … But his true originality lies deeper – Kansai is not so much a designer of clothes but an architect, with clothes built round the body in layers, wrapped round, looped and tied, and put on like a suit of armour. It's for this reason that we believe Kansai Yamamoto will have a massive impact on the world of fashion.'

3

+ David Bowie, Lady Gaga

4

> **Bowie's impact on fashion thanks to his radical individualism is still everywhere ... but it was meeting Kansai in those early days that helped him realize his vision and express his own individuality.**
>
> Victoria Broackes, curator

3
Yamamoto's legendary, industry game-changing debut fashion show in London in 1971, watched by the 24-year-old Bowie.

4
A model from Yamamoto's seminal 1971 show, which revolutionized catwalk presentations and set the wheels of his relationship with David Bowie palpably in motion.

Obliterating contemporary catwalk etiquette, the thrilling frenzy of fashion immersed in motion was not lost on then 24-year-old audience member David Bowie, for whom Yamamoto extravagantly mirrored his own obsessions with performance, music, theatre and identity – and, in particular, the swaggering, unbridled individualism that propelled him to pop-culture immortality long before his death in 2016. The landscape of twentieth-century pop culture would be virtually unrecognizable without Bowie's gender-bending, culture-splicing, status quo-sabotaging reveries; and his most significant chameleonic shift – into the messianic sci-fi guise of Aladdin Sane – could arguably not have been realized without the exotic futuristic frisson unleashed by the Bowie–Yamamoto partnership. 'Bowie's impact on fashion thanks to his radical individualism is still everywhere,' says Victoria Broackes, who co-curated the show 'David Bowie Is' (2013). 'Designers such as Gucci, Jonathan Saunders, Miu Miu and Richard Nicoll all cite Bowie as a huge influence on their recent work, but it was meeting Kansai in those early days that helped him realize his vision and express his own individuality.'

Tracking the origins of Yamamoto's own genesis, and its subsequent impact on stars from Bowie to Lady Gaga, reveals a story of cultural curiosity and taboo teasing, both in homage to and in rebellion against his Japanese heritage. Born in Yokohama, just outside Tokyo, he originally studied engineering but switched to a fashion apprenticeship at 21 years old, purely to impress women. His methodology was simple: the more individual a man's style, the more visible and impressive the man. Three years and a portfolio of illustrations later, he had won a national Japanese fashion competition (formerly won by design heavyweights Kenzo Takada and Yohji Yamamoto) and was inundated with magazine commissions for bespoke, thematic garments – a flattering scenario but one ultimately at odds with his personal agenda. Says Yamamoto, 'I wanted to do my own thing, and I began to wonder what I was making clothes for. Meanwhile, the hippie movement was happening in the US and Europe – changing my view of fashion. I was utterly intrigued and raring to go into the eye of the [hippie] typhoon.'

Kansai Yamamoto

Hungry for new influences and an environment more appreciative of a mentality that railed against the acquiescent serenity of Japan's traditional *wabi-sabi* aesthetic, Yamamoto travelled to London and New York in search of psychedelia. 'I was absolutely inspired by Japanese beauty, but it was more the violent rainbow colours, the Samurai warriors of the fifteenth and sixteenth centuries and the idea of *basara* or *kabuku*, which literally mean to lean out of balance, to slant, to deviate. That's what excited me,' says Yamamoto. The transition was well received; his own outré sense of style became his passport to Western cities, gaining him friendships, patrons and party invitations. 'I didn't know anyone in those cities when I initially arrived, so being stopped and asked questions about my clothes was the only real time I had any communication with anyone. I literally became my own canvas.'

On his first trip to London, walking down London's King's Road – then a mecca for Britain's most flamboyant fashion trendsetters – while boasting an afro hairstyle and full snakeskin jumpsuit, Yamamoto was approached by a photographer for *Life* magazine about a feature documenting the ten most fashionable men in the world. 'I thought, "Great, but am I tenth?" I don't want to take silver or bronze – how can I be number one?' he recalls.

5

I was absolutely inspired by Japanese beauty, but it was more the violent rainbow colours, the Samurai warriors of the fifteenth and sixteenth centuries and the idea of *basara* or *kabuku,* which literally mean to lean out of balance, to slant, to deviate. That's what excited me.

Kansai Yamamoto

Cultural contrasts became Yamamoto's main weapon. Another image of him taken just two years later, around the time of the 1971 show, depicts him with a shaved head reminiscent of an oriental monk, feathered Native American earrings, a tight red wrestler-style bodysuit and a pair of silver and red 'London' boots (which Bowie had had copied for him by the designer Freddie Burretti before meeting Yamamoto) – all his own designs. Broackes says: 'As was always the case with Bowie, he was in the right place at the right time, and I think he saw something in Kansai that could provide a sense of becoming. He had a very clear vision for all of his "characters", and sought to truly absorb himself in them, assuming their personas, rather than simply playing dress-up. David has an enormous input in anything he chooses to design or collaborate on, and Kansai, with his incredibly intricate, historically influenced yet original and theatrical designs, completely understood this need to create a character or realize a vision, and thus was the perfect partner. Bowie's own shows in this era were pronounced by one critic as "perhaps the most consciously theatrical rock shows ever staged", and some of this Bowie had learned from Kansai Yamamoto's own fashion show.'

6

+ David Bowie, Lady Gaga

7

That highly competitive capacity to forge fashion personae in the most attention-grabbing, extreme way found an affinity with artists beyond Bowie, too: Marc Bolan, Mick Jagger and Elton John all embraced his wild stylistic unorthodoxy during their glam-rock years; and in 2013 Yamamoto began creating custom looks for Lady Gaga. 'When she came to me, she said she wanted to be number one in both music and fashion,' he says. 'Even David only claimed he wanted to be number one in music.'

Prior to their first collaboration – on the Aladdin Sane tour of 1972–73, when Bowie could afford to ditch the copycat designs for real articles – Yamamoto insists he had no knowledge of his music. 'Music has never been that important to me. I couldn't live if I was blind but being deaf is not really a problem.' Indeed, the first time he saw Bowie, after agreeing to lend him his clothes but before any co-creation, was as Bowie was being lowered from the ceiling on to the stage of a show in New York while wearing Yamamoto's monochrome 'Tokyo Pop' PVC *kabuki* bodysuit. Prophetically, it was a garment Yamamoto had originally made for a woman; underneath, as was revealed to the audience in a suitably theatrical unveiling, was a one-legged knitted body stocking.

5,6
A young Yamamoto wearing his own designs in the 1970s - a stylistic calling card that became his 'passport into Western cities' and their influential fashion tribes. Image 5 is taken from *Life* magazine.

7
The Yamamoto-designed knitted bodystocking that Bowie wore in concert under the Tokyo Pop PVC bodysuit - a classic example of the duo's penchant for blurred boundaries and 'beautiful surprise'.

8 (overleaf)
Bowie in the Yamamoto-designed short kimono, a typically sexually ambiguous design, but one distinct from the more predictable gender-bending of his 1970s rock-star peers.

8

As was always the case with Bowie, he was in the right place at the right time, and I think he saw something in Kansai that could provide a sense of becoming. He had a very clear vision for all of his 'characters', and sought to truly absorb himself in them, assuming their personas, rather than simply playing dress-up.

Victoria Broackes

+ David Bowie, Lady Gaga

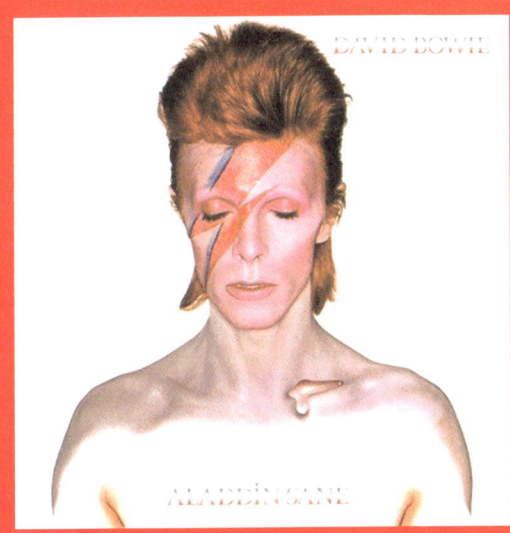

9

10

11

12

The pull was intoxicating. Both outsiders revelling in their self-imposed exiles (Yamamoto from the more restrictive aspects of traditional Japan, Bowie from the sanctified suburban normality of 1970s Britain), they were citizens of everywhere and nowhere at once. It was a meeting of minds that ignited an exhilarating cabaret of colliding cultures. 'Our tone, attitude and ambition towards gender and pushing boundaries, the way in which we wanted to go out into the world, were the same, but because of our mix of cultures with one player from the West and another from the East it crashed together almost like a chemical reaction, like cheese and miso soup, in a kind of beauty that generated an enormous amount of surprise,' says Yamamoto.

> **Our tone, attitude and ambition towards gender and pushing boundaries, the way in which we wanted to go out into the world, were the same, but because of our mix of cultures with one player from the West and another from the East it crashed together almost like a chemical reaction, like cheese and miso soup, in a kind of beauty that generated an enormous amount of surprise.**
>
> Kansai Yamamoto

9 (previous page)
The cover of Bowie's album *Aladdin Sane* (1973); the famous hairstyle was based on that worn by a female model from Yamamoto's seminal show in 1971.

10-12 (previous page)
Three key outfits from *Aladdin Sane*'s related tour (Bowie and Yamamoto's first major collaboration): wrestling boots based on Yamamoto's own wardrobe; the 'Woodland Creatures' leather playsuit, as surreal and ageless as it is gender-conflicted; and the 'Space Samurai Cape'.

13
Cover and pages from the poster-sized press book that accompanied Yamamoto's super-show of 2014, 'Hello Istanbul!'

The use of costume from traditional Japanese *kabuki* theatre – particularly when echoing that of the *onnagatas*, the male actors who assume female roles and dress as women – advertised that Bowie was an artist on whom his audience could rely as a portal to cultures, art and knowledge far beyond their own. More importantly, such costuming also transmitted the sexual ambiguity on which each of Bowie's pop personae had been built. A silk, short-skirted, white kimono suit worn onstage with glossy warrior-esque knee-high boots emphatically exuded a feminine allure but in a beautified version of the drag of his glam-rock peers, whose penchant for top hats and feather boas cut a more predictable picture of sexual vagary. The short leather 'Woodland Creatures' romper suit decorated with winged rabbits and surrealist black swirls is as ageless as it is gender-conflated – an asexual ode to pop music's greatest alien. Both the 'Space-Samurai' costume – a sweeping quilted cape stuffed with rows of black sequins – and a voluminous white cape emblazoned across the back with Japanese *kanji* characters presented a vision of an androgynous, even polymorphous, emperor – all-powerful in his supreme bizarreness. Even Ziggy Stardust's famous shock of razor-cut red hair, rendered immortal by the photographer Brian Duffy's 'lightning bolt' album cover for *Aladdin Sane*, was inspired by Yamamoto: it was derived from a leonine 'mane' of hair worn by one of the female models in his show of 1971.

The slippery landscape of gender continues to be fodder for Yamamoto's button-pushing sensibility. In one segment of his show 'Hello Istanbul!' (2014), male models wore long, veil-like facial coverings crafted from hundreds of old Japanese coins. Yamamoto explains that it was inspired not by a desire to break religious taboos but by an interrogation of survival – a combination of the mode in which Japanese farmers of both sexes historically hid their faces from the sun, how people are quarantined during disasters and the traditional disguise of Japanese *ninjas*. Nevertheless, the ambiguous symbolism inherent in the materiality of the pieces – mixing ancient and new, male and female (each veil appears bejewelled and enticing) – is Yamamoto to the core.

+ David Bowie, Lady Gaga

MERHABA

2014 yılı Türkiye ve Japonya'nın düzenli diplomatik ilişkiler kurmasının 90. Yıldönümü kutlaması 'HELLO İSTANBUL!!' etkinliğine hepiniz hoş geldiniz.
'HELLO ISTANBUL!!' 2 bölümden oluşmaktadır.
Birinci bölüm hep hayal ettiğim bir manzara . Cok renkli bir deniz etkinliği, hem Türk ve Japon çocukların hazırladıkları bayraklarla hem de geleneksel Japon denizci bayraklarıyla (Tairyo-bata) süslenen gemilerin Asya ve Avrupa'yı birleştiren İstanbul Boğazı'nda süzülmeleri.
Hazırlanan her bir bayrak bu iki ulusun dostluklarının daha da güçlü devam etmesi dileklerini taşıyacaktır.
Umarım İstanbullular bu Japon deniz festivali havasından keyif alırlar.
İkinci bölüm de bugün hazırladıklarımız.
Ayrı 2 katta gerçekleştirilecek bu gösteri sanırım moda defileler tarihinde bir ilk.
Karşılaştığımız tüm zorluklara rağmen özenle hazırladığımız bu koleksiyonun sizlere tüm güzelliğiyle ulaşmasını ümit ederim.
Bugün sunacağımız koleksiyonu dünyada lider Türk derisi ve son teknoloji Japon kumaşları kullanarak geleneksel tekniklerle beraber evren, doğa, hayvanlar, şehir ışıklarının parlaklığı ve geleneksel Japon giyimi gibi konulardan ilham alarak yarattık.
Ayrıca sizler için Japonya'daki engelli sanatçılarla birlikte, çivit boyalı kumaşlardan giysiler hazırladık. Çalışmalarını ilk defa gördüğümde, sıradışı fikirlerinden ve özgür yaklaşımlarında, ben derinden etkilendim. Eminim sizler de onların tutkularını ve güçlü enerjilerini hissedeceksiniz.
Ve son olarak, bu etkinliğin gerçekleşmesi için emek veren herkese kalpten şükranlarımı sunarım.
Şimdi, herkese iyi eğlenceler.

11 Ekim 2014, Cumartesi
The Marmara Esma Sultan

produced by **Kansai Yamamoto**

Türkiye – Japonya diplomatik ilişkilerinin kuruluşunun 90. Yılı anısına

HELLO ISTANBUL!!

While for Bowie the partnership solidified his status as the otherworldly overlord of pop culture, it was just as significant for Yamamoto. Bowie's emphasis on obstacle-smashing self-expression and, crucially, the power of stagecraft became the bedrock, two decades later, of Yamamoto's 'super shows' – mass-peopled fashion spectacles combining dance, music, gymnastics and often enormous venues such as Moscow's Red Square (and 120,000 Muscovites) in 1993; New Delhi's Nehru Stadium in 1997; and the Saitama Super Arena in Japan for a football World Cup qualifying event in 2006. He describes each show as 'a love letter to my audience, demonstrated with the full force of my energies', driven by a desire to create something astonishing and original that would provoke, prod and propel new ideas. The shows were, he says, galvanized by one very specific moment with Bowie: 'David was on stage, wearing what's basically only underwear. You can see almost everything; he's virtually naked. I was shocked, but when I saw his showmanship and that he didn't even care about being naked, I felt that I could do anything and break all restrictions and taboos in society, regardless of existing boundaries.'

14

A love letter to my audience, demonstrated with the full force of my energies.

Kansai Yamamoto

15

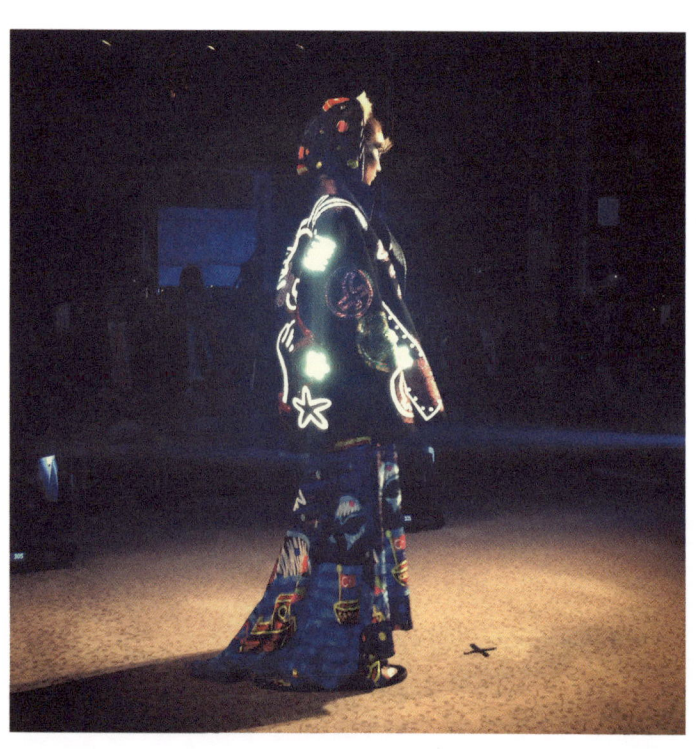

16

14
David Bowie as Ziggy Stardust in 1973, the performance that inspired-shocked Yamamoto into their initial collaboration.

15,16
Yamamoto's high-energy catwalk show 'Hello Istanbul!' (2014) featured pieces that merged high fashion with performance, and ancient references with modern technology.

17,18
The megastar Lady Gaga wearing Yamamoto: on the Tokyo subway (17) in 2014 in an outfit inspired by the erotic neon signs of the Shinjuku district; and on Japanese television in 2013, mixing his pieces with vintage Versace.

Lady Gaga – a pop star whose raison d'être, like Bowie before her, lies as much in performance art as it does in singing or dancing – is a logical ambassador for twenty-first-century Yamamoto. For a series of Japanese TV appearances in 2014, she wore an oversize metallic coat custom-designed by Yamamoto that was inspired by the erotic neon signs of Shinjuku in downtown Tokyo – after having mixed vintage Versace and Yamamoto on stage in Japan the previous year. Yamamoto suggests that further collaborations may be on the cards: 'My experience as a designer but also a producer means I can help artists to express themselves, to push through boundaries and elevate who they are.'

Now in his 70s, Yamamoto says he has no intention of slowing down, of relinquishing the creation of his own mythical beings, although he also refuses to confirm his direction: 'It could be a movie or maybe I'll just start a huge business conglomerate,' he says. But while vintage Yamamoto garments are still being sold by brands including the luxury e-tailer Farfetch, there will apparently be no reprisal of the Kansai Boutiques he had in New York, London and Paris during the 1970s. 'I want to challenge everything but I will never do anything twice,' he says. 'My heroes are those that have no fear of crossing borders, of pushing into new places.' His ultimate hero is in fact not a fellow creative but the late Japanese explorer Naomi Uemura – an adventurer renowned for doing solo what others had done only in large teams. He was the first man to reach the North Pole solo; the first person to raft the Amazon River alone; and the first, in 1984, to climb Mount McKinley in Alaska unaided, although he is believed to have died during the descent. Uemura's body was never found, making the already heroic figure something of a fabled being: a man–myth of folkloric significance and an easy-to-fathom vessel for Yamamoto's empathetic admiration.

17

18

Index

Page numbers in *italics* refer to the captions.

Abraham, Damian (Fucked Up) 111
Adam and the Ants 42, *113*, 118, 120
 Kings of the Wild Frontier (1980) 120, *121*
 Prince Charming (*Prince Charming*, 1981) 120
Aerosmith 144
Aether, Erevos 13
Aguilera, Christina: MTV Music Awards (2003) 128
Åkerlund, B. 10–19, 147
Åkerlund, Jonas 13, 14, 16
Albarn, Damon (Blur) 154
A.L.C. label (Lieberman) *101*
Allen, Lily: Sheezus tour (2014) *50*, 58
Allsopp, Robert 55, 58
Ambrose, June 174
America's Next Top Model TV show 184
Anderson, Brett (Suede) 154, 160
Andre 3000 (Outkast) 62
androgyny 85, 200
Ant, Adam (Adam and the Ants) 120
Ashish 108
Atwood, Colleen 191
Azalea, Iggy 66

'baby shower' dress (Goude and A. Lopez for Grace Jones) 86
'Back-to-School Mermaid' series (Marano for Azealia Banks) 108
Baker, William 20–9, *162*, *168*, 171
Banks, Azealia 108
Banton, Travis 134
Barker, Simon ('Six') 118
Beyoncé 14, 172, 174, 176, 181
 4 (2011) *173*, 176–7, *179*
 Beyoncé (2013) 14, *177*
 Dazed & Confused shoot (2011) *173*, *178*, *179*, 188
 The Gentlewoman cover (2012) 180
 Glastonbury Festival (2011) 176
 'Grown Woman' video (2013) *177*
 'Haunted' video (2013) 14
 'Independent Women' (with Destiny's Child, 2000) 174
 Mrs Carter tour (2013) 14
 O2 adverts 14
 L'Officiel magazine shoot (2011) *173*, 174, *175*, 176, *178*
 'Partition' video (2013) 14
 'Pretty Hurts' video (2013) 14
 'Run the World (Girls)' video (2011) 176, *179*, 180
 'Superpower' video (2013) 14

Björk 38, 66
 Debut (1993) 38, *39*
Blackwell, Chris 75
Blahnik, Manolo 96
Blame, Judy *8*, 22, 30–9, 43, 135
Blanco, Mykki 111
Blend magazine 61
Blige, Mary J. 96
 The Breakthrough (2005) 96
 Growing Pains (2007) 96
Blitz club, London 32, 42, 66, 154
Blitz magazine 124, *125*
Blow, Isabella 22
Blow Up club, London 154
Blur 154, 160
 'Coffee and TV' video (1990) *159*
BodyMap 34, *125*, 162, 164–8, 171
bodystocking (Yamamoto for David Bowie) *197*
Bolan, Marc 197
Bon Jovi, Jon 144
Bowery, Leigh 49, 77, 124, 167
Bowie, David 43, 58, 118, 134, 135, 188, *192*, 195, 202
 Aladdin Sane (1973) 200
 Aladdin Sane tour (1972–73) 195, *197*, *199*
 as Ziggy Stardust 58, 135, 200, *203*
Boy George 22, *32*, 33, 165, 167
 Grammy Awards (1984) *32*, 33
Britpop 153, 154–5, 158, *159*, *160*, 161
Broackes, Victoria (V&A) *192*, 195, 196
'Bromley Contingent' 118
Bruni, Carla 22
Bryant, Jeffrey 40–9, 54
Buffalo Crew 33, 39
Burns, Pete (Dead or Alive) 118
Burretti, Freddie 135, 196
Bush, Kate: Before the Dawn tour (2014) 55

Campbell, Naomi 22, 91
Candy, Brooke 71, 72, 77–8
 'Opulence' video (2014) 77, 78
'Captain Pugwash' jacket (Bryant for Pet Shop Boys) 47
Carbon Life ballet (Pugh, 2011) *50*, 55
Carmen Miranda dress (Wujek for Katy Perry) 185
Caroli, Constanze 137
The Cell (dir. Tarsem Singh, 2000) *19*, 141
Cha Cha club, London 32
Chalayan, Hussein 73
Chapman, Jake and Dinos 52, *53*
Cher 144, *145*

Cherry, Neneh 33, 34, 37, 167
 The Blank Project (2014) 39
 'Buffalo Stance' single and video (1989) 34
 'Everything' video (2014) 39
 'Manchild' video (1989) *34*, 37
 Raw Like Sushi (1989) *8*, 30, 34
chola culture 66, 101
Clark, Michael 162, 167
club scene
 London 32–3, 41, 42–3, 49, 66, *113*, 124, 154–5, 156, 162, 164, 165
 New York 82, 86, 94, 95, 104, 111, *142*, 144, 147, 156
Coachella festival (2009) *106*, 108
Cocker, Jarvis (Pulp) 154, 156, *159*, 167
Coldplay: 'Princess of China' video (with Rihanna, 2011) 151, 188
Cole, Marilyn 137
Color Code 71, 72, 79
 'I Like Dat' video (2014) 79
Combs, Sean (Puff Daddy) 94–5, 96
Conan the Destroyer (dir. Richard Fleischer, 1984) 85
Coon, Caroline 118
Costiff, Michael and Gerlinde 42, 43, *121*
Crisp, Quentin 156
Culture Club 33, 165, 167
Culture and Reality store, New York (Lieberman) 94
Cunningham, Rick 135
cupcake bra (Wujek for Katy Perry) *183*, 187
Currin, John 156, *159*
CuteCircuit 185
Cyrus, Miley 58, 59, 188
 Bangerz tour (2014) *57*, 58, 59
 as Hannah Montana 58

Daft Punk 108
dance pop 44, 96
'David Bowie Is' exhibition (2013), V&A 195
Dazed & Confused magazine 72, 73
 Beyoncé shoot (2011) *173*, *178*, *179*, 188
Deconstruction Records 23, 25
Deee-Lite 43
 'Groove Is in the Heart' (*World Clique*, 1990) 43
Destiny's Child 96, 174
 see also Beyoncé
Details magazine 125
Deuce 43, 44
Devlin, Es 45, 47, 50–9
Diesel 74, 77, *78*
disco 25, 65, 66, 85, 86, 125

Doran, Fee (Mrs Jones) 25
'Dress-Your-Gaga' paper doll cut-out book 42, *48*
Dune (dir. David Lynch, 1984) 59
Duran Duran 47, 132, 135, 141, 165
  'Planet Earth' video (1981) 141
  'Rio' video (1982) 141

East 17 (band) 44
electro-pop 25, 42, 53, 54, 69, 78, 108, 127, 188
Enlightened 108
Evangelista, Linda 22
Eve 99

The Face magazine 33, *160*
  Grace Jones cover (1987) 86
  Iggy Pop shoot (1986) 37
Farfetch 203
Fernandez, Franc 60–9
Ferry, Bryan 135, 137, 138, 165
  Boys and Girls (1985) 138, *139*
  'Let's Stick Together' video (1976) 138, *139*
  Olympia (2010) 138
  'Slave to Love' (*Boys and Girls*, 1985) *137*, 138, *139*
  see also Roxy Music
Fielding, David 47, 55
Fischerspooner 69
Flowered Up: *A Life with Brian* (1991) 155
Fonteyn, Margot 115
Formichetti, Nicola 49, 63, 70–9
Frankie Goes to Hollywood: 'Relax' (1983) 52
'French Correction' (Goude) 14, 82
Frischmann, Justine (Elastica) 154

Galliano, John 19, 135
Gaultier, Jean Paul 22, 29, 118, 127, 128, *129*, 188
gender-bending 33, 42, 85, 118, 124, 127, 131, 154, *192*, *195*, *197*, 200
  see also androgyny
Genest, Rico (Zombie Boy) 74
The Gentlewoman magazine: Beyoncé cover (2012) 180
Ghesquière, Nicolas 59
Gilford, Luke 69
Girls Aloud: 'Can't Speak French' (2012) *171*
glam rock 65, 127, 197, 200
Glastonbury Festivals 176
Goldfrapp, Alison: Head First tour (2010) 47
Goldsmith, Nick (Hammer & Tongs) 156, *159*

Gollings, Jo (Jo and Pat Skinny) 153
Goude, Jean-Paul 14, *20*, 25, 65, 80–91, 191
Grammy Awards *32*, 33, 73, 96, 105, 185
Green, CeeLo 16
Green, Martin 154
grunge 13, 140, 144, 154, 158
Grunwald, Eveline 137

The Haçienda club, Manchester 22
Hall, Jerry *133*, 137
Hammer & Tongs (Garth Jennings and Nick Goldsmith) 156, *159*
Hansen, Janet Cooke (Enlightened) 108
Harper's Bazaar magazine 90, *91*, 194, *195*
Harry, Debbie 147, 149, 151
Healy, Jeremy 135, 167
Heaven club, London 32, 42
Hedwig and the Angry Inch 127, 147
Hell club, London 42
'Hello Istanbul!' show (Yamamoto, 2014) 200, *201*, 203
Hinton, Jeffrey 167
hip-hop 34, 62, 63, 92, 94–6, 99, 101, 118, 180, 188
Hipgnosis 155
Holah, David (BodyMap) 125, 164, 167
Holland, Henry 105, 108
Holley, Patrick (Jo and Pat Skinny) 153
How, Jane 104
The Hunger (dir. Tony Scott, 1983) 65
Hynde, Chrissie (The Pretenders) 116, 125

i-D magazine 33, 124, *125*
  Lady Gaga cover *71*, 73
Ice T: *Cop Killer* (1992) 128
Iggy Pop
  The Face shoot (1986) 37
  Time Out cover (1996) 37
indie music 22, 23, 105, 140, 154
Inez & Vinoodh 74
Ishioka, Eiko 19, 141

J-pop 71, 72, 79, 101
Jacobs, Marc 90, *91*
Jagger, Mick 134, 197
Jay Kay (Jamiroquai) 23
Jay Z: Watch the Throne tour (2011–12) *50*, 53
Jennings, Garth (Hammer & Tongs) 156, *159*
John, Elton 197
Jones, Grace *20*, 25, 65, 81–90, *91*

'baby shower' performance (1979) 86
The Face cover (1987) 86
Island Life (1985) 82, 90
'My Jamaican Guy' (1982) *81*
New York magazine shoot (1978) 82
Nightclubbing (1981) 85
A One Man Show tour (1981) 85
Roseland Ballroom, New York (1978) 86, *91*
Slave to the Rhythm album and video (1985) 82, 86
'La Vie en Rose' (*Portfolio*, 1977) 86
'Walking in the Rain' (*Nightclubbing*, 1981) 85
Warm Leatherette (1980) 75
Jones, Kim 49
The Joy of Sex book 156
Jubilee (dir. Derek Jarman, 1978) 120, *121*
Juicy Couture 96
Jungle Fever book (Goude) *81*, 82

Kamen, Nick 135
Kansai Boutiques, New York 203
Kardashian, Kim 90
Karlsson, Anna-Karin *11*
Kawakubo, Rei 144
Kelela 65, *66*, 69
  'The High' (2014) 65, *66*
Kibu website 184
kimono suit (Yamamoto for David Bowie) *198*, 200
Kinky Gerlinky club, London 43
Klein, Steven 73, 74, 77, 90, *123*, 131
Knight, Nick 73, 74, 101, 116
Knode, Charles 141
Kraftwerk 25
Kravitz, Lenny 125
  'Are You Gonna Go My Way' video (1993) *123*, 125
  Let Love Rule (1989) 125
  Mama Said (1991) 125

LaChapelle, David 191
Lady Gaga 13, *48*, 49, 61, 63, 72–4, 78, 79, 90, *192*, *197*, 203
  'Alejandro' video (2009) 73, *74*
  'Bad Romance' video (2009) 63, 73, 74
  'Born this Way' video (2011) 73
  Grammy Awards (2011) 73
  i-D cover *71*, 73
  as Jo Calderone 73
  MTV Music Awards (2010) 63
  'Paparazzi' video (2009) 13, *17*
  Rolling Stone cover (2009) 149
  V magazine shoot (2009) 73

Lady Miss Kier (Deee-Lite) 43, 72, 167
Laleh: 'Colors' video (2015) 12, *13*
L.A.M.B. label (Stefani) 99, *101*
Lauper, Cyndi 44
Lawrence, Francis 73, *74*, 99
Le Snob label (Åkerlund) 19
Lear, Amanda 137
Leibovitz, Annie 94, 95, 174
Lieberman, Andrea 62, 92–101
LMFAO 16
Longpigs 153
  'Lost Myself' (1996) 155
  'She Said' (1995) 155
Lopez, Antonio 86
Lopez, Jennifer 92, 96
  'Get Right' video (2005) 96
  Grammy Awards (2000) 96
  'I'm Real' video (2001) 96
  'Jenny from the Block' video (2002) *92*, 96
  'Play' video (2001) 96
Louis Vuitton 47, 49, 59, 9
  spring-summer 2015 catwalk show (Devlin) 59, *59*
  'Series 3' exhibition (Devlin, 2015) *52*, 53
Love, Courtney 127
Lowe, Chris (Pet Shop Boys) 42, 43, 44, *45*, 46, 47, 54
L'Uomo Vogue magazine: Art for Freedom shoot (2014) 131
Lutens, Serge 115

Maal, Baaba 38
McDean, Craig *167*, 168
Mackie, Bob 144
McLaren, Malcolm 33, 42, 113, 115, 118, 120
McQueen, Alexander 23, 74, 77, 135
Madonna 16, 17, 19, 22, 72, 78, 111, 118, 123, 127–8
  American Life (2003) 127
  Blond Ambition tour (1990) 22
  Confessions tour (2001) 131
  'Don't Tell Me' video (2009) 128
  Drowned World tour (2001) 131
  'Frozen' video (1998) 127
  'Girl Gone Wild' video (2012) 128
  Hard Candy (2008) *13*, 17
  'Hung Up' video (2005) 128
  MDNA tour (2012) 131, 151
  MTV Music Awards (2003) 128
  Music (2000) 128, *129*
  'Nothing Really Matters' video (1999) *123*, 128, *129*, 188
  'Ray of Light' video (1998) 127–8
  Rebel Heart (2015) 127
  Reinvention tour (2004) 131
  Sticky & Sweet tour (2008) 131

Super Bowl halftime show (2012) 14, 16
Maison Martin Margiela see Margiela, Martin
Malakpour, Maryam and Marjan 184
Maliphant, Russell 162, 168
Marano, Anastasia 102-11
Margiela, Martin (Maison Martin Margiela) 38, 53, 60, 69
Marquee club, London 113
Martel, Diane 58, 59
Massive Attack 37
  'Day Dreaming' (1990) 35
  'Unfinished Sympathy' video (1991) 37
Matlock, Glen (Sex Pistols) 116
Matronic, Ana (Scissor Sisters) 65
'Meat Dress' (Fernandez for Lady Gaga) 61, 63
Memoirs of a Geisha book (Arthur Golden) 123, 128
Mensa, Vic: MTV Music Awards (2015) 62, 63
Met Ball gown (Wujek and CuteCircuit for Katy Perry) 185
M.I.A. 16, 103, 105, 108
  Coachella festival (2009) 106, 108
  Grammy Awards (2009) 105
  'Paper Planes' (Kala, 2007) 105
  Rebel Yell cover (Spin, 2008) 103, 105
Michael and Gerlinde's World: Pages from a Diary book (2013) 43, 121
Minaj, Nicki 16, 185
  American Music Awards (2011) 185, 185
Ministry of Sound club, London 154
Minogue, Kylie 20, 22, 23, 25, 26, 29, 167
  Aphrodite tour (2011) 162, 168, 171
  Body Language (2003) 26
  'Breathe' (1997) 23
  'Can't Get You Out of my Head' video (2001) 25
  'Did It Again' (1997) 23
  Fever (2001) 20, 25
  Fever tour (2002) 26
  Impossible Princess (1997) 23
  Intimate and Live tour (1998) 26
  Kiss Me Once (2014) 29
  KylieX2008 tour (2008) 20, 26, 29, 171
  Light Years (2000) 23, 25
  Showgirl tour (2005-6) 26
  'Spinning Around' video (2001) 25
  The X Factor (2012) 141

Minotaur heads (Devlin and Allsopp for Pet Shop Boys) 55
Missy Elliott: 'The Rain (Supa Dupa Fly)' video (1997) 66
Mitchell, Gayla 138
Miu Miu 99, 195
Miyake, Issey 82, 144
Mondino, Jean-Baptiste 30, 34, 38, 39
mood boards 14, 66, 101, 161
Mooney, Jordan (née Pamela Rooke) 112-21
Mooney, Kevin (Adam and the Ants) 120
Moss, Kate 22, 95, 138
Mossman, Katie 104
MTV 33, 52, 168
  Music Awards 62, 63, 128, 188
Mugler, Thierry 13, 14, 47, 74
Muller, Kari-Ann 137
Muller, Sophie 99

New Romantics 32, 33, 42, 43, 115, 118, 132
New Truth book (Fischerspooner, 2014) 69
new wave 81, 118, 121
  see also New Romantics
New York magazine: Grace Jones shoot (1978) 82
Nicopanda label (Formichetti) 77, 79
Nirvana 140
No Doubt 62, 99
  Rock Steady (2001) 99

L'Officiel magazine: Beyoncé shoot (2011) 173, 174, 175, 176, 178
On the Street book (Amy Arbus) 111
Outkast 62
'the outsider' in fashion design 60, 62, 69, 79, 200

Palladium club, New York 104
Paper magazine 71, 90
Parks, Alan (London Records) 158, 161
Pedzwater, Devin 105
performance art 13, 42, 49, 72, 77, 111, 124, 167, 195, 203
Perry, Katy 101, 183, 185, 187, 188
  California Dreams tour (2011) 183, 185
  'California Gurls' video (2010) 183, 185, 187
  'Dark Horse' video (2013) 185, 187, 188
  'E.T.' video (with Kanye West, 2011) 188, 189

GHD ads (2011) 191
  Grammy Awards (2014) 185
  MTV Music Awards (2013) 188
  One of the Boys (2008) 187
  Part of Me film (2012) 188
  Prism (2013) 69, 188
  'Roar' video (2013) 187
  Rolling Stone shoot (2011) 191
  Teenage Dream album and video (2010) 187, 188
  'Thinking of You' video (2009) 188
  'This Is How We Do' video (2014) 188, 191
  'Unconditionally' (Prism, 2013) 188
Pet Shop Boys 42, 44, 49, 53
  'Can You Forgive Her?' video (1993) 55
  Electric tour (2013-14) 45, 47, 54, 55
  Fundamental tour (2006-7) 47, 54
  London 2012 Olympics 50, 55
  A Man from the Future (2014) 54
  Pandemonium tour (2009-11) 41, 44, 45, 46, 54
  Performance tour (1990) 47
  'Was It Worth It?' video (1991) 43
Petri, Ray 33, 34, 37
Phillips, Arianne 122-31, 151
Phlemuns 66
Plaza store, London 134, 135
Pop, Iggy 125
pop music 16, 20, 22, 23, 44, 71
  see also dance pop; electro-pop; J-pop
Prada, Miuccia 74, 99
Price, Antony 33, 47, 132-41, 165
'Priceless' collection (Price for Topman, 2009-10) 139, 140, 141
Puff Daddy (Sean Combs) 94-5, 96
Pugh, Gareth 50, 55
Pulp 156, 158
  'Disco 2000' video (1995) 153, 156
  'Help the Aged' video (1997) 156, 159
  This Is Hardcore (1998) 156
punk rock 13, 32, 33, 42, 43, 53, 59, 78, 111, 113-21, 151

'Radiator/Flat-pack Jacket' (Bryant for Pet Shop Boys) 44, 45
rap 33, 53, 66, 71, 72, 77, 78, 94, 95, 105, 108, 111
rave 22, 104, 106, 108, 154
R&B 17, 65, 96, 111, 172, 173, 174, 179, 180

Reboot initiative (Formichetti and Diesel) 74
Reed, Lou: Transformer (1972) 138, 139
Reid, Jamie 118
Rhodes, Nick (Duran Duran) 141
Richter, Gerhard 54
Right Said Fred 44
Rihanna 188
  'Princess of China' video (Coldplay, 2011) 151, 188
  Rolling Stone cover (2011) 146, 147
  Vogue Italia cover (2009) 90
Riperton, Minnie: Adventures in Paradise (1975) 179, 180
rock music 13, 37, 62, 99, 103, 125, 132, 135, 143, 144, 147, 196
  see also glam rock; indie music
The Rocky Horror Picture Show (dir. Jim Sharman, 1975) 124, 125, 127
Rodeo Girl book (Lisa Eisner) 128, 129
The Rodin Project ballet (Maliphant, 2012) 168
Rolling Stone magazine 105, 128
  Katy Perry shoot (2011) 191
  Lady Gaga cover (2009) 149
  Rihanna cover (2011) 146, 147
  Women of Rock issue (1997) 127
Ross, Diana 85
Rotten, Johnny (Sex Pistols) 113, 118
Roxy Music 33, 47, 115, 132, 135, 138, 140, 141, 165
  'Angel Eyes' video (1979) 138
  Country Life (1974) 137, 137
  Flesh + Blood (1980) 137, 137
  For Your Pleasure (1973) 137, 137
  Roxy Music (1972) 135, 137, 137
  Siren (1975) 133, 137
  Stranded (1973) 137
  'Roxy Women' 134, 137

Salon, Philip 118
Sant'Angelo, Giorgio di 94
Santigold 108, 111
Savidge, Phill (Savidge & Best) 158
Schmidt, Michael 9, 142-51
Scissor Sisters 65, 140
Scott, Jeremy 23, 108, 142, 147
Seditionaries boutique, London (Westwood and McLaren) 42, 113, 116
Sex boutique, London (Westwood and McLaren) 113, 115, 116
Sex Pistols 113, 118
  Never Mind the Bollocks (1977) 118

Sexual Personae book (Camille Paglia, 1990) 22
Shadforth, Dawn 25
Shakira 185, *185*
Shears, Jake (Scissor Sisters) 65
Shoom club, London 154
Simmons, Tabitha *167*, 168
Siouxsie Sioux 118
skater style 62, 99
Skid Row 144
Skinny, Jo and Pat 152-61
Smashing club, London 154, 158
The Smiths 140
social media 49, 61, 63, 66, 72, 74, 101, 108, 147, 188, 191
social platforms 62, 66, 74, 101, 191
'Space-Samurai' costume (Yamamoto for David Bowie) 200
Sparro, Sam: 'Pink Cloud' video (2010) 61, 66, *66*
Spears, Britney
  Circus tour (2009) 171
  MTV Music Awards (2003) 128
  'Work Bitch' video (2013) 16, 151
Spin magazine 104-5, 108, *111*
  Rebel Yell cover (2008) *103*, 105
Spooner, Casey (Fischerspooner) 69
Spun (dir. Jonas Åkerlund, 2002) 13
Squeezebox! club, New York *142*, 144, 147
Stanley, Rod (*Dazed & Confused*) 179
Stefani, Gwen 62, 92, 99, 101
  'Let Me Blow Ya Mind' video (2001) *92*, 99
  Love. Angel. Music. Baby. (2004) 99, 101
  'Luxurious' video (2004) 101
  'Rich Girl' video (2004) 101
  The Sweet Escape (2006) 99
  'The Sweet Escape' video (2006) 101
  'What You Waiting For?' video (2004) 99
Stewart, Stevie 125, 162-71
  family 162, 164, *165*
Stirling Cooper store, London *134*, 135
Stock Aitken Waterman 23
Strange, Steve 33
'Straw Jacket' (Bryant for Pet Shop Boys) *41*, 44, 45
street style 33, 34, 53, 79, 94, 104, 105, 108, 116, 124, 144, 158
Studio 54 club, New York 82, 104, 156
Suede 154, 158, 160
  'She's in Fashion' video (1999) *160*
Super Bowl halftime shows *14*, 16

Tailly, Jenke-Ahmed 172-81
Taste Atelier (Tailly) 181
Taylor, John (Duran Duran) 141
Tennant, Neil (Pet Shop Boys) 42, 43, 44, 45, *46*, 47, 54
Terry, Helen 165, 167
Time Out magazine: Iggy Pop cover (1996) 37
'Tokyo Pop' bodysuit (Yamamoto for David Bowie) *192*, 197
Top of the Pops (TV show) 34, 105, 168
Topman *139*, 140, *141*, *160*, 161
Topolino 38
Trade club, London 42
Tunnel club, New York 104
Turlington, Christy 22
Turner, Tina 127, *142*, 144
  Foreign Affair (1989) *146*, 147

Uemura, Naomi 203

V magazine
  BodyMap shoot (2008) *167*, 168
  Lady Gaga shoot (2009) 73
Vauthier, Alexandre 176
Versace 108, *203*
Versus line (Versace) 108
Veruschka 94
The Verve 155
Vicious, Sid (Sex Pistols) *113*, 116
'Video-tape Cape' (Bryant for Pet Shop Boys) 47, *48*
A View to a Kill (dir. John Glen, 1985) 85
Visage 33
Vogue (US) 94, 95
Vogue Hommes Japan 73
Vogue Italia 104
  Rihanna cover (2009) 90
Von Teese, Dita 144, *145*

W magazine *123*, 131
Wainwright, Keith (Smile Salon) 115
Walker, Tim 191
Warhol, Andy 72, 120
Way, Sam 171
W.E. (dir. Madonna, 2001) 131
Weber, Bruce 44
West, Kanye 52, 53, 59
  'E.T.' video (with Katy Perry, 2011) 188, *189*
  Glow in the Dark tour (2008) 53
  Revel concert (Atlantic City, 2012) 53
  Touch the Sky tour (2005) 53
  Watch the Throne tour (2011-12) *50*, 53, 59
  Yeezus tour (2013) 53

Westwood, Vivienne 22, 33, 42, 104, 113, 115, 118
White, Vanna (*Wheel of Fortune*) 191
Who's Zoo ballet (Clark, 2012) 167
whoyouare.com (Åkerlund) 19
Williams, Sadie 79
Wilson, Dr Jonathan 22
Winston (drag queen) 43
Wire 52, 53
Wonderland (dir. James Cox, 2003) 184
'Woodland Creatures' romper suit (Yamamoto for David Bowie) 200
The World's Famous Supreme Team: 'Buffalo Gals' (1982) 118
Wujek, Johnny 182-91

X-STaTIC PRO=CeSS series (2001/2003) *123*, 131

Yamamoto, Kansai 43, 144, 188, 192-203
  fashion shows 194-5, 196, 200, *203*
Yarritu, David (ABC) 165, 167
Yates, Janty 141
Young, Will: 'Light My Fire' video (2002) 171
Young British Artists (YBA) 155

'Zonda' (Price) *134*, 135

Acknowledgements/Picture Credits

A special thanks to all the artists, agents, production and management teams whose unparalleled creative talent and generosity of time and spirit have made this book possible.

For their invaluable input:
Jonas Åkerlund, Victoria Broackes, Brooke Candy, Frances Corner, Michael Costiff, Michelle Egiziano, Casey Fischerspooner, Stuart Goddard, Deborah Harry, Kelela, Nick Knight, Lenny Kravitz, Madonna, Kylie Minogue, Tom Munro, Alan Parks, Devin Pedzwater, Barry Reynolds, Nick Rhodes, Phill Savidge, Dawn Shadforth, Gwen Stefani, Neil Tennant, Helen Terry, David Yarritu.

I would also like to extend heartfelt thanks to the following individuals for their invaluable advice, support and enthusiasm: Mayumi Aono, Yasuyuki Asano, Simon Barker (Six), Mike and Alison Baron, Alex Basch, Angela Becker, Kent Beldon, Murray Blewett, René Bosne, Sharon Cho, Ben Cox, Melissa Danny, Nathan Gale, Spilios Gianakopoulos, Lesley Henderson, Paul Jones, Virginie Laguens, Tracy Le Marquand, Rosie Lewis, Sean McGirr, Faye McLeod, Tessa Mansfield, Cassandra Maxwell, Jerry Morrone, Fumito Nakae, Yvette Noel-Schure, Evi Peroulaki, Gordon Richardson, Liz Rosenberg, Rona Siegel, Ayami Suda, Victoria Sullivan, Birgitta Toyoda, Thuy Tran, Sara Zambreno, Marco Zarczynski.

Katie Baron

t = top; b = bottom; l = left; r = right, c = centre

Richard E. Aaron/Redferns/Getty Images: 91b; Action Press/REX Shutterstock: 54r; © AF archive/Alamy: 19b, 32; Courtesy of B. Åkerlund: 14; Photos by Jonas Åkerlund: 19t; © Mario Anzuoni/Reuters/Corbis: 106; © William Baker: 7, 28 (all), 163; Courtesy of William Baker: 22, 26r, 29; Photograph by Simon Barker aka 'Six', from the book Punk's Dead (2011): 119bl; Photo by Katie Baron: 191t, 201, 202b; Matt Baron/BEI/REX Shutterstock: 116; Baron/Getty Images: 115; Photos by Pete Black: 98; © Mike Blake/Reuters/Corbis: 60b; Collage courtesy of Judy Blame: 33; Blitz, September 1986, Boy George by Paul Gobel: 124tl; Blitz, December 1986, 'Dead Trendy' by Gill Campbell: 124tr; Image courtesy of Jeffrey Bryant: 42, 44; Photo courtesy of Jeffrey Bryant, dancers Thomas Herron, Merri Holden in bouncing foil costumes, Pet Shop Boys Electric Tour 2013: 47b; Courtesy of Capitol, under license from Universal Music Enterprises, a Division of UMG Recordings, Inc.: 186, 187, 188t, c, 189, 190; Capitol Records/EMI: 146; Published by Carlton Books: 49b; Charisma Records: 119br; Michel Clementz/ABACA/PA Images: 50l, 58; Carolyn Cole/LA Times/Contour by Getty Images: 46; Roger Cummins/The AGE/Fairfax Media via Getty Images: 167; Published by Damiani: 69; Courtesy of Es Devlin: 51–54l, 55b–57, 59; Make-up: Michelle Diaz, photography: Jonny Coleman: 60t; Kevork Djansezian/Getty Images: 184t; Marko Djokovic/CROPIX/SIPA/REX Shutterstock: 40; Debi Doss/Redferns/Getty Images: 199bl; Courtesy of Lisa Eisner: 129; EMI: 199tl; Epic Records: 180l; Photographs © Gavin Evans: 36–37; Farrar Straus & Giroux. Courtesy of Jean-Paul Goude: 80l; Fascination Records/Universal Music Group: 171t; Courtesy of Franc Fernandez: 62, 63t, 64; Courtesy of Formichetti Japan: 71b, 79; Photo: Dana Fouras, dancer: Jennifer White: 169; Ian Gavan/Getty Images: 66; Geffen Records/Universal Music Enterprises, a Division of UMG Recordings, Inc.: 96t; Courtesy of Luke Gilford and Franc Fernandez: 60c, 68; Paul Gilham – FIFA/FIFA via Getty Images: 184br; Go Runway: 75, 142tr, br; © Jean-Paul Goude: 80c–82, 84, 86–91; Courtesy of Jean-Paul Goude. Island Records/Universal Music Enterprises, a Division of UMG Recordings, Inc.: 83, 85; Alastair Grant/AP/PA Images: 50r; Photo by Bauer Griffin: 168; © Bob Gruen/www.bobgruen.com: 149; Sharif Hamza/Trunk Archive: 173c, 178; Dave J. Hogan/Getty Images: 27, 176; Hulton Archive/Getty Images: 202t; i-D, no. 8, October 1982. Courtesy of Thomas Degen and Scarlett Cannon: 124bl; i-D, no. 14, April 1983. Photo by Nick Knight/Trunk Archive: 124br; Photography by Inez and Vinoodh: 78; Interscope Geffen A&M Records: 145t; Courtesy of Interscope Records, under license from Universal Music Enterprises, a Division of UMG Recordings, Inc.: 17, 63b, 74t, b, 93b, 99, 100b, 101, 127b; Island Records: 153; Island Records/Universal Music Enterprises, a Division of UMG Recordings, Inc.: 157, 158r, 159; ITV/REX Shutterstock: 118; Greg Kadel/Trunk Archive: 105r; Anna-Karin Karlsson campaign image. Photographer Ekaterina Belinskaya: 10; Jason Kempin/Getty Images: 45; Keystone/Getty: 195; © Douglas Kirkland/Corbis: 191br; Nick Knight/Trunk Archive. Vogue Hommes Japan vol. 5 © 2015 Condé Nast Japan: 72r; Jeff Kravitz/Getty Images: 73; © Annie Leibovitz/Contact Press Images: 95; Courtesy of Andrea Lieberman: 100t; Stephen Lovekin/Getty Images: 185b; Craig McDean/Art + Commerce: 166; Ken McKay/REX Shutterstock: 21; Photography by Alasdair McLellan, styling Jonathan Kaye, creative director Jop Van Bennekom. Image courtesy of The Gentlewoman: 181l; © Joan Marcus: 126t; Kevin Mazur/WireImage/Getty Images: 170, 182r, 185t; Frank Micelotta/Getty Images: 123t; Photo: Ari Michelson/Courtesy of Capitol, under license from Universal Music Enterprises, a Division of UMG Recordings, Inc.: 182l, 183; Mirrorpix: 114; Yui Mok/PA Archive/PA Images: 48; © Jean-Baptiste Mondino: 9, 31, 39; Portrait by Eddie Monsoon: 35; Mother Records: 154, 155; Moviestore Collection/REX Shutterstock: 13b; Tom Munro/2b management: cover; Tom Munro/Trunk Archive: 131b; Ilpo Musto/REX Shutterstock: 197; Leon Neal/AFP/Getty Images: 199br; Alexander Nemenov/AFP/Getty Images: 130b; Courtesy of Nicopanda: 77; Phil Noble/Reuters/Corbis: 55; Photography by Jason Nocito. Cover courtesy of SPIN Media LLC: 109; Nude Records: 160; One Little Indian Records. Photo © Jean-Baptiste Mondino: 38; PA Images: 113r; Courtesy of Paper magazine. Photo: Richard Bunbridge/Art + Commerce: 71t; © Parkwood Entertainment. Photo: Greg Gex: 173b, 177; Parlophone/Warner Music: 158l; Photograph Tina Paul/Camera Press London: 142tl; © Márton Perlaki: 111; © Pet Shop Boys Partnership. Photographer Eric Watson: 43t; © Photos 12/Alamy: 65r; Photography: Mark Pillai: 173t, 175, 179; Michael Putland/Getty Images: 198; Quarter Books: 156b; Wendy Redfern/Getty: 107; © Rhino Entertainment/A Warner Music Group Company: 12, 13t, 126b, 128b; Terry Richardson/Art Partner: 191bl; Terry Richardson/Art Partner. Vogue Hommes Japan vol. 5 © 2015 Condé Nast Japan: 72l; Herb Ritts/Trunk Archive: 142bl; Sheila Rock/REX Shutterstock: 112, 117; © Rolling Stone LLC 1992. All Rights Reserved. Used by Permission: 131t; © Rolling Stone LLC 1997. All Rights Reserved. Used by Permission: 127l; © Rolling Stone LLC 2011, 2009. All Rights Reserved. Used by Permission: 147, 148; Photo by Jordi Martín Romero: 47t; Franco Rubartelli/Vogue, © Condé Nast: 94; Photo by Albert Sanchez: 145b; Jun Sato/WireImage/Getty Images: 122, 130t; © Malick Sidibé. Courtesy of the artist and Jack Shainman Gallery, New York: 181r; Courtesy of Jo and Pat Skinny: 152, 156t, 161t; Courtesy of Slow Loris Publishing: 43b, 121b; Carter Smith/Art + Commerce: 92; Courtesy of Sony Music Entertainment: 76, 93t, 96b, 97, 120, 138tl, 171b, 180b; Courtesy of SPIN Media LLC. Photo by Lorenzo Bringheli/Trunk Archive: 110; Courtesy of SPIN Media LLC. Photo by Greg Kadel/Trunk Archive: 102; © Splash News/Corbis: 150t; Ray Stevenson/REX Shutterstock: 113l, 119l; Courtesy of Stevie Stewart: 164, 165; Dennis Stone/REX: 49t; © Masayoshi Sukita: 192, 199rt; Mark J. Terrill/AP/PA Images: 105l; Courtesy of Topman: 139t, 141, 161b; Michael Tran/FilmMagic/Getty Images: 188b; 20th Century Fox/Michael White Productions/The Kobal Collection: 125t; Courtesy of Virgin Records, under license from Universal Music Enterprises, a Division of UMG Recordings, Inc: 34, 123b, 125b, 133, 136, 137, 138tr, b, 139b; Mariano Vivanco/Trunk Archive: 71c; Courtesy of Tim Walker, B. Åkerlund and Robert Lussier: 18; Warner Music Group: 23–26l, 140, 150b; Kevin Winter/Getty Images: 65l; Ron Wolfson/Getty Images: 128t; Photos courtesy of Kansai Yamamoto: 192, 194, 196, 203l; © Jim Young/Reuters/Corbis: 15.

The publisher has made every attempt to trace and contact the copyright holders of all images reproduced in this book. It will be pleased to rectify any omissions in subsequent printings.